SPARKNOTES™

SAT Verbal Workbook

2004 Edition

Editorial Director Justin Kestler

Executive Editor Ben Florman

Director of Technology Tammy Hepps

Series Editor John Crowther

Managing Editor Vincent Janoski

Contributing Editors Matt Blanchard, Jennifer Chu

This edition published by Spark Publishing.

Spark Publishing
A Division of SparkNotes LLC
120 Fifth Avenue, 8th Floor
New York, NY 10011

03 04 05 06 07 SN 9 8 7 6 5 4 3 2 1

Please submit all comments and questions or report errors to www.sparknotes.com/errors

Library of Congress information available upon request

Printed and bound in Canada

ISBN 1-58663-957-9

Orientation

SAT Verbal Review

Practice Tests

General SAT Strategies

THE VERBAL PORTION OF THE SAT IS a multiple-choice test, with three timed sections. One of the verbal sections contains only reading comprehension questions, while the other two contain separate groups of sentence completions, analogies, and reading comprehension questions. In general, questions increase in difficulty as you progress through a group of same-type questions. All questions are worth the same number of points, and there are penalties for wrong answers. In this chapter, we will show you that the structure of the verbal SAT is very important to your success.

Imagine two children playing tag in the forest. Who will win—the girl who never stumbles because she knows the placement of every tree and all the twists, turns, and hiding spots, or the kid who keeps falling down and tripping over roots because he does not pay any attention to the landscape? The answer is obvious. Even if the other kid is faster and more athletic, the girl will still win because she knows how to navigate the landscape and use it to her advantage.

This example of tag in the forest is extreme, but it illustrates the point. The structure of the SAT is the forest. Taking the test is the game of tag.

Basic Rules

You should observe the following rules in every section of the SAT. Essentially, they are just common sense guidelines, but if you follow them, you will save time and cut down on careless errors.

Know the instructions for each section. The verbal SAT is timed, and you will definitely need every second. Don't waste time reading the instructions. Make sure you know the instructions so that you don't even have to glance at them on test day.

Use your test booklet as scratch paper. Some students feel as though they must keep their test booklets clean and pretty. There's no truth to that. When you finish with your test booklet, it just gets thrown away. Plus, writing on your test booklet can benefit you. If you need to write down a sentence to help you think through a problem, why not do it right next to the question? If you come to a question you want to skip and come back to later, mark it. (Do not make unnecessary marks on your answer sheet—it is definitely not scratch paper!)

Answer easy questions before hard questions. All questions are worth the same number of points regardless of difficulty, so it makes sense to answer the questions you find easy and less time-consuming first and the more difficult questions later. This way you'll be sure to accumulate more points. The structure of the test helps you to identify easy and difficult questions, as is explained in the "Order of Difficulty" section. And remember, you can skip around within a timed section. If you wanted to, you could answer all the easy sentence completions in a 30-minute verbal section, then skip over to the easy analogies, then go back to the moderate sentence completions, and so on.

Don't get bogged down. While taking seven minutes to solve a particularly difficult question may feel like a moral victory, it's quite possible that you could have used that same time to answer three other questions. Do not be scared to skip a question if it's giving you a lot of trouble—you can come back to it if you have time at the end.

Know when to guess. We will cover the specific strategies for guessing later.

Avoid carelessness. There are two types of carelessness, and both will cost you points. The first type of carelessness results from moving too fast. In speeding through the test, you make yourself vulnerable to misinterpreting the question, failing to see that the question contains some subtlety or extra nuance, overlooking one of the answer choices, or simply making a mathematical or logical mistake. So don't speed through the test. Make sure that you are moving quickly, but not so quickly that you become reckless.

The second type of carelessness results from lack of confidence. Do not simply assume out of frustration that you will not be able to answer a question without even looking at it. You should at least glance at every question to see if it's something you can answer. Skipping a question you could have answered is almost as bad as answering incorrectly a question you should have gotten right.

Be careful gridding in your answers. The scoring computer is unintelligent and unmerciful. If you answered a question correctly, but somehow made a mistake in marking your answer grid, the computer will mark that question wrong. If, somehow, you skipped question 5, but put the answer to question 6 in row 5, and the answer to question 7 in row 6, and so on, thereby throwing off your answers for an entire section . . . well, that would not be good.

Be very careful when filling out your answer grid. Many people will tell you many different ways that are the "best" way to fill out the sheet. We don't care how you do it as long as you're careful. We will give one piece of advice: talk to yourself. As you fill in the answer sheet, say to yourself: "number 23, B; number 24, E; number 25, A." Seriously. Talking to yourself will force you to look at the details and will increase your accuracy.

Answering SAT Multiple-Choice Questions

By now, you know that the SAT is a multiple-choice test. What you may not know is how the multiple-choice structure should affect your approach to answering the questions. Lucky for you, we're going to explain how.

Only the Answer Matters

A machine, not a person, will score your SAT. The scoring machine does not care how you came to your answers; it cares only whether your answers are correct and readable in little oval form. The test booklet in which you worked out your answers gets thrown in the garbage, or, if your proctor is conscientious, into a recycling bin.

The SAT has no partial credit, and no one looks at your work. If you get a question right, it doesn't matter if you did pristine work. In fact, it doesn't even matter whether you knew the answer or guessed. The multiple-choice structure of the test is a message to you from ETS: **we only care about your answers.** Remember, the SAT is your tool to get into college, so treat it as a tool. It wants right answers. Give it right answers, as many as possible, using whatever strategies you can.

Multiple-Choice and Scratch Work

Because the SAT is a timed test, and since your work doesn't matter, there's no reason to do more work than necessary to solve a problem. Speed matters on the SAT, so don't try to impress the test with excellent work. Do only what you have to do to ensure that you get the right answer and aren't working carelessly.

Multiple-Choice: You've Already Got the Answers

Even though this book covers the verbal SAT, here's an example of a simple multiple-choice math problem:

$$2 + 2 = ?$$

(A)	1
(B)	8
(C)	22
(D)	154
(E)	8006

It's immediately obvious that this is a bad question: all of the answers are wrong. You will never see a question like this on the SAT. Every SAT multiple-choice question will have exactly one correct answer. Again, obvious, but let's look at the implications of this fact.

When you look at any SAT multiple-choice question, the answer is already right there in front of you. Of course, ETS doesn't just give you the correct answer; they hide it among a bunch of incorrect answer choices. Your job on each question is to find the right answer. The important thing to realize is that a multiple-choice question is vulnerable to two separate methods :

- Find the **right answer**.

- Look at the answer choices and **eliminate wrong answers** until there's only one answer left—in other words, work backward.

Both methods have their advantages: you are better off using one in some situations. In a perfect scenario, when you are sure how to answer a question, the first method is clearly better than the second. Coming to a conclusion about a problem and then picking the single correct choice is a much simpler process than going through every answer choice and discarding the four that are wrong. However, when you are unsure how to solve the problem, the second method becomes more attractive: you should focus on eliminating the incorrect answer choices rather than trying to pick out the right answer.

You might be able to use the answer choices to lead you in the right direction, or to solve the problem through trial and error. You also might be able to eliminate answer choices through a variety of strategies (these strategies vary by question type; we'll cover them in the chapters dedicated to each specific type of question). In some cases, you might be able to eliminate all the wrong answers. In others, you might only be able to eliminate one, which will still improve your odds when you attempt to guess.

Part of your task in preparing for the SAT will be to get some sense of when to use the correct strategy. Using the right strategy can increase your speed without affecting your accuracy, giving you more time to work on and answer as many questions as possible.

Guessing on the SAT

Should you guess on the SAT? We'll begin to answer this question by posing another SAT question:

Ben is holding five cards, numbered 1–5. Without telling you, he has selected one of the numbers as the "correct" card. If you pick a single card, what is the probability that you will choose the "correct" one?

Okay, this isn't really an SAT question, and the answer choices aren't that important, though the answer is $\frac{1}{5}$. But the question does precisely describe the situation you're in when you guess blindly on any SAT question with five answer choices. If you were to guess on five multiple-choice questions with five answer choices, you would probably get one question right for every five guesses you made.

ETS took these probabilities into account when devising its system to calculate raw scores. As described in the introduction, for every right answer on the SAT, you get one point added to your raw score. For each answer left blank, you get zero points. For each incorrect multiple-choice answer you lose one-quarter of a point.

It's easy to figure out why ETS chose the wrong-answer penalties that it did. Let's look at each type of question and examine what its penalty value means.

Five-choice. If you guess blindly on a verbal question, probability dictates that you will get one question right for every four wrong. Since you get 1 point for your right answer and lose $\frac{1}{4}$ point for each wrong answer, you're left with $1 - 4 \times \frac{1}{4} = 0$ points. Guessing blindly for five-choice questions is a waste of time.

Intelligent Guessing

The numbers above show that the wrong-answer penalty renders any sort of blind guessing pointless. But what if your guessing isn't blind? Let's say you're answering the following sentence completion question:

In Greek mythology, Hades, the realm of the dead, is guarded by ---- dog.

(A)   an anthropomorphic
(B)   a protean
(C)   a sesquipedalian
(D)   a delicious
(E)   a sanguinary

It seems likely that you don't know the meanings of the words **anthropomorphic, protean, sesquipedalian,** or **sanguinary** since we purposely chose words that were more obscure than the vocabulary that appears on the SAT. But you probably do know the meaning of **delicious,** and can tell immediately that it does not fit correctly into the sentence (a delicious dog?). Once you've eliminated delicious as a possible answer, you only have to guess between four rather than five choices. Is it now worth it to guess? If you guess among four choices, you will get one question right for every three you get wrong. For that one correct answer you'll get 1 point, and for the three incorrect answers you'll lose a total of a total of $\frac{3}{4}$ of a point. $1 - \frac{3}{4} = \frac{1}{4}$, meaning that if you can eliminate one answer, then the odds of guessing turn in your favor: you become more likely to gain points than lose points.

The rule for guessing, therefore, is simple: if you can eliminate even one answer choice on a question, you should definitely guess. The only time you should ever leave a question blank is if you cannot eliminate any of the answer choices.

Guessing as Partial Credit

Some students feel that guessing correctly should not be rewarded with full credit. But instead of looking at guessing as an attempt to gain undeserved points, you should look at it as a form of partial credit. Let's use the example of the sentence completion about the dog guarding Hades. Most people taking the test will only know the word delicious, and will only be able to throw out that word as a possible answer, leaving them with a 1 in 4 chance of guessing correctly. But let's say that you knew that protean means "able to change shape," and that the dog guarding Hades was not protean. When you look at this question, you can throw out both "delicious" and "protean" as answer choices, leaving you with a 1 in 3 chance of getting the question right if you guess. Your extra knowledge gives you better odds of getting this question right.

Order of Difficulty

SAT questions are divided into groups. For example, in one of the 30 minute verbal sections, the 10 sentence completions are grouped together as questions 1–10, the 13 analogies are listed together as questions 11–23, and the 12 reading comprehension questions make up questions 24–35. Except for reading comprehension questions, all of these groups of questions are arranged by difficulty, from easiest to most difficult.

Making Decisions Based on the Order of Difficulty

Imagine that you are taking a test that consists of two questions. After your teacher hands out the test, and before you set to work, a helpful little gnome whispers to you from the corner, "The first problem is very simple, the second is much harder." Would the gnome's statement affect the way you approach the two problems? The answer, of course, is yes. For a "very simple" question, it seems likely that you should be able to answer it quickly and without much, or any, agonized second-guessing. On a "much harder" question, you will probably have to spend much more time, both to come up with an answer and to check your work to make sure you didn't make an error somewhere along the way.

And what about all the other students who didn't hear the gnome? They might labor over the first easy question, exhaustively checking their work and wasting time that they'll need for the tricky second problem. Then, when those other students do get to the second problem, they might not check their work or be wary of traps, since they have no idea that the problem is so difficult.

Because SAT questions are ordered by difficulty, it's as if you have that helpful little gnome sitting next to you for the entire test. The simple knowledge of question difficulty can help you in a variety of ways.

Knowing Where to Spend Your Time

As discussed earlier, you should try to avoid getting bogged down, and you don't have to answer questions in numerical order. In fact, in some situations it can be a good idea to skip an occasional question. Think about it: every question on the SAT is worth the same number of raw points, so what matters most on the test is answering as many questions correctly as possible. If skipping a question that's giving you trouble allows you the time to answer three other questions, then it's a good bargain.

How many questions you should skip depends entirely on your target verbal score. If you have a target score of 700 or higher, you need to answer every question, so there isn't much of a reason to skip around. But if, for example, your target score is a 550, you can afford to skip 2–3 questions in every group. In this case, if you encounter a sentence completion you just can't answer, don't spend a ton of time trying to figure it out. Skip it and move on to the next. If the sentence completions you find difficult happen to be the last one or two in the group, don't worry about leaving them behind, and move on to the analogies.

Please note that we are *not* suggesting that you skip all the questions in a group as soon as you hit one that you find difficult. Don't just assume that all questions appearing after a question that you find hard will be too hard for you. Sometimes, for whatever reason, a question will be hard for you even if the question after it is easy. The location of a question is a clue about its difficulty, but you shouldn't let the test dictate what you can and cannot answer simply based on its location. If you have a sense of how difficult a question probably is, and a similar sense of how many questions you can afford to skip, you should be able to make an informed decision about whether to skip a question or not. But make sure that your decision is informed: at least try to glance at every question in a group to see if you might be able to answer it.

Knowing When to Be Wary

Most students answer the easy SAT questions correctly. Only some students get moderately difficult questions right. Very few students get difficult questions right. What does this mean to you? It means that when you are going through the test, you can often trust your first instincts on an easy question. With difficult questions, however, you should be much more cautious. There is a reason most people get these questions wrong: not only are they more difficult, containing more sophisticated vocabulary or mathematical concepts, they are also often tricky, full of enticing wrong answers that seem as if they must be correct. But because the SAT orders its questions by difficulty, the test tips you off about when to take a few extra seconds to make sure you haven't been fooled by an answer that only *seems* right.

Pacing

The SAT presents you with a lot of questions and not that much time to answer them. As you take the test, you will probably feel some pressure to answer quickly. As we've already discussed, getting bogged down on a single question is not a good thing. But rushing too quickly isn't any good either. In the end, there's no real difference between answering very few questions and answering lots of questions incorrectly: both will lead to low scores. What you have to do is find a happy medium, a groove, a speed at which you can be both accurate and efficient and get the score you want.

Setting a Target Score

The previous paragraph sure makes it sound easy. But how do you actually go about finding a good speed? First, before anything else, you should recognize that you absolutely do not have to answer every question on the test. Remember, the SAT is your tool to help you get into one of the schools of your choice, and it probably won't take a perfect score to get you there. You should set a target score, and your efforts should be directed toward gaining that score.

In setting a target score, the first rule is always this: be honest and realistic. Base your target score on the schools you want to go to and have a realistic chance of getting into. Talking to a college counselor can help you gauge how reasonable your choices are. You can also gauge your expectations by your first practice test. If you score a 450 on the first verbal practice test, it's foolish to set your target score at 750. Instead, your target should be about 50–100 points higher on each section than your score on your first practice test. That's a total of 100–200 points higher for the whole test.

If you reach your target score during preparation, give yourself a cookie or some other treat and take a break from working. But just because you hit your target score doesn't mean you should stop working altogether. In fact, you should view reaching your target score as a clue that you can do better than that score: set a new target 50–100 points above your original, pick up your pace a little bit, and skip fewer questions. By working to improve in manageable increments, you can slowly work up to your top speed, integrating your new knowledge of how to take the test and the subjects the test covers without overwhelming yourself by trying to take on too much too soon. If you can handle working just a little faster without becoming careless and losing points, your score will certainly go up. If you meet your new target score again, repeat the process.

Your Target Score Determines Your Overall Strategy

Your target score can, and should, deeply affect your strategy. If you want to get a 500 on the verbal section of the SAT, your strategy will differ significantly from that of someone aiming for a 700. A person who wants a 700 must work fast and try to answer almost every question. He or she must be able to work very quickly without carelessness. A person looking to score a 600 does not have to answer every question. In fact, that person probably shouldn't try to answer every question. So, what's the moral? Adjust your pacing to the score you want. The chart below shows the approximate raw scores necessary to achieve certain scaled target scores on each section of the SAT.

Verbal	
Target Score	Raw Score
800	78
750	72
700	66
650	59
600	51
550	42
500	34
450	27
400	20

If your target score is a 500 on verbal, you need a raw score of 34. Think about what this means. There are a total of 78 possible raw points on the verbal SAT. To get a 500, you need to get a little less than half of those points. In other words, you need to answer a little less than half of the questions correctly (assuming you don't answer any questions wrong). If we take into account that you probably will answer at least a few questions incorrectly, then you know that you need to get a few more than half of the questions right. Even so, a little over half only constitutes the easy and moderate questions on the test. You could probably get a 500 without answering a single difficult question—this realization should help you pace yourself accordingly. Instead of rushing to answer as many questions as possible, spend the time you need to avoid errors and make sure you'll hit your target.

Knowing the Clock

When you take both your practice tests and the real SAT, you should be aware of the clock. You should not become obsessed with the clock and lose time by constantly glancing at those terrible ticking seconds, but you should have a sense of the time to keep yourself on proper pace.

We recommend that you always take practice tests with the clock. Since your proctor will enforce the time on the real SAT strictly, you should do the same on your practice tests. By using the clock on practice tests, you will learn to manage your time and become more familiar with taking the test as the clock ticks down to zero.

Luck

If you have lucky clothes, or any other lucky items, you might as well wear them, carry them, twirl them over your head and dance beneath them: do whatever works. A little luck never hurt anyone.

The Verbal SAT

T HE THREE VERBAL SECTIONS OF THE SAT contain 78 questions in total:

- 19 Sentence completions

- 19 Analogies

- 40 Reading comprehension

The following three chapters are devoted to analyzing, breaking down, and explaining the strategies that will help you do your best on each of these three question types.

Before getting to the specifics, though, it is best to discuss the verbal section as a whole. This chapter focuses on the general skills and strategies you need to succeed on the verbal section.

Vocabulary and the Verbal SAT

The verbal SAT claims to test your facility with language. This is sort of true: the analogies, sentence completions, and reading comprehension questions gauge your ability to form relationships between individual words, to understand words in context, and to comprehend written passages. Even so, these questions test your vocabulary far more extensively than they do any other verbal or literary skill. All of the analogy and sentence completion questions test vocabulary, and about one fifth of reading comprehension questions do too. If you know the vocabulary used in a particular question, not only will you have a better chance of answering the question correctly, your speed will also increase, allowing you to answer more questions and spend more time focusing on difficult questions. On the SAT, knowing your vocabulary can pay off in a big way.

The SAT's emphasis on vocabulary makes it a rather poor test of verbal or literary skills, but that doesn't mean that the stress on vocabulary makes those sections more difficult. After all, it's easier to learn vocabulary words than it is to develop your critical-reading skills. Furthermore, the SAT often reuses words from test to test. As part of this guide, we have included a list of the 1000 most common words to appear on recent SATs. Study the list. When you go through a practice test and come upon a word you don't know, write the word down and learn it.

It's unlikely that you'll be able to remember the exact meaning of every single word you try to learn, but it isn't so improbable that you'll get a sense of all those words. For example, even if all you can remember about a word is that it expresses something negative, that information can go a long way toward helping you get the right answer.

General Verbal SAT Strategies

The verbal half of the SAT is made up of three sections. Two of those sections are 30 minutes long and include analogies, sentence completions, and reading comprehension questions. The other section is 15 minutes long and contains one reading comprehension passage and its corresponding questions. The analogies and sentence completions are roughly organized from easiest to most difficult, but reading comprehension questions are not ordered by difficulty.

The only thing that's important on the SAT is getting as many answers correct as you possibly can. Getting the hard questions right earns no more points than correctly answering the easy questions. And answering the easy questions is much easier than answering difficult ones. Given this, it seems wise to devise a strategy that ensures that you get to see, and answer, all of the easier questions.

Answer Easy Questions First

Let's say you're in the 30-minute verbal section that has 10 sentence completions followed by 13 analogies, and a reading comprehension passage. Answer the sentence completions first. When you hit a question that's too difficult, skip it and move on to the next question. Do *not* skip out of the sentence completion section entirely. On this first run through, at least look at every question to see whether you think you can answer it. If you do skip a question, mark it in some way so that you can go back to it. Once you've gone through the sentence completions, skipping where necessary, move on to the analogies and do the same thing. After the analogies, turn to the reading comprehension, read the passage, and answer every question you can. Finally, go back to the questions you've skipped and see if you can figure out the answers or eliminate some answer choices and put yourself in a good position to guess.

Know Your Strengths

If you take a couple of practice tests before the test date, you'll start to get a feel for your SAT verbal strengths. If you're best at analogies, go back to the analogy group and give the hard ones another shot. If you are least good at sentence completion questions, return to those last. By refusing to follow the order in which the test presents itself and instead making certain you answer all the questions you can, you tailor the SAT to your strengths. And the closer the test fits your strengths, the better you'll do.

The Verbal SAT

Sentence Completions

Sentence Completions

THE SAT INCLUDES 19 SENTENCE COMPLETIONS, broken into two groups—one of 9 questions and one of 10. The two groups of sentence completions will appear on the two 30-minute verbal sections. In each case, the sentence completions will appear first, before the analogies and reading comprehension.

Sentence Completion Instructions

You should be comfortable with the test instructions before you arrive on test day. Here are the instructions for the sentence completions. Learn them.

Each sentence below has one or two blanks, each blank indicating that something has been omitted. Beneath the sentence are five words or sets of words labeled A through E. Choose the word or set of words that, when inserted in the sentence, <u>best</u> fits the meaning of the sentence as a whole.

Example:

Medieval kingdoms did not become constitutional republics overnight; on the contrary, the change was ----.

(A)   unpopular
(B)   unexpected
(C)   advantageous
(D)   sufficient
(E)   gradual   Correct Answer: (E)

Anatomy of a Sentence Completion

As described in the instructions you just read (if you didn't, go read them!), every sentence completion includes a sentence with one or two blank spaces and five possible answer choices that have either one or two words. Below are examples of each.

One-Word Completion

Bel Biv Devoe was a terrible rap and R&B group in the early '90s; its music was dull and its lyrics ----.

(A)   excellent
(B)   new
(C)   poor
(D)   loud
(E)   fresh

Two-Word Completion

Though out of water seals lumber around and look ---- , within the sea they move smoothly and ---- .

(A)   cute..wonderfully
(B)   sleek..purposefully
(C)   ungainly..slowly
(D)   cruel..quickly
(E)   awkward..gracefully

While looking at the structure and format of SAT sentence completions, you should recognize two important facts:

1. The sentences are logical and contain all the information necessary to define the word that fits in the blank.

2. All of the answer choices are grammatically correct. The correct choice will be the word that makes the most sense. In other words, don't be fooled into picking an answer simply because it makes grammatical sense.

These two guidelines are important. The first makes it clear that you should almost always be able to figure out the gist of the missing word or words. If you understand the vocabulary in the sentence, you should be able to deduce if a missing word should have a positive or negative connotation and what it should probably mean. The second fact just tells you that all the words in the answer choices will sound right, since they are all grammatically correct. Choose your answers by meaning, not by sound.

Decoding Sentence Completions

Sentence completions are not just pure vocabulary tests. To figure out the right answer, you have to decode the sentence to understand how it's functioning. "Decoding a sentence" might sound difficult, but it's something you do every day. For example, when you a hear a sentence such as "Usually I am happy, but . . ." you immediately know that the second half of the sentence will go something like "I am not happy right now." On hearing the word "but" in relation to the initial statement, you realize that the second half will contradict the first half. This intuitive thought process is what we mean by decoding the sentence.

Let's apply the decoding technique to the two examples above. In the one-word example about Bel Biv Devoe, there are no words like "but," so the first and second part of the sentence must agree—if Bel Biv Devoe is a terrible singing group, then their voices must be *poor*. For the two-word example sentence about seals, you can decode it by realizing that the initial word, "though," implies that the two halves of the sentence will oppose each other. In other words, what is true in the first half will be the opposite in the second half: though seals might lumber and look *awkward* on land, they move smoothly and *gracefully* in the water.

Sentence Flow and Hinge Words

Think of a simple sentence. Actually, forget it. We'll give you a simple sentence:

> The scientists' research confirmed their theories.

This sentence has a single flow or direction: it expresses a single idea from the beginning to the end. Now consider a variation of this sentence:

> Though the scientists' research confirmed their theories, many people refused to believe them.

In this second sentence, there are two flows: the half of the sentence before the comma states a fact, and the half of the sentence after the comma states a different fact that is *in opposition* to the first. The flow of the sentence changed.

Now let's say that the second sentence was an SAT sentence completion with, for the sake of simplicity, only two possible answers:

> Though the scientists' research confirmed their theories, many people ---- to believe them.

(A)   began
(B)   refused

We already know that the answer is *refused,* but pretend for a moment that you don't. How could you figure out the answer? We'll answer this question by writing out a sentence in which *began* actually would make sense:

> The scientists' research confirmed their theories, and many people ---- to believe them.

These two sentences differ by only two words: the first sentence begins with "though," while the second sentence replaces the "though" with an "and" in the middle. The addition or subtraction of the "though" and the "and" completely change how the sentence functions. We call such words "hinge words" because, just as a hinge determines whether a door is open or closed, hinge words determine the flow of the sentence. The sentence about the scientists with the hinge word "though" is a contrasted sentence—there is a change of direction between the first and second halves. The second sentence with the hinge word "and" is a straight or direct sentence with a single flow.

As you can see, being able to identify hinge words is a vital part of decoding a sentence. You should also notice that there are two types of hinge words: those such as "and" that signal a sentence will continue in the same direction, and those like "though," which signal that a sentence will change direction.

Hinge words that signal a direct flow in a sentence:

and	*because*	*since*	*so*	*thus*	*therefore*

Hinge words that change the flow of a sentence:

but	*though*	*although*	*while*	*rather*	*instead*
unless	*despite*	*however*	*nevertheless*	*notwithstanding*	

Identifying hinge words to help you determine the flow of the sentence is one of the best methods for answering sentence completions. Learning to identify hinge words should be one of your first tasks in preparing for the sentence-completion portion of the SATs.

Answering Sentence Completions

The process for answering one-blank and two-blank sentence completions is quite similar, but there are some important differences. We will therefore treat the two types separately.

Answering One-Word Sentence Completions

There is a definite process you should follow when answering one-blank sentence completions.

1.Read the question (without looking at the answers). In this initial reading, you should try to get a sense of the sentence. Look for hinge words and identify the sentence's flow. You might want to circle or otherwise mark the hinge words. Locate where the blanks fit into the sentence's flow. Does the blank fit into the single flow of the sentence? Is the blank set against the flow of the rest of the sentence by a hinge word? Let's look at the example about Bel Biv Devoe:

> Bel Biv Devoe was a terrible rap and R&B group in the early '90s; its music was dull and its lyrics ---- .

In this sentence, there are no obvious hinge words. Still, the second half of the sentence seems to flow directly from the first. The first half of the sentence says Bel Biv Devoe was "terrible" and the second half says that its music was "dull." The two halves of the sentence agree. The blank fits into a flowing sentence.

Next, figure out *what* the blank is referring to or describing within the sentence, and then *how* the sentence refers to or describes that thing. In the sentence about Bel Biv Devoe, the blank refers to Bel Biv Devoe's lyrics. The sentence also gives you the information that Bel Biv Devoe was a bad group with bad music. Since the sentence contained no change-of-direction hinge word, it seems safe to assume that BBD's lyrics will also be described negatively.

2.Read the question again (still without looking at the answers). Once you've decoded the sentence, read through it again and try to come up with your own answer to fill in the blanks. This answer can be either a single word or a description of the meaning of the word that should fill the blank. By anticipating what type of word will fill the blank before looking at any of the answers, you are making sure that you don't fall for any of ETS's tricky wrong answers.

> Bel Biv Devoe was a terrible rap and R&B group in the early '90s; its music was dull and its lyrics ----.

In reading this sentence through the second time, after decoding it and realizing that the two halves of the sentence agree, you could come up with the following:

> Bel Biv Devoe was a terrible rap and R&B group in the early '90s; its music was dull and its lyrics *bad*.

By inserting "bad" into the blank, you certainly haven't generated the word that *is* the correct answer (bad isn't even one of the answer choices), but you have come up with a word that defines, explains, or provides a synonym for the right answer.

If the sentence is difficult and you can't come up with a distinct word or phrase, at least try to determine whether each blank is positive or negative. Often, even that much information can show you the correct answer or help you to eliminate wrong answers.

3. Look through the answers and pick one. Now that you have a good sense of what kind of word should fill the blank, go through the answers. Find the answer that fits with the word or idea you've decided should fill the blank.

> Bel Biv Devoe was a terrible rap and R&B group in the early '90s; its music was dull and its lyrics *bad*.
>
> (A) excellent
> (B) new
> (C) poor
> (D) loud
> (E) fresh

Obviously, the only answer with a meaning similar to "bad" is **(C) poor.**

4. Try the answer out in the sentence. Once you've chosen a word, plug it into the sentence and try it out. If it works, you're set. If it doesn't, go back to the sentence and check to see that you decoded it correctly.

5. Guessing. If you cannot come to a decisive correct answer, you can still guess, which you should do if you can eliminate at least one answer choice. When you've gotten to this point in the process, you should at least have a sense of whether the word that fills a blank should have a positive or negative connotation. Use this information to eliminate answer choices.

Though the method described above seems extensive, once you're comfortable with the process, you should be able to fly through each step in a few seconds.

Answering Two-Word Sentence Completions

Two-word sentence completions are probably somewhat more intimidating to you than the one-word variety, since you have two blanks to fill. However, the process you follow to solve them should not be all that different.

1. Read the question (without looking at the answers). Just as with one-blank sentence completions, read through the sentence, identify the hinge word if there is one, and determine how the blanks fit in the sentence and what each refers to.

2. Read the question again (still without looking at the answers). Again, just as with one-blank sentences, try to anticipate the connotation of the words that will fit in the blanks.

3. Look through the answers and pick one. This step might actually be easier in two-blank sentences than one-blank sentences because you can eliminate an answer choice if just one of the words in the pair doesn't fit. In other words, two-blank questions offer you twice as many opportunities to eliminate an answer choice.

4.Try the answer out in the sentence. Same as with one-word sentence completions.

5.Guessing. Same as with one-word sentence completions.

When dealing with two blanks, you are more likely to be tempted to choose words based on what they mean in a vacuum rather than on their function within the sentence. In other words, you should not focus on the relationship between the two words in the answer pairs. You should focus on how each word needs to function in the sentence. If you come to the conclusion that a sentence contrasts, you might be tempted to choose words that are antonyms, or one word that has a positive connotation and one that has a negative connotation. But that could lead you to the wrong answer. Instead of choosing two words that contrast each other, you should choose words that make the *entire sentence* change direction.

> Tired of war and finally becoming hopeful that a(n) ---- might be a real possibility, the two factions redoubled their efforts to hammer out a settlement that would end their years of ----.

After reading this sentence carefully, you should realize a few things:

The first half and the second half of the sentence are *directly* related: the hope of *something* in the first half of the sentence is exactly what pushed the two sides to try to create a settlement that will end *something*. There is no hinge word or situation that might make the two sides of the sentence contrast.

Once you realize that the sentence is direct, you can infer the following:

- Both factions are tired of war (meaning both want to end the war).

- They each see the possibility of accomplishing *something* that is related to being "tired of war."

- Because they are tired of war, the two sides "redouble their efforts to hammer out a settlement" that ends their *something*.

With this information, you should have a good sense of how to answer the question:

- Since both sides are tired of war and want it to end, what would they be "hopeful" about? The prospect of peace, most likely.

- In order to bring about this peace, the two sides try to create a settlement that will end their years of *something*. If the two factions have been fighting, what might characterize their last few years? Something angry and violent.

Plug these words into the sentence:

Tired of war and finally becoming hopeful that a(n) *something peaceful* might be a real possibility, the two factions redoubled their efforts to hammer out a settlement that would end their years of *something angry and violent.*

(A)   battle..enmity
(B)   chamber..lawfulness
(C)   agreement..friendship
(D)   truce..hatred
(E)   tryst..romance

As you scan the answers and try to match them with the words or phrases that you think define the right answers, you can quickly throw out (A) because a battle isn't peaceful; (B) because a chamber makes no sense in this sentence; (C) because the two sides would not have had years of friendship if they were at war; and (E) because tryst and romance are words to describe a love affair, not the hope of ending a war. That leaves choice **(D),** and if you plug in the answers, you'll see that it is an effective practice. Notice, however, that to create this direct sentence, we used two words that are themselves opposite: **truce** and **hatred.** It's not the relation between the words themselves that matters, but how those words function in the sentence. In this example, we needed to find the two words that would fit the direct flow of the sentence in which the hope of peace led to the end of anger and violence. Remember, sentence completions are about vocabulary in context. Your job is to find the words that make the sentence work.

The Five Types of Sentence Completions

The better you are at identifying and decoding a sentence, the more quickly and accurately you will be able to answer sentence completions. We have compiled a list that describes the five main types of sentence completions.

1. One-Word Direct Sentences

One-word direct questions are the simplest kind of sentence completion, and are also the most common. About 6 of the 19 sentence completions on the SAT will be of this type. In one-word direct sentences, the sentence has a single flow of argument, and the word you choose to fill the blank must fit within that flow. One-word direct sentences come in two variations, each just as common as the other. The first type of one-word direct is just a simple sentence with a word left out. The second type of one-word direct involves two clauses set off from each other by a semicolon, colon, or comma. Usually, the first half of the sentence contains the blank, and the second half describes the word that goes in the blank.

Simple Sentence

The first type of one-word direct is just a simple sentence with a word left out:

> The ---- undergrowth of the jungle made it difficult for the explorers to remain on a straight path without using their machetes.
>
> (A) slight
> (B) limp
> (C) dense
> (D) standard
> (E) green

The correct answer is **dense**; the undergrowth made it difficult for the explorers to stay on the path, meaning the undergrowth was impenetrable or dense.

This example was fairly easy. The more difficult sentences of this type usually involve harder vocabulary and describe more sophisticated concepts, but the structure of the sentence is rarely more complicated.

Semicolon

> Big John Stud was a ---- wrestler; all of the other wrestlers in the WWF were hesitant to pit themselves against his great might.
>
> (A) minor
> (B) troubled
> (C) fearsome
> (D) tall
> (E) serviceable

In this sentence, the phrase "all of the other wrestlers in the WWF were hesitant to pit themselves against his great might" makes it clear that Big John Stud must be super-tough or **fearsome.** Note that this kind of sentence is particularly easy to decode. Your job is to figure out what kind of wrestler Big John Stud is, and the second half of the sentence gives evidence that describes precisely what kind of wrestler Big John Stud is. The example above used a semicolon; below you'll find examples of this type of question using commas and colons.

Colon

> Listeners were constantly amazed by the president's ---- speeches: he seemed unable to put together a coherent sentence.
>
> (A) excellent
> (B) lengthy
> (C) inarticulate
> (D) dogged
> (E) efficient

If the president is "unable to put together a coherent sentence," then his speeches must be very bad, or **inarticulate.**

Comma

Many sports fans considered the 1998 Yankees to be a(n) ---- team, one unbeatable by any other team in the league.

(A) middling
(B) destructive
(C) artistic
(D) quiescent
(E) invincible

An "unbeatable" team is **invincible.**

In rare instances, the structure of this type of sentence might be flipped, with the blank appearing after the semicolon, colon, or comma. In that case, the clause before the semicolon, colon, or comma provides the description or definition of the word needed to fill the answer blank.

One-Word Direct Practice Questions

1. During the hottest part of the day, lions move ---- and sleep in the shade.

   (A) furiously
   (B) contentedly
   (C) languidly
   (D) alertly
   (E) comically

2. The ---- hunting instinct of owls stems from their ability to see in the dark.

   (A) predatory
   (B) nocturnal
   (C) elegant
   (D) brilliant
   (E) terrifying

3. Professor Popkin explained Einstein's theory so thoroughly that to have any questions after his lecture would be ----.

   (A) implausible
   (B) prerequisite
   (C) candid
   (D) gratuitous
   (E) obsolete

4.   Renouncing material comforts, ascetics ---- luxuries in their surroundings.

      (A)   maintain
      (B)   enjoy
      (C)   denounce
      (D)   provide
      (E)   eschew

5.   When the pilot, thinking that he had flown across the Atlantic Ocean, instead landed in California, he realized he had made a(n) ---- and shocking error.

      (A)   extremely bad
      (B)   very difficult
      (C)   somewhat probable
      (D)   possibly understandable
      (E)   totally excusable

6.   ---- attempts to censor unpopular ideas, the First Amendment to the U.S. Constitution forbids the suppression of speech.

      (A)   enhancing
      (B)   subtracting
      (C)   considering
      (D)   vitiating
      (E)   stupefying

7.   Appealing to viewers' emotions, a frequent trick of advertising, can support ---- claims.

      (A)   negligent
      (B)   important
      (C)   malevolent
      (D)   specious
      (E)   militant

8.   Stan's ---- jokes and crude remarks offended his friends; they thought he was vulgar rather than funny.

      (A)   delightful
      (B)   ribald
      (C)   morbid
      (D)   pretentious
      (E)   exquisite

9.   The delegate could not decide whether he agreed or disagreed with the resolution; this ---- caused him to abstain when the roll call vote was taken.

      (A)   certainty
      (B)   equivalence
      (C)   insanity
      (D)   contradiction
      (E)   ambivalence

10. The signs for a successful ski trip were ----: the weather forecaster said more snow was probable.

    (A)   efficient
    (B)   propitious
    (C)   dogmatic
    (D)   ominous
    (E)   strident

One-Word Direct Answers

1. **(C)** One-Word Direct   *Easy*
The words surrounding the blank in the sentence indicate that the missing word describes the way in which lions move. When they are not moving, they are sleeping, so the correct word would not describe much activity. Thus, you can eliminate *furiously* and *alertly*. While *contentedly* might be a possibility, it describes a mood rather than an action. *Comically* tells more about the viewer's reaction than the lion's movement. *Languidly*, meaning "slowly and sluggishly", is the best choice.

2. **(B)** One-Word Direct   *Easy*
Although all of the choices could correctly describe the way in which owls hunt, the sentence relates to their ability to see in the dark, so *nocturnal* is the best answer.

3. **(D)** One-Word Direct   *Moderate*
If the explanation were complete, further questions would be unnecessary. *Prerequisite* means "required in advance", so it can be eliminated. While *implausible* indicates something "unbelievable", it suggests a criticism of the question. *Candid* means "truthful", and *obsolete* means "out-of-date". Neither of these fits the sentence's meaning. *Gratuitous*, meaning "uncalled for", is the best choice

4. **(E)** One-Word Direct   *Difficult*
You may not know the word *ascetics*, but the first part of the sentence tells you that they renounce material comforts. Therefore, *maintain, enjoy,* and *provide* contradict the meaning of *ascetics*. *Denounce* means "condemn", but the context of the sentence suggests that the blank refers to an action that ascetics take rather than something they say. *Eschew*, meaning "to avoid or to shun", is therefore the best answer.

5. **(A)** One-Word Direct   *Easy*
What kind of error was it? Clearly a serious one, and flying in the opposite direction from that intended would not be expected of an airplane pilot. Therefore, the error could not be *probable*, *understandable*, or *excusable*. It may be *difficult* to make such

an error, but the tone of the sentence indicates the correct word should indicate disapproval, so *extremely bad* is the best choice.

6. **(D)**   One-Word Direct   *Difficult*
The second half of the sentence tells you that the First Amendment forbids suppression of speech, so the blank in the sentence should be filled with a word that describes an action that tends to prevent that suppression. *Enhancing* has an opposite meaning. *Stupefying*, which means "amazing", does not make sense. *Considering* is too vague. *Subtracting* could make sense, but "to forbid" something is not "to subtract it from" something else. Thus, *vitiating*, which means "to weaker or lessen in force", is the best choice.

7. **(D)**   One-Word Direct   *Difficult*
Since the appeal to emotions is described as a *trick*, the sentence indicates that a negative word should be inserted to describe the claims. *Important* and *militant* will not fit. While *malevolent*, meaning "evil", is negative, it is too strong a word to refer to advertising. *Negligent* means "careless", but if the advertisers are using deliberate tricks, they are not careless. *Specious*, which means "appearing true or attractive but actually false", is the best answer.

8. **(B)**   One-Word Direct   *Easy*
Since the jokes are crude and offensive, words with positive connotations cannot fill the blank, so *delightful* and *exquisite* are incorrect. Of the remaining choices, neither *pretentious* nor *morbid* agrees with the second part of the sentence, which describes the jokes as vulgar. *Ribald*, meaning "characterized by sexual humor", is the correct answer.

9. **(E)**   One-Word Direct   *Moderate*
The words surrounding the missing word in the sentence suggest that the missing word represents uncertainty. *Certainty, equivalence,* and *insanity* can therefore be eliminated. Being unable to decide between two alternatives is not a *contradiction*. Thus, *ambivalence*, meaning "having opposing feelings or thoughts about a subject", is the correct answer.

10. **(B)**   One-Word Direct   *Moderate*
Skiers are obviously delighted to hear a snowy forecast. Therefore, words with negative connotations, such as *ominous, dogmatic,* and *strident*, are not correct answers. Although *efficient* has a positive connotation, its meaning does not fit the context of the sentence. Therefore, *propitious*, meaning "favorable", is the best answer.

Sentence Completions

2. One-Word Contrast Sentences

On average, SAT tests include about four one-word contrast sentences. In this type of sentence completion, the single blank stands in contrast to some other clause in the sentence. There are two types of one-word contrast sentences: those that include hinge words and those that don't. We will give examples of each.

One-Word Contrast with a Hinge Word

If you are familiar with hinge words and can identify them when necessary, this type of sentence should be easy to recognize. Once you've identified the sentence as a one-word, hinged contrast, you know immediately that the word that fits in the blank must somehow stand in opposition to another part of the sentence. All you have to do then is determine which phrase or idea the blank contrasts.

> Carlita thought her pranks were ----, but her former friends found her actions annoying and juvenile.
>
> (A)   hilarious
> (B)   angry
> (C)   colossal
> (D)   trite
> (E)   new

Here, the hinge word, "but," clearly sets the feelings of Carlita's former friends against her own sentiments. Therefore, if Carlita's former friends find her pranks annoying and juvenile, you should, without even looking at the answer choices, know that Carlita finds her pranks good, or funny, or something similar. The correct answer is **hilarious.**

> Although the radical youth of the '60s saw rock music as embodying the desire for peace and love, many conservatives saw the music as a threat that ---- the moral values of America.
>
> (A)   embraced
> (B)   revitalized
> (C)   undermined
> (D)   justified
> (E)   displayed

Clearly the vocabulary in this sentence is more difficult than that in the easy question about Carlita. The sentence also deals with concepts and issues that are more sophisticated than those in the easy sentence. Even after you recognize "although" as a hinge word and see that the second half of the sentence must oppose the first half, it still might take a little effort to figure out what the opposition to "embodying the desire for peace and love rather than war" might be.

In attempting to answer this question, the first thing you should realize is that the "desire for peace and love rather than war" is a positive thing, and so the radical youth of the '60s saw rock music as a good thing. Once you recognize this, it should be simple, given the hinge word "although," that the conservatives saw rock music differently—as a negative thing, a "threat."

With this knowledge, you are ready to look at the answer choices. Embrace, answer (A), means to support and show love, which is clearly not what the conservatives feared rock music might do to American moral values. Similarly, conservatives would have been happy with rock music if they saw it as revitalizing (renewing or giving strength to) or displaying American moral values, but the conservatives described in the sentence are not happy. The word justified (meaning "demonstrated to be correct or valid") doesn't fit well within the sentence; the conservatives might see the existence of rock music as a justification for increased stress on morals, but they wouldn't see rock music itself as justifying morals. That leaves only **undermined,** which creates the proper negative connotation needed in the second half of the sentence to stand in contrast to the first half.

Of the five answer choices in the question we just answered, the correct answer was the only word that had a *negative* connotation. To embrace, revitalize, display, or justify are all either positive or neutral actions. Undermining someone or something, in contrast, is a negative action. That we picked the sole negative word in order to get the proper negative sense might seem perfectly correct and logical, but you must be cautious here. Remember that your goal is not to pick an individual word whose connotation opposes the first half of the sentence, but to pick a word that will make the *entire* second half contrast the first. For example, what if the sentence above had been:

> Although the radical youth of the sixties saw rock music as embodying the desire for peace and love, many conservatives saw the music as ---- anarchy and the overthrow of the American government.

In the previous example, the conservatives saw music as threatening something that they loved: moral values. The music therefore had to be doing something negative to those values. But in this example, the second half of the sentence discusses things the conservatives feared: "anarchy and the overthrow of the American government." In order for it to make sense that the conservatives dislike rock music in this sentence, the rock music must be doing something *positive* for "anarchy and the overthrow of American government." But it's not as simple as, "The conservatives hate rock music, therefore rock music must be doing something negative." You must always examine the word in the context of the sentences in which it appears.

One-Word Contrast Without a Hinge Word

Some sentences can create a contrast relationship without using hinge words. Without such an identifying marker, these contrast sentences are harder to identify. For example:

Once a(n) ---- theory, the notion that the earth revolves around the sun is now accepted by virtually everyone.

(A) terrific
(B) pleasant
(C) esteemed
(D) beloved
(E) controversial

The sentence describes two different reactions to the "theory" at different times: at one time the world reacted a certain way, and now it reacts another way. Together, "once" and "now" describe a change through time that necessitates a contrast between the two halves of the sentence. In this example, the contrast to everyone accepting the theory could be that either no one believes in the theory or that many people dispute it. The only answer that works is **controversial.**

In general, when a sentence describes more than one point in time, it is usually a contrast sentence.

One-Word Contrast Practice Questions

1. Although he had not expected to play that day, the relief pitcher ---- to the manager's request to face one batter, and fortunately, he struck him out.

    (A) conceded
    (B) preceded
    (C) acceded
    (D) impeded
    (E) succeeded

2. In spite of the social ---- placed on women in her time, the heroine of *The Awakening* decided to live an autonomous life.

    (A) contraries
    (B) freedoms
    (C) choices
    (D) constraints
    (E) mortality

3. Helena felt that the play was absorbing, but Mark thought that the production was ----.

    (A) romantic
    (B) excessive
    (C) delightful
    (D) inexcusable
    (E) insipid

4. Countries with underdeveloped economies may possess a(n) ---- of natural resources yet suffer from a scarcity of manufactured goods.

   (A)   rarity
   (B)   amount
   (C)   plethora
   (D)   paucity
   (E)   inadequacy

5. The United States Supreme Court may interpret the Constitution, but it cannot ---- any of the provisions of the Bill of Rights.

   (A)   initiate
   (B)   consolidate
   (C)   intimidate
   (D)   abrogate
   (E)   interpolate

6. Osteoporosis occurs when bones ----; however, medication may help to rebuild lost bone mass.

   (A)   atrophy
   (B)   flourish
   (C)   terminate
   (D)   proliferate
   (E)   descend

7. While most of the speech expounded ideas at great length and with much detail, its conclusion was ----.

   (A)   precise
   (B)   exaggerated
   (C)   pithy
   (D)   moderate
   (E)   inordinate

8. The Piltdown Man, originally considered a significant discovery, turned out to be a hoax as ---- by Sir Arthur Conan Doyle and his friends.

   (A)   admitted
   (B)   concocted
   (C)   admired
   (D)   precluded
   (E)   designated

9. Mark Twain's irony reveals the characters' ---- when Huck Finn professes to believe the claims of the self-styled Duke and King.

   (A)   maleficence
   (B)   guile
   (C)   humor
   (D)   veracity
   (E)   candor

10.   Carl delights in solitude; no one who knows him would describe him as ----.

(A)   charitable
(B)   conscientious
(C)   contented
(D)   philosophical
(E)   gregarious

One Word Contrast Answers

1.   **(C)**   One-Word Contrast   *Easy*
The second half of the sentence indicates that the pitcher did participate in the game, so the blank requires a word that means "agreed to". While *conceded* means "to agree", it implies a change in one's opinion. *Preceded* means "occurred before" something else; *impeded* means "obstructed", and *succeeded* means "to have accomplished" something. *Acceded* is therefore the best choice.

2.   **(D)**   One-Word Contrast   *Difficult*
Even if you are not sure of the meaning of the word *autonomous*, *in spite of* indicates that something prevented the heroine from living in that way. *Freedoms* and *choices* are opposites of "preventing something from occurring". *Mortality*, meaning "death", does not make sense in the sentence. Thus, *constraints*, meaning "restrictions", is the best answer. Although *contraries*, meaning "contrasting ideas", is a plausible choice, it is not as precise a choice as *constraints*.

3.   **(E)**   One-Word Contrast   *Easy*
The hinge word *but* indicates that Mark's view was the opposite of Helena's. Her view was positive, so *romantic* and *delightful* can be eliminated. *Absorbing* means "interesting or fascinating". While *excessive* and *inexcusable* are negative words, they do not directly contrast the meaning of *absorbing*. *Insipid*, meaning "dull and boring", is the best choice.

4.   **(C)**   One-Word Contrast   *Moderate*
The hinge word *yet* suggests that the missing word means the opposite of "scarcity". While *amount* indicates a quantity, it is a general word; the amount could be small or large. *Plethora*, meaning "abundance or excess", is a better answer. *Poverty* and *inadequacy* are more similar in meaning to *scarcity* than contrasting.

5.   **(D)**   One-Word Contrast   *Difficult*
The word *but* indicates that correct choice should contrast with *interpret* in some way. *Intimidate* refers to a person, so it is not a good choice. To *initiate* is "to begin"; to *interpolate* is "to add material to"; *consolidate* means "unify". These meanings are dif-

ferent from *interpretation*, but they are not contrasts. *Abrogate*, meaning "to abolish or nullify", is the most direct contrasting word.

6. **(A)** One-Word Contrast   *Moderate*
If the bones need to be rebuilt, the correct choice means "to wear away". *Flourish* and *proliferate* have opposite meanings. While *terminate* and *descend* contain a diminishing meaning, they are not precise in context. *Atrophy*, meaning "to wither away or shrink", is the best choice.

7. **(C)** One-Word Contrast   *Moderate*
The hinge word *while* indicates a choice that means the opposite of long-winded. *Inordinate* means "exceeding moderate limits", so it is a synonym rather than an opposite. *Exaggerated* also implies something that carries on at length. While *precise* and *moderate* might describe a speech that was not very detailed, *pithy*, because it means "concise and to the point", is the best answer.

8. **(B)** One-Word Contrast   *Easy*
Although there is no hinge word, the sentence indicates that a development that was once perceived to be significant was a hoax. The verb that belongs in the blank should mean "inventing something false". The hoaxers would not *admit* or *admire* or *designate* that the discovery was a fake. To *preclude* means "to prevent", which would be the opposite of what was done. *Concoct*, meaning "to make up or invent", is the correct choice.

9. **(B)** One-Word Contrast   *Difficult*
There is not a hinge word, but the correct choice has a meaning that is opposite of "something believable". *Veracity* and *candor*, meaning "truthfulness and frankness", could not be correct. While their claims might provoke laughter when the reader sees that they are untrue, *humor* would not apply to the characters. *Maleficence* means "evil", and while the claims were false, that detail does not necessarily make the characters wicked. *Guile*, meaning "deceit and trickery", is the best choice.

10. **(E)** One-Word Contrast   *Moderate*
Although there is not a hinge word, it is clear that the correct choice describes someone who does not enjoy solitude, which means "to be alone". *Charitable, conscientious, philosophical,* and *contented* can either describe a person who does not enjoy solitude or someone who enjoys it. *Gregarious*, meaning "friendly and sociable", is the only possible answer.

3. Two-Word Direct Sentences

Two-word direct sentence completions contain two blanks that fit into the same flow of argument. About three of the sentence completions on the SAT will be two-word direct.

A good clue that a two-blank sentence is a direct sentence is the presence of same-direction hinge words such as *and, because, since, so,* and *therefore.* Another good way to determine if a sentence is direct is to ask yourself, "Does one part of the sentence happen because of another part of the sentence?" If the answer is yes, the sentence is probably direct. If the answer is no, if one part of the sentence happened *despite* the situation or facts described in the other part of the sentence, then the sentence as a whole is probably a contrast. Two-word direct sentences can come in a few forms:

Simple Statements

Creating a hypothesis involves ---- a great deal of data and identifying ---- that explain the data's distribution.

(A) studying..patterns
(B) defying..issues
(C) seeing..plateaus
(D) raising..structures
(E) encountering..plans

Simple statements define a single thing, in this case the creation of a hypothesis; the two words you use must make that definition correct. In this case the answer is **studying . . patterns** because creating a hypothesis demands studying data and interpreting the patterns that the data form.

Blanks Appearing Near Each Other

The ---- conditions ---- even the intrepid explorer, who never again ventured out into the tundra.

(A) destructive..angered
(B) gorgeous..moved
(C) harsh..terrified
(D) appalling..enveloped
(E) serene..pleased

The answer is **harsh . . terrified.** In looking at the question, you should see that the two blanks help define a situation that directly caused the intrepid explorer never to venture into the tundra again.

Distant Blanks

Well known as a man who was ---- even when under the heaviest fire, the general was as
---- as a person could be.

(A)   composed..tremulous
(B)   helpless..efficient
(C)   frigid..warlike
(D)   serene..unflappable
(E)   grave..humorous

As you can see in this example, many two-word direct sentences of this form actually use one blank as the key to understanding the other. In this sentence, the clause before the comma describes the general when under fire. The second half of the sentence then uses the first half to justify an assertion about the general's character. In other words, there's no way we can come to an understanding of the general's character if we don't know how the general acted under heavy fire, and the word that describes the general's behavior under fire is a blank!

Frustrating, right? Not really. If the first blank describes behavior generally characteristic of the general, then the two words you choose must go together. You can immediately throw out *composed . . tremulous, helpless . . efficient,* and *grave . . humorous* because all three contain words that are antonyms. *Frigid . . warlike* just doesn't make much sense together or in the sentence, so you can throw that choice out too, leaving you with **serene . . unflappable,** the correct answer.

Sentences in which one blank actually contains the word crucial to knowing what should fill the other blank are not particularly difficult. But in those first moments they might scare you a little, since the key word seems to be hidden. Simply knowing that these types of questions exist will help you answer them with ease.

Two-Word Direct Questions

1.   Both ---- and ----, Hilary was known as the schoolyard bully.

(A)   aggressive...contentious
(B)   optimistic...forceful
(C)   passive...impolite
(D)   robust...peaceful
(E)   serene...cheerful

2.   Kim's ---- note-taking was merely a ---- to conceal a lack of interest in the lecture.

(A)   instantaneous...habit
(B)   profuse...facade
(C)   sloppy...stratagem
(D)   profligate...pattern
(E)   careless...means

3.   The ---- at the diplomat's funeral consisted of ---- for her efforts to maintain world peace.

    (A)   rhetoric...cheers
    (B)   speeches...condemnation
    (C)   elegy...kudos
    (D)   prayers...compliments
    (E)   hymns...tributes

4.   The demonstrators tried to behave with ---- and ---- in order to avoid confrontations with local authorities.

    (A)   pathos...despair
    (B)   rectitude...etiquette
    (C)   contention...anger
    (D)   pacifism...hostility
    (E)   forbearance...fortitude

5.   The ---- environments of slum housing ---- Jacob Riis's campaign for the reformation of these conditions.

    (A)   horrific...provided
    (B)   appalling...instigated
    (C)   disgusting...pursued
    (D)   appealing...goaded
    (E)   admirable...supported

6.   Struggling to win an election, the representative argued that comments suggesting that he had accepted a bribe were ---- and ----.

    (A)   scandalous...logical
    (B)   unjustified...illegal
    (C)   fallacious...fabricated
    (D)   corrupt...credible
    (E)   criminal...potable

7.   Because Iago deceived him, Cassio was ---- helpful, and he became ---- in Iago's plot to destroy Othello.

    (A)   unwittingly...complicit
    (B)   extremely...inutile
    (C)   posthumously...useful
    (D)   noxiously...responsible
    (E)   virulently...inured

8.   ---- suggestions aided the playwright in revising a ---- of the dialogue in the first act, much of which he had disliked but had been unable to decide how to change.

    (A)   Helpful...line
    (B)   Complex...mandate
    (C)   Hackneyed...quantity
    (D)   Maudlin...pittance
    (E)   Trenchant...preponderance

Sentence Completions

9. James Baldwin and other African-American writers were ---- when predicting, in their works, the disorders that would ---- if civil rights legislation did not pass.

    (A) pessimistic…evanesce
    (B) prescient…ensue
    (C) omniscient…slacken
    (D) dissonant…promulgate
    (E) magnanimous…fulminate

10. Darwin's theories are not ----; portions of them have been challenged, even by ---- of evolution such as Steven Jay Gould.

    (A) complete…lackeys
    (B) inviolate…proponents
    (C) inexplicable…detractors
    (D) mesmerizing…masters
    (E) santimonious…critics

Two-Word Direct Answers

1. **(A)** Two-Word Direct   *Easy*
If Hilary is a bully, both blanks must be inserted with words whose meaning refers to someone who is bold and likes to argue. *Optimistic*, *passive*, *peaceful*, and *cheerful* are not attributes of a bully, so all of the choices containing those words can be quickly eliminated, even if the other word in the choice is appropriate. *Aggressive…contentious* is consequently the only possible answer.

2. **(B)** Two-Word Direct   *Easy*
Since Kim wanted to disguise her lack of interest in the lecture, the second blank should be filled by a word that suggests trickery or deceit. *Habit*, *pattern*, and *means* do not have that connotation. The word to complete the first blank should mean "something that suggests that one is paying attention". *Sloppy* has an opposite connotation, so even though a *stratagem* is a clever or underhanded scheme, this is not a correct choice. *Profuse*, meaning "in great quantity", and *facade*, a deceptive appearance or attitude, is the best choice.

3. **(C)** Two-Word Direct   *Moderate*
Since maintaining world peace is a praiseworthy goal, the word that belongs in the second blank should have a positive connotation, so the choice including *condemnation* can be eliminated. The portion of a funeral ceremony in which the deceased is spoken about is not part of the *prayers* or *hymns*, eliminating those two responses. While *rhetoric…cheers* is a logical answer, *rhetoric* sometimes has negative connotations, and it is inappropriate to cheer at a funeral. An *elegy*, a speech given in praise of a deceased per-

son, is the best choice for the first blank, and *kudos*, for the second blank, means "praise for an achievement".

4. **(E)** Two-Word Direct   *Moderate*
The words that belong in the blanks should be characteristics that do not provoke confrontation. *Contention* and *anger* would provoke a strong reaction. *Pathos* and *despair* both mean "sadness", but the demonstrators' personal emotions are irrelevant to a confrontation. *Rectitude* means "moral rightness", so this word looks like a possible answer, but *etiquette* is "correct behavior in social situations" and would not refer to a demonstration. *Pacifism* would clearly be correct, but the other word in this choice, *hostility*, contradicts *pacifism*.
  Choice E uses *forbearance*, which means "restraint in making demands or voicing disapproval", and *fortitude*, or strength, can refer to physical or moral steadfastness or courage.

5. **(B)** Two-Word Direct   *Easy*
Since the situation required reform, the first word must have negative connotations. *Horrific, appalling*, and *disgusting* could all be correct. The *horrific* environments might have *provided a reason* for his campaign, but they could not logically provide the campaign itself, nor could *disgusting* environments *pursue* a campaign. *Appalling*, so bad as to be shocking, and *instigated*, urged or goaded to begin something, is therefore the correct answer.

6. **(C)** Two-Word Direct   *Moderate*
All of the choices for the first word are possible answers, so the best way to choose an answer is to focus on the second word. Since the sentence indicates that the charges were denied, *logical* and *credible* can be eliminated. *Potable*, meaning "safe to drink", can also be eliminated, since it does not make sense in context. Of the remaining answers, to simply make an accusation is usually not *illegal*. The remaining choice, *fabricated*, made up or invented, and *fallacious*, incorrect or misleading, is correct.

7. **(A)** Two-Word Direct   *Difficult*
Deceived indicates that Cassio did not know what was happening. *Posthumously* means "after death", so it would not make sense in the first blank. *Noxiously*, harmfully, and *virulently*, poisonously, would make Cassio's actions unhelpful, and would thus contradict the sense of the sentence. *Extremely* and *compliant* looks like a good choice; even if one is deceived, the deceiver may make use of him. *Inutile*, however, means "not useful". *Unwittingly*, meaning "unknowingly", and *complicit*, meaning "acting as an accomplice in a wrongful act", is the correct choice.

8.   **(E)**   Two-Word Direct   *Moderate*

Maudlin can be eliminated, because if the suggestions were helpful, they would not be weakly sentimental. *Hackneyed* means "unoriginal and trite", so that choice also is incorrect. The suggestions could have been *helpful, complex,* or *trenchant,* so the key is to look at the choices for the second word. *Line* can be eliminated, because much of the dialogue needed to be changed. *Mandate* means "a command or an order" and does not make sense in the sentence. *Trenchant,* articulate and clear-cut, and *preponderance,* superior in quantity, or most, is the best answer.

9.   **(B)**   Two-Word direct   *Difficult*

Predict suggests that the writers saw into the future, which is exactly what *prescient* means. *Ensue* means "to follow or result from". The writers may have been *pessimistic,* but if the civil disorders *evanesced,* they evaporated. *Omniscient,* meaning "all-knowing", is too absolute to describe their writings. *Dissonant,* which means "out of tune with popular opinion", might be a good choice if these writers were in the minority, but the sentence does not indicate whether or not that was the case. The second word of this choice, *promulgate,* to proclaim, does not fit the context. *Magnanimous,* meaning "generous", would not describe the writers' knowledge of the future; however, *fulminate,* meaning "to explode", might be a good choice.

10.   **(B)**   Two-Word Direct   *Difficult*

The key to the correct choice is the phrase *even by* in the second half of the sentence, which refers to those who agree with portions of Darwin's theories. Thus, choices using *critics* and *detractors* as the second word can be eliminated. Because of the second half of the sentence, the missing word in the first half must mean something like "those who find the theory at least partially valid". *Complete* is not a good choice, because if it were complete, no criticism would be required. *Mesmerizing* means "completely enthralling or hypnotic", and again, this would be interpreted as "not subject to criticism". In the correct choice, *inviolate* means "secure from assault", and *proponents* refer to those who advocate a theory.

4. Two-Word Contrast Sentences

Like one-word contrast sentence completions, two-word contrast sentences have some sort of internal shift in direction, where one side of the sentence is set against the other. These contrasts are usually marked by change-of-direction hinge words. In some instances, the contrast is created by progression in which what was true *back then* is no longer the case *now*. Below are examples of hinge word and non-hinge word two-word contrast sentence completions.

About five of the sentence completions on the SAT will be of this type.

Two-Word Contrasts with a Hinge Word

We'll give examples of an easy and a difficult hinge-word question. Notice that difficult questions have more advanced vocabulary *and* more sophisticated ideas.

> Although the lives of the highest officials of the oppressive government are filled with luxury and ----, the general populace lives in terrible ----.
>
> (A)   pain..joy
> (B)   splendor..poverty
> (C)   love..friendship
> (D)   comfort..cruelty
> (E)   anger..corruption

With the obvious hinge word of "Although," this sentence clearly sets the living experience of the "highest officials" against that of the "general populace." The word "luxury," used in reference to the life of the high officials, functions as a clue and makes it clear that their life is good and filled with riches—the general populace must be poor and unfortunate. As you go through the answers, the only one that fits is **splendor . . poverty.**

> Faulkner's use of intense, adjective-filled language in his novels is now accepted as an essential aspect of his style and a product of his literary ----; but when his fiction was first published, many critics often ---- his style as needlessly ornate.
>
> (A)   proclivities..extolled
> (B)   descrimination..praised
> (C)   abilities..examined
> (D)   genius..decried
> (E)   bombast..enlightened

Obviously, this sentence is slightly longer, a little more grammatically complex, and involves more sophisticated vocabulary and concepts than the previous example did. However, the basic method for finding an answer is the same. The presence of the word "but" in the sentence should tell you that this is a contrast sentence, and you should then realize that the response of the early critics to Faulkner's work is very different from the modern response. Further, the words "essential aspect of his style" in the clause about the modern response and the words "needlessly ornate" in the clause about the early critics should give you the sense that the modern response is positive while many early critics responded negatively to Faulkner's style.

Therefore, the word that fills the first blank must allow the first clause to be positive, while the word for the second blank should make the second clause negative. You can eliminate *proclivities . . extolled* and *descrimination . . praised* because "extolled" and "praised" are positive actions in which critics who saw flaws in Faulkner's work would not engage. *Bombast . . enlightened* can also be thrown out since its words just don't make sense in the sentence. That leaves (C), *abilities . . examined,* and **(D), genius . . decried.** (D) is a much better choice, since "examined" in (C) doesn't fit the context of the sentence.

Two-Word Contrasts Without a Hinge Word

Non-hinge contrast sentences are much less common than hinged ones. Those that you do come across will almost always be difficult. Such non-hinged sentences usually focus on time and how things have changed through time.

> The student found it ironic that the medieval belief that bathing was bad for one's ---- actually helped to create the ---- conditions that resulted in plagues and epidemics.

(A) behavior..superb
(B) relations..specific
(C) development..ideal
(D) standards..unfortunate
(E) well-being..unsanitary

The word "irony" as it is used in this sentence should function as a clue that the way people acted or thought actually had the opposite effect than the one they expected. You should also have a good idea that the first blank discusses issues of disease or health since the second half of the sentence says that beliefs about *something* "ironically" brought about "plagues and epidemics." With that knowledge, you should quickly be able to pick out **well-being . . unsanitary** as the correct answer, since only this choice deals with issues of health or well-being, while also logically filling the second blank with the word "unsanitary."

Two-Word Contrast Questions

1. In western movies, the villains are sometimes ----, contrasting with the bold and ----hero.

    (A) pusillanimous…steadfast
    (B) bold…shaky
    (C) virile…manly
    (D) immoral…pretentious
    (E) calculating…ignorant

2. Stories of a flood destroying the world are ---- in ancient cultures, but few of them ---- the event to an angry god.

    (A) rare…conceed
    (B) shocking…sacrifice
    (C) trivial…relate
    (D) ubiquitous…attribute
    (E) lengthy…contribute.

3. Trying to cheer up a sick friend may ---- the situation rather than providing ----.

    (A) exacerbate…solace
    (B) terminate…companionship
    (C) satiate…anxiety
    (D) provoke…solicitude
    (E) enlighten…tremors

4. To some audiences, Shakespeare's language may seem ----, but his characters and themes nevertheless ----.

   (A) confusing...procreate
   (B) grandiose...levitate
   (C) archaic...resonate
   (D) magnanimous...jibe
   (E) affected...concur

5. Although the Fifth Amendment to the U.S. Constitution ---- being forced to testify against one's self, those who ---- this privilege are often criticized.

   (A) recommends...petition against
   (B) provokes...violate
   (C) instigates...amend
   (D) exhorts...regurgitate
   (E) proscribes...invoke

6. Rather than resulting from ---- fate, the actions of a tragic hero ---- his downfall.

   (A) querulous...rebuke
   (B) considerate...reward
   (C) capricious...precipitate
   (D) deliberative...conclude
   (E) amusing...maintain

7. To avoid conviction, Galileo ---- his disfavored views that had caused him to be put on trial, yet legend suggests that he ---- that action by whispering "but the Earth does move."

   (A) rescinded...repeated
   (B) propounded...quelled
   (C) promulgated...formulated
   (D) recanted...revoked
   (E) announced...invented

8. Originally thought to be a(n) ---- for people who suffer from back pain, the drug provided only a(n) ---- of relief and had some dangerous side effects.

   (A) miracle...plethora
   (B) advance..excess
   (C) disappointment...minimum
   (D) panacea...modicum
   (E) indication...surplus

9. Jeered and ---- at its premier in 1913, Stravinsky's music for the ballet "The Rite of Spring" today ---- the spirit of modernism.

   (A) cheered...delights
   (B) reviled...embodies
   (C) detonated...thrills
   (D) assaulted...coerces
   (E) lauded...dissimulates

10.   An irony in *Great Expectations* is that Magwitch's ---- gifts to Pip cause him to squander his
        fortune, reducing him to ----.

    (A)   consummate...solitude
    (B)   beneficial...conviviality
    (C)   frugal...beggary
    (D)   munificent...penury
    (E)   generous...opulence

Two-Word Contrast Answers

1.   **(A)**   Two-Word Contrast   *Easy*
Contrasting with, the hinge, indicates the negative qualities of the villain and the positive ones of the hero. *Virile* and *manly* can be eliminated; both are positive and are synonyms. *Immoral* is negative, but *pretentious*, meaning "faking behavior to impress others", does not describe a hero. *Bold* and *shaky* express the positive quality of the villain and the negative quality of the hero. *Calculating* can be positive or negative, but the missing word for the second blank, *ignorant*, is not a positive attribute. *Pusillanimous*, meaning "cowardly", and *steadfast*, meaning "strength in upholding one's principles", is the best choice.

2.   **(D)**   Two-Word Contrast   *Easy*
The hinge word, *but*, indicates a contrast between the word describing flood stories and the first blank, and the idea in the second half of the sentence that *few* of them do whatever fits in the second blank. *Rare* can be eliminated because it means the same as *few*. *Trivial* means "something small and unimportant". *Lengthy* describes a characteristic of the stories, so it does not contrast with *few*. These observations leave two choices for the first blank. Although the stories might have been *shocking*, the choice for the second blank, *sacrifice*, does not make sense, because sacrifices were material objects, not stories. The only possible answer is *ubiquitous*, which means "widespread" or "appearing to be everywhere", and *attribute*, which means "to give credit to or assign cause".

3.   **(A)**   Two-Word Contrast   *Moderate*
Rather than implies that trying to cheer the person up does not work. Therefore, the first blank requires a negative word, and the second blank requires a positive one. Answers C and E can be eliminated, because *anxiety* and *tremors* are not positive. *Terminate* means "to end a situation", but the sentence does not suggest that either the friendship or the illness would come to an end. To *provoke* means "to cause someone to react"; thus, it would not make sense, even though *solicitude* will fit in the second

blank. *Exacerbate* means "to increase the severity of something", and *solace* means "comfort". These words fit the blanks.

4. **(C)** Two-Word Contrast   *Moderate*
The contrast is between language of the past and reactions in the present. *Confusing* can describe a modern audience's reaction to Shakespeare's language, but *procreate*, meaning "to have children", does not make sense. *Grandiose* language, which means "exaggerated", may work, but *levitate*, meaning "rise in the air", does not fit the sentence.

    Magnanimous means "generous", and while Shakespeare's language may be described in that way, this choice will not provide a contrast between past and present. The language may seem *affected*, used simply to create an elevated impression, but that will not *concur*, which means "to agree with modern audiences". In the correct answer, *archaic* means "outdated", and *resonate* means "to create a profound emotional impact in an audience".

5. **(E)** Two-Word Contrast   *Moderate*
The hinge word, *although*, indicates that something is legal, according to the U. S. Constitution event, even though it is criticized. The second blank must mean something like "use." Thus, *violate* and *amend* can be eliminated. *Petition*, meaning "to ask for formally", is a possibility, as is *regurgitate*, "to repeat what one has heard without thinking about it". The tricky part is that the first missing word should make reference to something that the Constitution permits one to do. However, what it permits is something that one can *not* be forced to do, so a negative word is needed. Therefore, *recommends* can be eliminated, and so can *exhorts*, meaning "advises strongly". *Proscribes*, meaning "forbids", and *invoke*, meaning "to call on" or "call for", is the only possible answer.

6. **(C)** Two-Word Contrast   *Difficult*
The second half of the sentence needs a word meaning "to cause directly". The hinge word, *rather*, indicates that the first missing word means something like "accidental". *Considerate* and *reward* do not provide this contrast. Neither do *deliberative* and *conclude*.

    Querulous, meaning "complaining", and *rebuke*, meaning "to scold", also do not fit. Since the subject is tragedy, *amusing* can not be a possibility. *Capricious*, meaning "based on a whim", and *precipitate*, to cause, especially to cause suddenly, is the correct choice.

7. **(D)** Two-Word Contrast   *Difficult*
Even though *yet* indicates that there is a contrast between the meaning of the two halves of the sentence, the correct answer involves two words with a similar meaning. He did something to avoid conviction, and then he contradicted what he had done.

Since the views were *disfavored*, he would have to deny them. *Rescinded* and *repeated* do not have similar meanings. If he *propounded* the beliefs, he argued for them, which does not make sense if they were disfavored. *Promulgated* and *formulated* have similar meanings, "to argue for or set forth ideas", but they contradict the sense of the sentence. *Announced* and *inverted* do not make sense in the sentence. *Recant* means "to renounce views formerly held", and *revoke* means "to take back", and is therefore the correct answer.

8. **(D)** Two-Word Contrast   *Moderate*
There is not a hinge word, but the second half of the sentence suggests that the drug did not function as intended. It caused side effects, and because it did not help people who suffered back pain, the second missing word should be a one that indicates a lack of quality. *Plethora*, *surplus*, and *excess* can be eliminated. Of the remaining choices, if the drug was a *disappointment*, there would be no contrast, so *disappointment* and *minimum* can be eliminated. *Panacea*, meaning "a cure for all ills or problems", and *modicum*, a small amount, is the best choice.

9. **(B)** Two-Word Contrast   *Difficult*
Although there is not a hinge word, the context of the sentence makes it clear there is a contrast between the unfavorable reaction when the ballet was first presented and the favorable criticism of it now. The word in the first blank must have negative connotations, so *cheered* and *lauded*, meaning "praised", can be eliminated. *Detonated* means "exploded", but it would be the criticism that was explosive, not the music. *Assaulted* would be a good choice, but the word for the second blank, *coerces*, means "forces", and it does not describe what the music does. In the correct choice, *reviled* means "criticized with strong language", and to *embody* is to represent in material form.

10. **(D)** Two-Word Contrast   *Difficult*
The word "irony" indicates that the missing words describe a situation in which the opposite of what was intended is the result. The words *squander*, meaning "to use wastefully", and *reduce* are further clues. If Pip squandered a fortune, he does not have money left. *Opulence* means "wealth", so that choice can be eliminated. *Conviviality* means "sociability", and although a person who became poor might become sociable, it would not be ironic if *beneficial* gifts caused that result. *Frugal* means "stingy", so there would be no irony if the gifts resulted in *beggary*. It would be ironic, though, if *munificent* gifts, meaning "extremely generous" ones, led to *penury,* or extreme poverty.

5. Other Types of Sentence Completions

There are some types of sentence completions that do not fit into any of these categories. Luckily, these "other" sentence completions aren't all that common: almost 90 percent of all sentence completions will fit into the categories we've described above. Also, you can be sure that only two-word completions make up the "other" category. All one-word completions will either be direct or contrast.

Because they can vary quite widely, there is no way to provide you with examples of *all* of these other sentence completions. But rest assured that these other sentences are just as decodable as the sentences we've just covered. If you follow the standard procedure, paying attention to hinge words and tracking the flow of a sentence, you should be able to figure out how the two blanks function and relate within the sentence. Once you've done that, you'll be able to choose the words that correctly fill the blanks, or, if the vocabulary gives you trouble, you'll at least be able to eliminate answers that are obviously wrong and guess from among the remaining choices.

Other Questions

1.   The plots of romantic comedies are ----; boy and girl always meet and feel either instant --- or immediate disharmony, misunderstandings follow, and an unexpected plot twist brings the couple together.

    (A)   fungible...rapport
    (B)   predictable...dislike
    (C)   surprising...affection
    (D)   misanthropic...distraction
    (E)   mendacious...contempt

2.   When the ---- waiter asked the diners every few minutes if they needed anything, their annoyance at these interruptions caused him to ---- his tip.

    (A)   helpful...increase
    (B)   obsequious...forfeit
    (C)   dimunitive...surrender
    (D)   irate...establish
    (E)   conscientious...enlarge

3.   As a child, Maya Angelou found the adult world ----, and her confusion wasnot ---- when she reached adolescence.

    (A)   chaotic...multiplied
    (B)   lucid...succored
    (C)   incomprehensible...alleviated
    (D)   poignant...substantiated
    (E)   understandable..removed

4.   The American legal system requires each state to provide attorneys for criminal defendants who cannot afford to hire them, but ---- procedures to ensure representation of ---- have not been adopted nationally.

   (A)   generous...peasants
   (B)   unequal...citizens
   (C)   proportional...philanthropists
   (D)   uniform...indigents
   (E)   ineffective...dissidents

5.   Wishing to remain anonymous, the heroine of the play, disguised as a man, ---- the harlequin not to ---- her true identity.

   (A)   challenges...indicate
   (B)   requires...conceal
   (C)   orders...obscure
   (D)   permits...illuminate
   (E)   implores...divulge

Other Answers

1.   **(A)**   *Moderate*
The word "always" is the clue to this question. It suggests that the plots repeat themselves. In the second half of the sentence, *or* indicates that the missing word means the opposite of "disharmony". Thus, *dislike, distraction* and *contempt* can be eliminated. Of the two remaining choices, *surprising...affection* will not work, because if the plots were surprising, they would not always be the same. In the correct choice, *fungible* means "interchangeable", and *rapport* means "mutual understanding".

2.   **(B)**   *Easy*
If the diners were annoyed, they would not give the waiter a tip. Thus, *increase* and *enlarge* can be eliminated, because these words are positive, and yet, the waiter's behavior could only *establish* his tip in a negative way.

   Surrender might be a good choice, but describing the waiter as *diminutive*, or very small, is unrelated to his actions. His *obsequious,* or excessively compliant, comments caused him to *forfeit* his tip, to give up what he otherwise would have deserved.

3.   **(C)**   *Easy*
The second half of the sentence indicates that the confusion she experienced as a child continued as she grew older. So, it was not *removed.* That her confusion was not *multiplied* suggests that it got no worse, so this is a possible answer. *Substantiated* means "proven to be so by evidence", which does not make sense when applied to *confusion.* *Succored* means "to give help to one in need", which does not fit the context. For the

first blank, *incomprehensible* is the word closest in meaning to *confused*, and *alleviated*, meaning "reduced in severity", is the best choice for the second blank.

4. **(D)**   *Moderate*

The clue to the second blank is in the first part of the sentence. For what kind of people are states required to provide attorneys? They must provide them for those who can not afford them. Thus, *philanthropists*, people who give a great deal of money to charity, can not be correct. The word *peasants* does not apply to any recognized group of Americans. *Dissidents* are people with views different from established ones, and they are not necessarily poor, while *citizens* can be of any economic status. *Indigents*, people with little or no money, is the only possible choice. The second half of the sentence implies that the procedures are not national; rather, they differ from state to state, so they are not *uniform*.

5. **(E)**   *Easy*

Because the heroine wants her disguise to be kept a secret, she wants it to remain hidden. Therefore, she would like to conceal or obscure her identity.

To *challenge* the other character would imply a contest between them. If she *forbid* him not to *illuminate* it, he would be forced to reveal it, which is the opposite of the sentence's meaning. She *implores*, or strongly begs, that he not reveal something secret or *divulge* who she is.

Don't Know the Vocabulary? There's Still Hope

There may be some questions for which you simply don't know some of the vocabulary included in the answer choices or in the sentence. While this can be frustrating, you should not immediately write off these questions as unanswerable. First, even if you don't know the precise meaning of a vocabulary word, you may have a sense of whether it has a positive or negative connotation. In that case, you might very well be able to go through the sentence and figure out what type of word (positive or negative) needs to be used to fill the blank. It's quite possible that only one word out of all the answer choices might fit the type of word you need. More likely, though, you'll be able to eliminate some of the answer choices based on the criteria of positive or negative connotation, which will put you in a strong position to guess.

If the sentence completion is simply too hard, or if you think that it will take you a tremendous amount of time to eliminate even a few answer choices, then you should skip the question, marking it as one you might want to return to. The time you spend answering that question would be better used answering several easy and moderate analogy or reading comprehension questions.

Sentence Completion – Unit Test

1. The boss gave Marcie the promotion because of her ----; she always gets the job done quickly.

   (A) expedience
   (B) laboriousness
   (C) reticence
   (D) frugality
   (E) pathos

2. During his speech, Alex continuously wiped sweat off of his brow, signaling his ----.

   (A) ambivalence
   (B) brashness
   (C) tactfulness
   (D) agitation
   (E) tranquility

3. Aspirin has recently been lauded as a ----; many experts believe that it can ---- all sorts of illnesses.

   (A) blight...exacerbate
   (B) plague...exaggerate
   (C) panacea...alleviate
   (D) paregoric...induce
   (E) pandemic...incite

4. Drinking one alcoholic drink per day is strongly ---- by many doctors for its health benefits.

   (A) advocated
   (B) dictated
   (C) forbidden
   (D) disallowed
   (E) banned

5. Rita was obviously ---- about her last boyfriend's behavior; she shredded his picture into tiny pieces and muttered under her breath after their breakup.

   (A) incensed
   (B) apprehensive
   (C) apathetic
   (D) ignorant
   (E) sentimental

6. The ballet teacher ---- her students often; she would not accept ---- effort.

   (A) pampered...strenuous
   (B) placated...arduous
   (C) patronized...minimal
   (D) lambasted...trivial
   (E) persecuted...minute

7.   Many people were ---- when the quiet, prudent science teacher suddenly eloped.

    (A)   flabbergasted
    (B)   petulant
    (C)   affable
    (D)   indifferent
    (E)   disinterested

8.   Sheri has always been ----; her last high test score ---- her brilliance.

    (A)   inane...belied
    (B)   astute...underscored
    (C)   ostentatious...disproved
    (D)   ingenious...miscast
    (E)   boorish...reiterated

9.   Running is a ---- sport; as a result, runners often experience ---- effects of running, such as shin splints, twisted ankles, and knee problems.

    (A)   lackadaisical...euphoric
    (B)   rigorous...deleterious
    (C)   arduous...admirable
    (D)   leisure...unfortunate
    (E)   taxing...gratifying

10.   Because Miss Jones never married and has five cats, many take her for a(n) ---- old maid.

    (A)   fastidious
    (B)   atypical
    (C)   obstreperous
    (D)   bellicose
    (E)   obtuse

11.   Although the students liked the new professor, they found his class to be ---- because of its weekly tests, quizzes, and lengthy papers.

    (A)   facile
    (B)   pedantic
    (C)   bovine
    (D)   arduous
    (E)   animated

12.   Because of his bad behavior toward women, attendance at wild parties, and excessive drinking, Chris was known as a ----.

    (A)   rapscallion
    (B)   clergyman
    (C)   knight
    (D)   dandy
    (E)   youngster

13. At first, the stylish, trendy store was a(n) ---- success, serving hundreds of customers each day; however, after its prices soared, it lost its appeal.

(A) marginal
(B) moderate
(C) modest
(D) immense
(E) reasonable

14. Margie kept hearing ---- noises in her house; however, she thought she was ---- until a rat scampered across the floor one evening.

(A) commonplace…deluded
(B) extraordinary…foolhardy
(C) daunting…cognizant
(D) astounding…intuitive
(E) foreign…discerning

15. John could tell from the look of ---- on Bonnie's face that she was not happy to see him.

(A) consternation
(B) nonchalance
(C) ignorance
(D) felicity
(E) incredulity

16. A job in which one is paid solely on commissions can often be ----, since income is never guaranteed.

(A) tenuous
(B) consoling
(C) opportune
(D) rigid
(E) astounding

17. Because of her downcast eyes and shy smile, Nancy is viewed as ---- by most people.

(A) lugubrious
(B) demure
(C) ingenious
(D) raucous
(E) derisive

18. The seasoned employees did not appreciate the young man's ---- attitude.

(A) compliant
(B) unpretentious
(C) amicable
(D) perfidious
(E) reputable

19. Lara could not get used to the ---- northern weather; the snow never seemed to ----.

    (A) blustery...dissipate
    (B) temperate...commence
    (C) balmy...evaporate
    (D) moderate...cease
    (E) tempestuous...accrue

20. Although the speaker had ---- ideas, he could not seem to organize them and was described by many listeners as ----.

    (A) intriguing...discombobulated
    (B) vapid...eloquent
    (C) pedantic...loquacious
    (D) base...glib
    (E) spirited...voluble

21. Scientists have recently stated that *acrylimide*, a chemical found in some fried foods, may be ---- to the development of fetuses, causing cancer later in life.

    (A) detrimental
    (B) salutary
    (C) amicable
    (D) advantageous
    (E) salubrious

22. Ryan has one very --- habit: he always picks his nose in public.

    (A) hale
    (B) robust
    (C) noxious
    (D) cultivated
    (E) refined

23. Nat King Cole was a(n) ---- jazz singer whose voice still echoes on radio today; interestingly, he always ---- the many cigarettes he smoked each day as his secret.

    (A) mediocre...hailed
    (B) phenomenal...credited
    (C) incompetent...praised
    (D) groveling...lauded
    (E) liminal...extolled

24. Stress during pregnancy ---- the risk of early delivery; such women may deliver on or before 37 weeks of pregnancy.

    (A) modifies
    (B) exacerbates
    (C) decimates
    (D) alleviates
    (E) denigrates

25. Lucy often blames her lack of friends on her ----, although she is not extremely overweight.

    (A)   comeliness
    (B)   gauntness
    (C)   corpulence
    (D)   svelteness
    (E)   fecundity

26. Joe is a(n) ---- actor who always keeps his audiences entertained; however, he only lands ---- roles that do not pay his bills.

    (A)   brilliant…acclaimed
    (B)   inane…scant
    (C)   inept…grandiose
    (D)   adroit…paltry
    (E)   apt…glamorous

27. Sally has a(n) ---- nature; she seems to float in and out of rooms without people noticing her.

    (A)   ephemeral
    (B)   stolid
    (C)   garrulous
    (D)   ghastly
    (E)   obsequious

28. Lorna always thought that raising children would be ---- since her own mother raised six children with seemingly no effort; however, she told me that it is the most ---- task she has ever performed.

    (A)   facile…minute
    (B)   uncomplicated…severe
    (C)   leisurely…eccentric
    (D)   laborious…perplexing
    (E)   harrowing…ghastly

29. Alan always chooses the most ---- Halloween costume each year; last year he was Dracula, and he frightened everyone out of their wits with his fangs, fake blood and generally ---- appearance.

    (A)   benign..comely
    (B)   ghastly..gory
    (C)   ostentatious..radiant
    (D)   macabre..celestial
    (E)   titillating..naive

30. Mark realized too late that Anna's intentions were ----; she tricked him before he knew what had happened.

    (A)   benevolent
    (B)   virtuous
    (C)   perfidious
    (D)   insolent
    (E)   mundane

Sentence Completions

Answers and Explanations

1. **(A)** One-Word direct   *Moderate*

The clue word "quickly," suggests that the missing word is a synonym of this word. So, *laboriousness* would not work since it implies slow labor, and neither would *reticence,* since it means "slow to do something". Likewise, *frugality* has nothing to do with speed, and *pathos*, or sympathy, does not either. So, the correct answer is (A), expedience.

2. **(D)** One-Word direct   *Moderate*

Because wiping sweat off of one's brow usually signals nervousness, the word that fits in the blank should be one with a similar meaning. Thus, *ambivalence* can be eliminated since it means "confusion about an issue". Likewise, *brashness* may be deleted as a possibility since it implies boldness. *Tactfulness* and *tranquility* may also be eliminated as choices since the speaker is neither mannerly or at peace. The correct answer is then (D), *agitation*.

3. **(C)** Two words   *Moderate*

Because of the clue word "lauded," one can expect the blanks to be filled with positive words. Thus, choices (A), (B), and (E) may all be eliminated since they refer to worldwide diseases. Choice (D) may also be eliminated since *paregoric* refers to an opium tincture. Thus, the correct answer is (C), *panacea*, meaning "remedy or cure-all".

4. **(A)** One-Word direct   *Easy*

Because having one drink a day has health benefits, it may be assumed that doctors want patients to consume one drink per day. Thus, answers (C), (D), and (E) may be eliminated. Answer (B) seems like a good choice, but most doctors would not have *dictated* that a patient do anything. Thus, (A), *advocated*, meaning "suggested", is the best answer.

5. **(A)** One-Word direct   *Moderate*

Since Rita's behavior suggests anger, a synonym of that emotion would likely fit in the blank. Thus, (B), (C), (D), and (E) can quickly be eliminated since they do not suggest anger. The correct choice is (A), *incensed*.

6. **(D)** One-Word direct   *Moderate*

The ballet teacher obviously pushes her students to do their best. Thus, the first words, *pampered*, *placated*, and *patronized* must rule out (A), (B), and (C) as possible answers. Answer (E) can be ruled out because it is too harsh. A good teacher would never have *persecuted* her students. Thus, (D), *lambasted...trivial*, meaning "to assault verbally...unimportant", is the correct answer.

7. **(A)** One-Word direct   *Moderate*
Because her actions are surprising, the answer should reflect people's stunned reaction. Thus, (D) and (E) may be immediately ruled out since these words mean "not surprised". Also, (B) may be eliminated since a *petulant*, or angry, reaction would not fit the situation. (C) may be done away with, as well, since the people were not necessarily *affable*, or agreeable, to such an occurence. Thus, (A), *flabbergasted*, is the correct answer.

8. **(B)** Two words   *Moderate*
Since the sentence states that Sheri is brilliant, the first blank should have a word that means the same as the word "brilliant." (A), *inane*, meaning "stupid", (C), *ostentatious*, meaning "pretentious", and (E), *boorish*, meaning "rude", can all be eliminated because none of these mean "brilliant." Answer (D) can be deleted as an option because of the word *miscast*. Thus, the correct answer is (B), *astute* (clever) *...underscored*.

9. **(B)** Two words   *Moderate*
The construction of this sentence implies a relationship between the type of sport that running is and the physical effects it wreaks on the body. Thus, (A), (D), and (E) may be eliminated since running and its effects are not properly paired. Answer (C) will not work, because injuries such as those listed are not *admirable*. Thus, the answer is (B), *rigorous* (demanding)..*deleterious* (harmful).

10. **(A)** One-Word direct   *Easy*
Because Miss Jones is described as a stereotypical old maid, it seems that a typical descriptor would fit in the blank. So, (B), (C), *obstreperous*, meaning "noisy", (D), *bellicose*, meaning "warlike", and (E), *obtuse*, meaning "dense or dull", can all be eliminated since they would not be logical answers. The correct answer is (A), *fastidious*, meaning "particular" or "given to routine".

11. **(D)** One-Word direct   *Moderate*
The major clue in this sentence is the list of the assignments and tasks that the class requires. Since there are so many requirements, one might assume that the class is difficult. Thus, the most logical answer would be (D), *arduous*. Unfamiliar vocabulary may include these words: *facile* (easy), *pedantic* (showing off one's knowledge), and *bovine* (cow-like).

12. **(A)** One-Word direct *Moderate*

Because of his bad behavior, one would expect the answer to be descriptive of a man with such behavior. Thus, *knight, youngster*, and *clergyman* can be immediately eliminated. *Dandy* might seem to be a good answer, but it is more descriptive of a man who is very concerned with dress and social appearances. So, *rapscallion*, (A), is the best answer.

13. **(D)** One-Word direct *Easy*

Because this store serviced hundreds of customers when it first opened, one might assume that it experienced more than a *marginal, moderate, reasonable*, or *modest* success. It was an *immense* success, (D).

14. **(B)** Two words *Moderate*

Answer (A) may be eliminated since the sounds are apparently not *commonplace*, or everyday sounds. (C), (D), and (E) may be removed as choices, too, because the second word in each pair does not describe the woman's skepticism of what she hears. However, (B) does. Thus, the answer is *extraordinary…foolhardy*.

15. **(A)** One-Word direct *Moderate*

Since Bonnie does not look happy to see John, the word that fits in the blank has something to do with sadness or anger. Thus, *felicity*, or happiness, can be ruled out, as can *nonchalance*, or indifference. *Ignorance* can also be eliminated since someone showing ignorance would probably be neither happy nor sad. Also, *incredulity* may be removed since it simply means that something is "not believable" and "only intimates surprise". So, the correct answer is (A), *consternation*, meaning "anger".

16. **(A)** One-Word direct *Moderate*

It stands to reason that a job worked solely on commission would be uncertain. Thus, the word that fits in the blank is most likely a synonym of the word "uncertain." *Consoling* and *opportune* can quickly be eliminated, as they are positive words, and such a job would certainly have its ups and downs. *Astounding* does not make sense in the sentence and can be removed as an option. Likewise, a job based on commission would not be *rigid*, or predictable, so that choice may be eliminated. Clearly, the answer is (A), *tenuous*, meaning "uncertain."

17. **(B)** One-Word direct *Moderate*

Because of her mannerisms, Nancy might be described as shy. So, *raucous*, meaning "loud and noisy", can be ruled out as an answer. Also, *lugubrious*, meaning "mournful", can be eliminated. Likewise, *ingenious* and *derisive* may be removed as options because they do not logically link with shyness. So, the correct answer is (B), *demure*, or shy.

18. **(D)** One-Word direct   *Moderate*
(A), (B), (C), and (E) may be ruled out as answers since seasoned employees would have no problem with a person described in friendly and respectable terms. The correct answer, then, is (D), *perfidious*, meaning "dishonest."

19. **(A)** Two words   *Moderate*
(B), (C), and (D) may be ruled out since these adjectives do not usually describe snowy, cold conditions. *Tempestuous* is tempting, but its partnered word, *accrue*, does not make sense. So, the answer is (A).

20. **(A)** Two words   *Moderate*
(B), *vapid*, meaning "boring", (C), *pedantic*, or showing off one's knowledge, and (D), *base*, which means "of the lowest level", may be ruled out as answers since the speaker obviously has interesting content and the first words of each of these pairs contradicts that notion. (E) does not work because of the last word, *voluble*, meaning "talkative." Disorganized and talkative are not synonyms; thus, answer (A) is correct.

21. **(A)** One-Word direct   *Easy*
(B), (C), (D), and (E) may be eliminated since all of them suggest that this chemical is harmless or even healthy for fetuses. Thus, (A), *detrimental*, meaning "harmful", is the correct answer.

22. **(C)** One-Word direct   *Moderate*
(A) and (B) may be eliminated since both of these words mean "healthy", and this habit certainly is not a healthy one. (D) and (E) may also be removed as options since both of these choices mean "mannerly." So, answer (C), *noxious*, meaning "disgusting", is the correct answer.

23. **(B)** Two words   *Moderate*
Because Cole's songs are still played on the radio today, one may assume that he was a very popular singer. Thus, all of the pairs may be eliminated, except for (B), since they make light of his talent or cast him as a mediocre singer. So, the correct answer is (B). Unfamiliar vocabulary may include these words: (D), *groveling*, which means "crawling", and (E), *liminal*, which pertains to threshold.

24. **(B)** One-Word direct   *Moderate*
(A) may be ruled out because of the evidence in the sentence that suggests that stress increases the possibility of premature labor. (C), (D), and (E) may also be eliminated because all of these words mean that stress reduces the likelihood of premature labor. Thus, (B), *exacerbates*, meaning "to make worse", is the correct answer.

25. **(C)**   One-Word direct   *Easy*
Since that the sentence suggests that Lucy is large, or at least thinks she is overweight, the word that fits in the blank must be a synonym for obesity. Thus, (C) is the correct answer.

26. **(D)**   Two words   *Maximum*
(B) and (C) may be eliminated because context clues indicate that Joe is a good actor. (A) and (E) may also be removed, because they do not fit exactly into the context of the last blank. The word needed concerns a low-paying job. Thus, (D), *adroit*, meaning "clever", is the correct answer.

27. **(A)**   One-Word direct   *Moderate*
The clues in this sentence are that Sally seems to "float" and that no one notices her. Thus, her presence is fleeting, and she is (A), *ephemeral*.

28. **(B)**   Two words   *Moderate*
Since Lorna relies on her mother's own experience in raising children, she expects her own childrearing to be the same way. Thus, the first blank must be filled with a word meaning "easy." So, (D) and (E) may be omitted as answers. (B) is the best answer, because Lorna finds the task to be (B), *severe*, rather than *uncomplicated*.

29. **(B)**   Two words   *Moderate*
(A), (C), and (E) may be eliminated because one of the two words does not fit the idea of Halloween and Dracula. (D) looks good, at first, because of the word *macabre*, meaning "gory", but the word *celestial*, meaning "heavenly", does not work. So, the correct answer is (B).

30. **(C)**   One-Word direct   *Moderate*
(A), (B), and (E) are not compatible with out contextual clue, "tricked." Insolent might be a consideration, but it does not fit with a person who likes to deceive others. Thus, the correct answer is (C), *perfidious*, which means "faithless."

Analogies

T HE SAT INCLUDES 19 ANALOGIES, broken into two groups—one of 6 questions and one of 13. The two groups of analogies will appear on the two 30-minute verbal sections. In each case, the analogies will appear after the sentence completions and before the reading comprehension questions.

Analogy Instructions

Don't waste time reading the analogy instructions during the test. Instead, learn them now. Here are the instructions, as they appear on the SAT:

> Each question below consists of a related pair of words or phrases, followed by five pairs of words or phrases labeled A through E. Select the pair that <u>best</u> expresses a relationship similar to that expressed in the original pair.
>
> Example:
>
> CRUMB : BREAD ::
>
> (A)   ounce : unit
> (B)   splinter : wood
> (C)   water : bucket
> (D)   twine : rope
> (E)   cream : butter   Correct Answer: (B)

Format and Structure of an Analogy

The idea behind analogies is simple. ETS gives you two capitalized words that are related in some way, but you have to figure out their relationship. Then you have to go through a list of five other pairs of words and find the pair that has the same relationship as the capitalized pair. Every analogy will have the same format as the example below:

HAPPY : SMILE : :

(A)   friendly : milk
(B)   angry : lawnmower
(C)   loving : elevator
(D)   sad : frown
(E)   smart : intelligence

HAPPY : SMILE :: is the original pair of words, what we will call the "stem pair" from here on. The colon between the words means, "is related to." The double colon after the stem words means, "in the same way as." When you read the analogy above, you should read it as "HAPPY is related to SMILE in the same way as . . .", or you can shorten the sentence and just say, "HAPPY is to SMILE as . . ." Working through the analogy: "HAPPY is to SMILE as **sad** is to **frown.**

There are two structural issues of analogies that can affect the answer: the order of words in a stem or answer pair; and the parts of speech used in the analogies.

Word Order

In SAT analogies, the order of words in a pair is important. Let's say, for example, that the question above actually looked like this, with the answer pair in (D) flipped around:

HAPPY : SMILE ::

(A)   friendly : milk
(B)   angry : lawnmower
(C)   loving : elevator
(D)   frown : sad
(E)   smart : intelligence

Answer (D) was the correct answer in the last example, but is it now? Is HAPPY related to SMILE in the same way as *frown* is related to *sad*? No. When you look for the correct answer to an analogy, the answer you choose must not only contain words that relate to each other in the same way as the stem pair, but the two words of the answer pair must also follow the same *order* as the stem pair. In the example above, therefore, there is no correct answer (don't worry, every real SAT analogy will have a correct answer).

The SAT will definitely try to use word order to trick you during the test. Often the test will provide an answer pair that has the same association as the stem pair, except the answer pair will be flipped in the wrong direction. Be careful.

Parts of Speech

The parts of speech found in a stem pair will always be mirrored in the answer pairs. If, for example, both of the stem words are nouns, then every answer pair will be made up of two nouns. If the stem pair has a noun and a verb, then the answer pairs will always be a noun and a verb:

NOUN : NOUN ::

(A) noun : noun
(B) noun : noun
(C) noun : noun
(D) noun : noun
(E) noun : noun

NOUN : VERB ::

(A) noun : verb
(B) noun : verb
(C) noun : verb
(D) noun : verb
(E) noun : verb

Knowing this facet of analogy structure can help you on more difficult questions. ETS occasionally includes words that can function as more than one part of speech. Take a look at the following example:

COMPOUND : BUILDING ::

(A)   heart : life
(B)   trial : jury
(C)   forest : tree
(D)   tennis : ball
(E)   razor : hair

The word "compound" is most commonly used as a verb meaning "to combine," and your instinct will probably be to try to make a relation between the verb compound and the noun "building." If you were to do so, you wouldn't find an answer that fits among the answer choices. Instead, you should notice that all of the answer pairs follow the format NOUN : NOUN, meaning the stem pair must also be NOUN : NOUN. As a noun, compound means a group of buildings protected by a wall. The answer is **(C)**: just as a COMPOUND is composed of many BUILDINGS, so is a **forest** composed of many **trees.**

Answering Analogies: Making Sentences

Everyone from the test preparation companies to the College Board agrees: making a sentence that defines the specific relationship between the stem words is the single best way to answer an analogy. Once you have the sentence, you can easily test an answer choice by replacing each stem word with the corresponding word from the answer pair. Let's go back to the first example:

HAPPY : SMILE ::

(A)   owl : milk
(B)   lawnmower : anger
(C)   love : elevator
(D)   sad : frown
(E)   college : intelligence

A good sentence for this analogy is, "When people are happy, they smile." If you look at each of the answer choices, the only one that fits is **(D)**, "When people are sad, they frown."

Few of the analogies on the SAT will be quite this easy. Let's try one that's harder:

LIMB : BODY ::

(A)   eyes : view
(B)   cast : bone
(C)   branch : tree
(D)   surgery : injury
(E)   blade : grass

A sentence for this analogy is: a LIMB is part of a BODY. If you try out each of the answer pairs, you'll quickly see that only one fits your sentence: a **branch** is part of a **tree.**

Write the Most Specific Sentence Possible

The truth is, while the sentence "a limb is part of a body" turned out to be good enough for the last example, it wasn't actually the *best possible* sentence. The best possible sentence would have been more specific: "a limb is part of a body that extends from the main trunk."

As you'll see in the next example, having the most specific possible sentence can at times be very important:

METER : DISTANCE ::

(A)   runner : race
(B)   mile : exhaustion
(C)   hourglass : time
(D)   quart : volume
(E)   summer : heat

You might be tempted to make the following sentence for this analogy: A METER measures DISTANCE. As you searched for the answers you would come upon, "An **hourglass** measures **time**," fitting your sentence perfectly. And if you then happily put down (C) as your answer, you'd have gotten the question wrong. Woe is you! If you had only chosen a better, more specific sentence, none of this would have happened. For instance, if you came up with the more specific sentence: A METER is a single unit of DISTANCE measurement," then *hourglass* : *time* doesn't fit, since an hourglass isn't a unit of time. But **quart : volume** does fit perfectly, since a quart is a single unit of volume measurement.

Knowing When Your Sentence Is Good Enough

There's a simple way to determine whether the sentence you've created is specific enough: go through every answer pair. If more than one answer pair fits with your sentence, then go back and modify the sentence so that it's more specific.

In the case of LIMB : BODY, the sentence was good enough even though it wasn't very specific; you were still able to whittle down the answer choices to one possibility. For METER : DISTANCE, you had to make the sentence more specific.

In other words, don't sweat it. Come up with a sentence and try it out. If multiple answer choices fit the sentence, go back and make your sentence more specific. If no answer choices fit the sentence, check to see if you made it too specific, or if you somehow misjudged the relation between the stem words. You should definitely not waste time trying to come up with the perfect sentence.

As you practice analogies, don't just focus on getting them right. Think about the process of getting them right. Did you come up with a good enough sentence the first time? Did you have to try a number of sentences, meaning the questions took you more time? If you pay some attention to the sentences you come up with for each question you encounter, you will train yourself to create better sentences in the future.

Types of Analogies

There are a variety of ways in which words can be related. Luckily for you, the SAT seems only partially aware of this fact: a few relationships appear on the test much more frequently than others. Creating a sentence to define a relationship becomes easier when you recognize an analogy as a particular *kind* of analogy—becoming familiar with the different sorts of analogies is therefore a very good idea.

The following table outlines, in order of frequency, the twelve most common types of analogies found on the SAT:

Type	Example
Function / Purpose	CHAINSAW : TREE *the function of a chainsaw is to cut a tree*
Part / Whole	PETAL : FLOWER *a petal is part of a flower*
Characteristic Action	DOCTOR : SURGERY *a doctor characteristically performs surgery*
Relative Size and Degree	DRY : ARID *an arid place is very dry*

Analogies

Type	Example
Type	CANAL : WATERWAY *a canal is a type of waterway*
Characteristic Location	CAR : GARAGE *a car is typically parked in a garage*
Attribute	NOVICE : EXPERIENCE *lack of experience defines a novice*
Descriptive Pair	TEXTURE : ROUGH *a texture feels rough*
Cause & Effect	CAST : MOVEMENT *the effect of a cast is to stop movement*
Lack	PAUPER : MONEY *a pauper lacks money*
Characteristic Use	FISHERMAN : ROD *a fisherman uses a rod*
Other	About $\frac{1}{6}$ of SAT analogies fall into this category.

Though we've given you this list, we have to be honest—the science of categorizing SAT analogies is not perfect. Some categories do overlap slightly. However, if you become comfortable with these categories and are able to identify whether a particular analogy fits into one of them, it will usually make creating a sentence much simpler. And the better you are at creating a good sentence, the faster and more accurately you will be able to move through the two analogy sections.

1. Function / Purpose

Function analogies relate an object and the purpose for which it is used. A very simple example would be CHAINSAW : TREE—the purpose of a chainsaw is to cut down trees. Almost all function analogies follow the model of CHAINSAW : TREE, in which the analogy is NOUN : NOUN and the sentence you produce includes a verb that describes how one noun functions by acting upon the other. In the CHAINSAW : TREE example, the verb you have to supply is "cut down." However, we've found a few instances of NOUN : VERB function analogies, such as CHAINSAW : CUT. In these instances, the sentence you produce would be something more general, such as, "The purpose of a chainsaw is to cut."

NOUN : NOUN Example

LAMP : LIGHT ::

- (A)   elevator : skyscraper
- (B)   lever : machine
- (C)   microphone : amplifier
- (D)   mentor : guidance
- (E)   honey : food

The correct answer is **(D).** The function of a LAMP is to provide LIGHT, just as the function of a **mentor** is to provide **guidance.**

NOUN : VERB Example

LIE : DECEIVE ::

- (A)   truth : cheat
- (B)   speech : communicate
- (C)   payment : save
- (D)   hand : sort
- (E)   eye : glance

The correct answer is **(B).** The function of a LIE is to DECEIVE, just as the function of **speech** is to **communicate.** The only answer choice that should have given you trouble here is (E). But while an eye can glance, glancing is not the function of an eye; seeing is the eye's function.

Function/Purpose

1.   PEN : WRITE ::

- (A)   merger : isolate
- (B)   ruse : scam
- (C)   certification : expurgate
- (D)   orator : speak
- (E)   dye : blanch

2.   AWARD : RECOGNIZE ::

- (A)   assessment : simulate
- (B)   battle : stimulate
- (C)   imitator : emulate
- (D)   aid : encumber
- (E)   extraction : incorporate

3.   LOBBYIST : INFLUENCE ::

- (A)   confirmation : verify
- (B)   megaphone : silence
- (C)   protest : manipulate
- (D)   precedent : evolve
- (E)   barricade : pass

Analogies

4.   POSTPONEMENT : DELAY ::

   (A)   interloper : deliberate
   (B)   renovation : repair
   (C)   declaration : proclaim
   (D)   ration : proliferate
   (E)   argument : concur

Answers and Explanations

1.   **(D)**   Function/Purpose   *Easy*
"The function of a PEN is to WRITE" is the best sentence you can make with with this stem pair. Similarly, the function of an *orator* is to *speak*. In choices (A) and (E), the meaning of the first word is opposite in function or purpose of the second word; in choice (A), *merger* means "to join", and (D), *blanch,* means "to take the color out of". Choice (B) is a pair of synonyms rather than a function or purpose relationship, and choice (C) does not have a meaningful or necessary relationship: *certification* means "approval or authorization" while *expurgate* means "to remove objectionable parts" or "to censor".

2.   **(C)**   Function/Purpose   *Easy*
"The function of an AWARD is to RECOGNIZE someone or something" is the best sentence you can make with with this stem pair. Similarly, the function of an *imitator* is to *emulate* someone or something. In choices (A) and (B), the word pairs do not have meaningful or necessary relationships. Choices (D) and (E) contain pairs of opposite functions; in choice (D), *encumber* means "to weigh down", and in (E), *extraction* means "the removal of something".

3.   **(A)**   Function/Purpose   *Easy*
"The function of a LOBBYIST is to INFLUENCE something" is the best sentence you can make with this stem pair. Similarly, the function of a *confirmation* is to *verify*, or approve, of something, . In choices (B) and (E), the meaning of the first word is opposite in function or purpose of the second word. The word pairs in choices (C) and (D) do not have meaningful or necessary relationships.

4.   **(B)**   Function/Purpose   *Difficult*
"The purpose of a POSTPONEMENT is to DELAY something" is the best sentence you can make with this stem pair. Similarly, the purpose of a *renovation* is to *repair* something. The word pairs in choices (A) and (D) do not have meaningful or necessary relationships; in choice (A), an *interloper* is an intruder, while *deliberate,* in this choice, is used as a verb, "to consider something". In choice (D), *proliferate* means "to grow rap-

idly". The words in choice (C) have a meaningful relationship, but one is not the purpose of the other; the pair in choice (E) are opposite in purpose.

2. Part / Whole

There are three types of part/whole analogies, all of which are related. The first involves a particular thing and a larger structure or entity completely composed of a number of the original things. Consider an example like SOLDIER : ARMY—an army is made up of many soldiers. The second involves a thing and a larger structure of which that thing is a part, though that larger entity is not composed entirely of the original thing. For example, TOE : FOOT. The third is very similar to the second, but it involves a further spatial dimension. For example, ROOF : HOUSE—a roof is the part of a house *located at the top of the house.*

Type 1 Example

TREE : FOREST ::

(A)   broccoli : vegetable
(B)   album : music
(C)   actor : troupe
(D)   forum : speaker
(E)   inquisitor : question

The correct answer is **(C)**. A FOREST is made up of many TREES, just as a **troupe** is made up of many **actors.**

Type 2 Example

PETAL : FLOWER ::

(A)   eyes : view
(B)   nose : head
(C)   seedling : plant
(D)   surgery : injury
(E)   blade : grass

The correct answer is **(B)**. A PETAL is part of a FLOWER (though the flower is not made up entirely of petals), just as **nose** is a part of the **head.**

Type 3 Example

ROOF : HOUSE ::

(A)   plateau : landscape
(B)   door : entrance
(C)   status : hierarchy
(D)   summit : mountain
(E)   surfeit : resources

Analogies

The correct answer is **(D)**. The ROOF is the highest part of a HOUSE, just as the **summit** is the highest part of a **mountain**.

Part/Whole

1.   STRING : VIOLIN ::

    (A)   ball : tennis
    (B)   thorn : barb
    (C)   hammer : wrench
    (D)   leaf : trunk
    (E)   faucet : water

2.   EYE : FACE ::

    (A)   container : vessel
    (B)   hanger : shirt
    (C)   enigma : class
    (D)   grape : raisin
    (E)   screen : television

3.   STORY : PLOT ::

    (A)   memory : reminiscence
    (B)   fortitude : stamina
    (C)   meal : dessert
    (D)   dog : leash
    (E)   endowment : fund

4.   COLUMN : PORTICO ::

    (A)   sovereign : monarch
    (B)   charade : cloak
    (C)   soap : cleanse
    (D)   membrane : cell
    (E)   threshold : pragmatism

Answers and Explanations

1.   **(E)**   Part/Whole   *Easy*
"A VIOLIN needs STRINGS in order to be played" is the best sentence you can make with this stem pair. Similarly, the game of *tennis* needs a *ball* in order to be played. Choice (B) is a pair of synonyms, and while choices (C), (D), and (E) have meaningful relationships; however, the first word in each of them is not needed by the second in order to complete the action.

2.   **(E)**   Part/Whole   *Moderate*
"An EYE is part of a FACE" is a logical sentence that can be made from this stem pair. Similarly, a *screen* is part of a *television*. Choice (A) is a pair of synonyms. Choice (B) is

a pair of words that can be used in the same context, but a *hanger* is not part of a *shirt*. In choices (C) and (D), the words have no necessary or meaningful relationship. Unfamiliar vocabulary may include *enigma*, which is a puzzle.

3. **(C)** Part/Whole   *Moderate*
"A STORY contains a PLOT" is a logical sentence that can be made from this stem pair. Similarly, a *meal* contains a *dessert*. Choices (A) and (B) are pairs of synonyms; in choice (C), *fortitude* and *stamina* mean "strength" or "endurance". The words in choice (D) can be used in the same context, but a *dog* does not contain a *leash*. In choice (E), the function of *endowment* is to *fund* something.

4. **(D)** Part/Whole   *Difficult*
"A COLUMN is part of a PORTICO," which is(a series of columns), is a logical sentence that can be made from this stem pair. Similarly, a *membrane*, or thin layer, is part of a *cell*. Choice (A) is a pair of synonyms meaning "a ruler". The word pairs in choices (B) and (E) have no necessary or meaningful relationship; a *charade*, (B), is the representation of a word in riddling verse or dramatic action, while *pragmatism*, (E), is the practical approach to problems. In choice (C), the function of *soap* is to *cleanse* something.

3. Characteristic Action

Characteristic action analogies in the form NOUN : NOUN relate something and what that thing (or being) typically does. In the examples below, note that not only is the vocabulary harder for the difficult example, the relation between the stem words is also more sophisticated.

Easy Example

NOVELIST : BOOK ::

(A) house : roof
(B) tailor : needle
(C) weaver : cloth
(D) unicorn : horn
(E) scientist : laboratory

The correct answer is **(C)**. A NOVELIST makes a BOOK, just as a **weaver** makes **cloth.**

Difficult Example

ICONOCLAST : CONVENTION ::

(A) tailor : robe
(B) sycophant : love
(C) pariah : friendship
(D) anarchist : government
(E) fireman : safety

The correct answer is **(D).** An ICONOCLAST dislikes and fights against CONVENTION, just as an **anarchist** dislikes and opposes **government.**

Sometimes you might see characteristic action analogies in the form ADJECTIVE : VERB. In these cases, the adjective describes a person or thing, and the verb is something that person or thing characteristically does.

DISSATISFIED : COMPLAIN

(A) pleased : tolerate
(B) ungrateful : enliven
(C) friendly : ridicule
(D) curious : inquire
(E) generous : pacify

The correct answer is **(D).** A DISSATISFIED person COMPLAINS, just as a **curious** person **inquires.**

Characteristic Action

1.   MARTYR : SUFFERS ::

(A) rector : rests
(B) jockey : rides
(C) follower : guides
(D) abstainer : imbibes
(E) tourist : subsidizes

2.   MOTORIST : DRIVE ::

(A) submissive : assert
(B) zealot : customize
(C) recluse : prove
(D) jailer : incarcerate
(E) spectator : perform

3.   BENEFICIARY : RECEIVE ::

(A) narrator : obviate
(B) zoologist : animate
(C) apostle : engage
(D) raconteur : segregate
(E) philanthropist : give

4.   MOB : RIOT ::

    (A)   despot : acquiesce
    (B)   participant : refrain
    (C)   journalist : report
    (D)   advocate : evade
    (E)   thespian : bore

5.   CENSOR : EXPURGATE ::

    (A)   enigma : elucidate
    (B)   itinerant : provoke
    (C)   assembly : isolate
    (D)   journeyman : demolish
    (E)   spy : infiltrate

Answers and Explanations

1.   **(B)**   Characteristic Action   *Easy*
"A MARTYR is one who SUFFERS" is a logical sentence than can be produced formed with this stem pair. Likewise, a *jockey* is one who *rides*. The pairs in choices (A) and (E) are not related in any manner; a *rector*, or a clergyman, is not necessarily one who *rests*, while and *subsidizes*, or to furnish with money, is not the function of a *tourist*. The words in choices (C) and (D) are pairs of opposite actions. Unfamiliar vocabulary may include *abstainer*, one who refrains from some action, and *imbibes*, which means "to drink."

2.   **(D)**   Characteristic Action   *Easy*
"A characteristic action of a MOTORIST is to DRIVE" is the most likely sentence that can be constructed with this stem pair. In the same way, a characteristic action of a *jailer* is to *incarcerate*, which means "to put in prison". Choices (A) and (E) are pairs of opposite characteristic actions, while the word pair in choices (B) and (C) have no meaningful or necessary relationship. Unfamiliar vocabulary may include the following: a *zealot* is a fanatic, and a *recluse* is a hermit or someone who leads a secluded life.

3.   **(E)**   Characteristic Action   *Moderate*
"A characteristic action of a BENEFICIARY is to RECEIVE" is the mostly likely sentence that can be constructed with this stem pair. In the same way, a characteristic action of a *philanthropist* is to give, for a *philanthropist* is one who typically gives support to an organization. Choices (A), (C), and (D) have no meaningful or necessary relationships; unfamiliar vocabulary may include *obviate*, which means "to prevent or make unnecessary", and *raconteur*, which means "a storyteller". Choice (B) seems to imply a logical relationship if you associate *zoologist* with a zoo and *animate* with animals, but *animate* actually means "lively."

4.   **(C)**   Characteristic Action   *Difficult*

"A characteristic action of a MOB is to RIOT" is the mostly likely sentence that can be constructed with this stem pair. In the same way, a characteristic action of a *journalist* is to *report*. Choices (A), (B), and (E) are pairs of opposite characteristic actions. Unfamiliar vocabulary may include these words: in choice (A), *despot* means "tyrant," and *acquiesce* means "to agree"; in choice (E), a *thespian* is an actor. The word pair in choice (D) has no meaningful or necessary relationship; *advocate* means "to be in favor of," while *evade* means "to avoid."

5.   **(E)**   Characteristic Action   *Difficult*

"A characteristic action of a CENSOR is to EXPURGATE," or remove objectionable material, is the most likely sentence that can be constructed with this stem pair. In the same way, a characteristic action of a *spy* is to *infiltrate*, which means "to enter unobtrusively." Choices (A) and (C) are pairs of opposite characteristic actions; in (A), *enigma* is a puzzle, while *elucidate* means "to make clear." The word pairs in (B) and (D) have no meaningful or necessary relationships; in (B), an *itinerant* is a wanderer.

4. Relative Size and Degree

This type of analogy describes a thing or state of being and a second thing or state of being that is similar but smaller or larger in size or degree.

Easy Example

POKE : PUNCH ::

(A)   murmur : shout
(B)   crouch : smack
(C)   lose : win
(D)   groan : hurt
(E)   stink : smell

The correct answer is **(A).** A POKE is a much weaker touch than a PUNCH, just as a **murmur** is much weaker sound than a **shout.** You might have been tempted by the answer choice *stink : smell*, but that choice is not best answer because the relationship between stink and smell is one of type, not degree. A stink is a bad smell.

Difficult Example

LUDICROUS : SILLY ::

(A)   monstrous : skyscraper
(B)   brackish : messy
(C)   conscientious : moralistic
(D)   spurious : rotten
(E)   emaciated : thin

The correct answer is **(E)**. To be LUDICROUS is to be extremely SILLY, just as to be **emaciated** is to be extremely **thin**.

Relative Size and Degree

1.   HATE : DISLIKE ::

    (A)   embellish : adorn
    (B)   berate : scold
    (C)   emulate : imitate
    (D)   absolve : condemn
    (E)   annihilate : preserve

2.   EMACIATED : THIN ::

    (A)   useless : ineffective
    (B)   contentious : susceptible
    (C)   solemn : serious
    (D)   exhausted : tired
    (E)   fickle : perpetual

3.   RESISTANT : IMPERVIOUS ::

    (A)   exemplary : abysmal
    (B)   fallacious : honest
    (C)   exorbitant : excessive
    (D)   futile : ineffectual
    (E)   gregarious : hackneyed

4.   NIHILISM : REJECTION ::

    (A)   flammable : combustible
    (B)   incontrovertible : indisputable
    (C)   decorous : unpromising
    (D)   gallant : reckless
    (E)   noxious : harmful

5.   LUCID : UNDERSTOOD ::

    (A)   opaque : transparent
    (B)   pervasive : omnipresent
    (C)   perfunctory : thorough
    (D)   gullible : convinced
    (E)   pedantic : devastated

Answers and Explanations

1.   **(B)**   Relative Size and Degree   *Easy*
"To HATE something is to DISLIKE it intensely" is the best sentence that can be made with this stem pair. Similarly, to *berate* is to *scold* intensely. In choices (A) and (C), the word pairs are synonyms, while the choices in (D) and (E) are antonyms.

2. **(D)** Relative Size and Degree   *Moderate*

"Someone who is EMACIATED is extremely THIN" is the best sentence that you can make with this stem pair. Equally, someone who is *exhausted* is extremely *tired*. Choices (A) and (C) offer pairs of synonyms; the words in choice (B) have no logical relationship, because *contentious* means "argumentative or quarrelsome." The words in choice (E) are antonyms, because *fickle* means "inconstant" while *perpetual* means "everlasting."

3. **(C)** Relative Size and Degree   *Moderate*

"To be IMPERVIOUS is to be RESISTANT to something completely" is the best sentence that can be made with this stem pair. Similarly, to be *exorbitant* is to be completely *excessive*. The word pairs in choices (A) and (B) are antonyms; *exemplary* means "outstanding," while *abysmal* means "hopeless or wretched," and *fallacious* means "deceptive or misleading." The words in choice (D) are synonyms that mean "useless"; the pair in choice (E) do does not share a necessary or meaningful relationship, because *gregarious* means "friendly" while *hackneyed* means "commonplace."

4. **(B)** Relative Size and Degree   *Difficult*

"NIHILISM is total and absolute REJECTION" is the best sentence you can make with this stem pair. Equally, something that is *incontrovertible* is totally and absolutely *indisputable*. Choices (A) and (E) are pairs of synonyms, and the pairs in (C) and (D) share no necessary or meaningful relationship, because in choice (C), *decorous* means "correct," while in choice (D), *gallant* means "noble or brave."

5. **(D)** Relative Size and Degree   *Difficult*

"Something that is LUCID is easily UNDERSTOOD" is the best sentence that can be made with this stem pair. Similarly, someone who is *gullible* is easily *convinced*. In choices (A) and (C) are pairs of antonyms, and the words in choice (C) are synonyms. The words in choice (E) do not share a necessary or meaningful relationship, because *pedantic* pertains to parade parading one's education.

5. Type

In type analogies, one stem word names a category into which the other typically fits. For the moderately difficult type questions, the relation between the two words may be a little more complicated. For example, in the stem pair NIGHTMARE : DREAM, a nightmare is a bad or ominous kind of dream. The SAT almost never includes difficult type analogies.

Easy Example

BANANA : FRUIT ::

(A)   lung : organ
(B)   grape : raisin
(C)   crab : lobster
(D)   ocean : land
(E)   slope : mountain

The correct answer is **(A)**. A BANANA is a type of FRUIT, just as a **lung** is a type of **organ.**

Moderate Example

EMOTION: ANGUISH ::

(A)   fascination : frenetic
(B)   dossier : categorized
(C)   cabbage : vegetative
(D)   sensation : burning
(E)   compensation : financial

The correct answer is **(D)**. ANGUISH is an intense and unpleasant type of EMOTION, just as **burning** is an intense and unpleasant type of **sensation.**

Type

1.   MOLAR : TOOTH ::

(A)   hammer : nail
(B)   ballad : song
(C)   hemisphere : oxygen
(D)   bridge : highway
(E)   trail : jury

2.   WATER : LIQUID ::

(A)   paddock : horse
(B)   winter : snow
(C)   particle : fascia
(D)   edifice : building
(E)   cumulus : cloud

3.   PANCREAS : ORGAN

(A)   pistol : gun
(B)   proponent : cause
(C)   stalemate : deficit
(D)   option : preference
(E)   journey : voyage

4. BESTOWAL : GIFT

   (A)   reprobate : sage
   (B)   dimension : inertia
   (C)   parliament : government
   (D)   camaraderie : amity
   (E)   enthusiasm : apathy

Answers and Explanations

1. **(B)** Type   *Easy*
"A MOLAR is a type of TOOTH" is the simplest sentence that can be constructed with this stem pair, just as a *ballad* is a type of *song*. While the vocabulary in choices (A) and (D) have meaningful relationships, *hammers* and *bridges* are not types of *nails* or *highways*. In choice (C), there is no necessary or meaningful relationship within the word pair, and in choice (E), it would be easy to misread *trail* for trial and assume a meaningful relationship between these words.

2. **(D)** Type   *Easy*
"WATER is a type of LIQUID" is the best sentence that can be made with this stem pair. Similarly, *cumulus* is a type of *cloud*. In choice (A), a *paddock* can contain a *horse*; however, a *paddock* is not a type of *horse*. The same is true for choice (B). In choice (C), there is no meaningful or necessary relationship between *particle* and *fascia*, which can be an architectural term meaning "a broad band". The words in choice (D) are synonymous.

3. **(A)** Type   *Moderate*
"A PANCREAS is a type of ORGAN" is the simplest sentence that can be constructed with this stem pair, just as a *pistol* is a type of *gun*. While the vocabulary in choices (B) and (D) have meaningful relationships, one is not a type of the other. In choice (C), the word pair has no meaningful or necessary relationship; a *stalemate* is a deadlock. The words in choice (E) are synonymous.

4. **(C)** Type   *Difficult*
"A BESTOWAL is a type of GIFT" is the best sentence that can be made with this stem pair. Similarly, *parliament* is a type of *government*. In choice (A), the words have no necessary or meaningful relationship, because *reprobate* means "corrupt," while *sage* pertains to wisdom. In choice (B), the words have no meaningful or necessary relationship, because *inertia* means "a lack of motion". In choice (D), the words in each pair are synonyms meaning for friendship, while the words in choice (E) are antonyms.

6. Characteristic Location or Event

In this type of analogy, one of the stem pair words describes a typical location or event at which the other word can be found. These analogies are generally simple. Only rarely will you find one in the difficult last third of an analogy group.

> HORSE : STABLE ::
>
> (A)   rider : saddle
> (B)   heart : blood
> (C)   street : lamp
> (D)   view : window
> (E)   guest : hotel

The correct answer is **(E).** A HORSE stays in a STABLE, just as a **guest** stays in a **hotel.**

Characteristic Location

1.   CABOOSE : TRAIN ::

    (A)   telephone : pole
    (B)   integer : vastness
    (C)   head : hat
    (D)   precipice : fissure
    (E)   hand : arm

2.   BARK : TREE ::

    (A)   organ : viscera
    (B)   sock : shoe
    (C)   throng : crowd
    (D)   enamel : tooth
    (E)   freezer : ice

3.   STOVE : KITCHEN ::

    (A)   battery : cell
    (B)   tree : forest
    (C)   aquarium : fish
    (D)   monument : shrine
    (E)   cottage : bungalow

4.   RENAISSANCE : EUROPE ::

    (A)   aria : opera
    (B)   enhancement : criteria
    (C)   umbrage : resentment
    (D)   easel : canvas
    (E)   vial : urn

Answers and Explanations

1.   **(C)**   Characteristic Location   *Easy*
"A CABOOSE is located at the end of a TRAIN" is the best sentence that can be made with this stem pair. Similarly, your *hand* is located at the end of your *arm.* The first words in choices (A), (C), and (D) are not located at the end of the second word. The words in choice (B) share no meaningful or necessary relationship; an *integer* is a number.

2.   **(D)**   Characteristic Location   *Easy*
"BARK is located on the outside of a TREE" is the best sentence you can make with this stem pair. Likewise, *enamel* is located on the outside of a *tooth.* The first words in choices (A), (B), and (E) are not located on the outside of the second word. The words in choice (C) are synonyms. Unfamiliar vocabulary may include *viscera*, which means "internal organs."

3.   **(B)**   Characteristic Location   *Moderate*
"A STOVE is located in a KITCHEN" is the best sentence you can make with this stem pair. Likewise, a *tree* is located in a *forest.* The first words in choices (A) and (C) are not contained in the second word. The words in choices (D) and (E) are synonyms.

4.   **(A)**   Characteristic Location   *Difficult*
"The RENAISSANCE occurred in EUROPE," just as an *aria* occurs in an *opera.* The first words in choices (B) and (D) do not occur in the second word. The words in choices (C) and (E) are synonyms.

7. Attribute

In attribute analogies, one word describes an integral characteristic of the other word. Attribute analogies often involve difficult vocabulary and can be quite subtle.

DICTATOR : POWER ::

(A)   priest : congregation
(B)   mathematician : energy
(C)   neophyte : inexperience
(D)   tyrant : wrath
(E)   creator : benevolence

The correct answer is **(C).** An attribute of a DICTATOR is POWER, just as an attribute of a **neophyte** is **inexperience.** Another way to write this sentence would be,

"A dictator could not be a dictator if he did not have power, just as a neophyte could not be a neophyte if he was not inexperienced."

Attribute

1. ASTUTE : OBTUSE ::

    (A) assiduous : industrious
    (B) culpable : sinister
    (C) subversive : unbridled
    (D) austere : lenient
    (E) adversarial : antagonistic

2. BRIEF : PROTRACTED ::

    (A) insipid : radical
    (B) commodious : cramped
    (C) undulated : rippled
    (D) terse : ordered
    (E) urbane : refined

3. VARIETY : HOMOGENEOUS ::

    (A) humility : haughty
    (B) unobtrusiveness : inconspicuous
    (C) cautiousness : prudent
    (D) acrimony : prosperous
    (E) vitriolic : caustic

4. SLOTH : INDOLENT ::

    (A) depravity : didactic
    (B) indecision : tenacious
    (C) connoisseur : conciliatory
    (D) tact : inconsiderate
    (E) generosity : munificent

Answers and Explanations

1. **(D)** Attribute   *Moderate*

"Being ASTUTE is not a characteristic of someone who is OBTUSE" is the best sentence you can make with this stem pair. Likewise, being *austere*, or strict, is not a characteristic of someone who is *lenient*. In word pairs (A), (B), and (E), the first word is an attribute of the second word. In choice (C), the word pair has no meaningful or necessary relationship. Unfamiliar vocabulary may include the following: *assiduous*, which means "diligent," and *culpable*, which means "guilty."

2. **(B)** Attribute *Moderate*

"Being BRIEF is not a characteristic of something that is PROTRACTED" is the best sentence you can make with this stem pair. Likewise, being *cramped* is not characteristic of being *commodious*, or spacious. In choices (A) and (D), the word pairs have no meaningful or necessary relationship. By definition, in choice (C), something that is *undulated* is *rippled*. Choice (E) presents a pair of synonyms.

3. **(A)** Attribute *Difficult*

"Having VARIETY is not a characteristic of something that is HOMOGENEOUS" is the best sentence you can make with this stem pair. Likewise, having *humility* is not a characteristic of someone who is *haughty*, which means "proud or arrogant." In choices (B) and (E), the word pairs are synonyms; *vitriolic* and *caustic* mean "corrosive or biting." In choice (C), *cautiousness* is characteristic of someone who is *prudent*, or careful, and in choice (D), the word pair has no meaningful or necessary relationship; *acrimony* means "harshness or bitterness of language."

4. **(E)** Attribute *Difficult*

"SLOTH is a characteristic of someone who is INDOLENT" is the best sentence you can make with this stem pair. Likewise, *generosity* is a characteristic of someone who is *munificent*. In word pairs (A) and (C), there is no meaningful or necessary relationship. In choices (B) and (D), the words are antonyms. Unfamiliar vocabulary may include these words: (A), *depravity,* means "corruption," while *didactic* means "intended to teach"; (B), *tenacious,* means "stubborn"; in (C), a *connoisseur* is an expert, while *conciliatory* means "gaining good will."

8. Descriptive Pair

Description analogies are unlike any other type. Description analogies come in the form ADJECTIVE : NOUN, in which the adjective modifies or describes the noun in some specific way. The answer pair must contain an adjective that modifies a noun in a similar way. Note that this type of analogy isn't so much about a relation between the words—it's more about the suitability of the adjective as a descriptor of the noun.

GUTTURAL : SOUND ::

(A)   economical : money
(B)   bombastic : speech
(C)   scattered : pilgrims
(D)   coarse : texture
(E)   gradual : slope

The correct answer is **(D).** A GUTTURAL SOUND is rough, just as a **coarse texture** is rough.

Descriptive Pair

1. WAX : WICK ::

   (A) lemon : pitcher
   (B) mattress : pillows
   (C) nucleus : boundary
   (D) dinghy : yacht
   (E) screen : partition

2. EDEMATOUS : ENLARGED

   (A) unconstrained : corroded
   (B) vigorous : lethargic
   (C) innocuous : nonmalignant
   (D) organic : embryonic
   (E) fervent : indifferent

3. SUPERFLUOUS : REPETITIOUS

   (A) resonant : analytical
   (B) abundant : scarce
   (C) superficial : erroneous
   (D) abandoned : disowned
   (E) perceptive : inconsiderate

4. KEEN : SHREWD ::

   (A) turbulent : innovative
   (B) mocking : sarcastic
   (C) vague : assorted
   (D) unsettled : unperturbed
   (E) ardent : desultory

Answers and Explanations

1. **(B)** Descriptive Pair *Moderate*
"Something made of WAX and a WICK is descriptive of a candle" is the best sentence that you can make with this stem pair. Similarly, something that is comprised of a *mattress* and a *pillow* is descriptive of a bed. In choices (A) and (C), the words in the pairs do not have a meaningful or necessary relationship. In choice (D), the word pair has a relationship of degree, and in choice (E), the words in the pair are synonyms.

2. **(C)** Descriptive Pair *Moderate*
"Something that is EDEMATOUS and ENLARGED is swollen" is the best sentence that you can make with this stem pair. Likewise, something that is *innocuous* and *nonmalignant* is benign, or harmless. The words in choices (A) and (D) do not have meaningful or necessary relationships. Choices (B) and (E) contain pairs of antonyms.

3.   **(D)**   Descriptive Pair   *Difficult*

"Something that is SUPERFLUOUS and REPETITIOUS is redundant," or need-lessly wordy. Similarly, something that is *abandoned* and *disowned* is renounced or given up. In choices (A) and (C), the words in the pairs do not have a meaningful or necessary relationship. In choices (B) and (E), the word pairs are antonyms.

4.   **(B)**   Descriptive Pair   *Difficult*

"Something that is KEEN and SHREWD is sagacious or wise" is the best sentence you can make with this stem pair. Likewise, something that is *mocking* and *sarcastic* is satirical. The words in choices (A) and (C) do not have meaningful or necessary relation-ships. Choices (D) and (E) contain pairs of antonyms. Unfamiliar vocabulary may include these: *turbulent*, which means "stormy"; *innovative*, which is creative; *unperturbed*, which means "calm"; *ardent*, which is "fiery"; and *desultory*, which is "random."

9. Cause and Effect

In cause and effect analogies, one word is an action, result, or situation that the other word creates or stops. Such analogies can follow one of three forms: NOUN : NOUN; VERB : NOUN; or VERB : ADJECTIVE.

In NOUN : NOUN cause and effect analogies, one of the nouns is an object that causes or stops the second noun:

BANDAGE : BLOOD ::

(A)   cable : bridge
(B)   cast : injury
(C)   fort : army
(D)   dam : river
(E)   pacemaker : heart

The correct answer is **(D)**. A BANDAGE stops the flow of BLOOD, just as a **dam** stops the flow of a **river.**

In VERB : NOUN cause and effect analogies, the verb describes an action commit-ted upon the noun, somehow causing the noun to be changed:

SHEAR : SHEEP ::

(A)   grade : paper
(B)   peel : apple
(C)   herd : cattle
(D)   punish : law
(E)   emancipate : freedom

The correct answer is **(B)**. To SHEAR a SHEEP is to remove its outer covering, just as to **peel** an **apple** is to remove its outer covering.

In VERB : ADJECTIVE cause and effect analogies, the verb describes an action, and the adjective describes the effect of the verb:

EXPAND : LARGE ::

- (A)   abridge : short
- (B)   spread : slim
- (C)   answer : correct
- (D)   destroy : miniscule
- (E)   garble : clear

The correct answer is **(A).** When you EXPAND something, you make it LARGER, just as when you **abridge** something you make it **shorter.**

Cause and Effect

1.   FUNGI : DECAY ::

- (A)   sweat : exercise
- (B)   activity : immobility
- (C)   laughter : tickle
- (D)   emergence : rain
- (E)   heartbeat : pulse

2.   FLOOD : RAIN ::

- (A)   waves : ocean
- (B)   avalanche : snow
- (C)   desert : heat
- (D)   storm : squall
- (E)   thaw : cold

3.   CARELESSNESS : ACCIDENT ::

- (A)   quandary : predicament
- (B)   dissonance : harmony
- (C)   disagreement : argument
- (D)   languor : exhilaration
- (E)   hindrance : deterrent

4.   EARTHQUAKE : SEICHE ::

- (A)   fire : heat
- (B)   melancholy : commemoration
- (C)   bewilderment : disorientation
- (D)   advancement : culmination
- (E)   volatility : stability

Analogies

Answers and Explanations

1. **(E)** Cause and Effect *Easy*
"FUNGI causes DECAY" is the best sentence you can make with the stem pair. Similarly, your *heartbeat* causes your *pulse*. In choices (A), (C), and (D), the first word does not cause the second word. Choice (B) contains a pair of words that are opposite in meaning.

2. **(B)** Cause and Effect *Moderate*
"A FLOOD is caused by too much RAIN" is the best sentence you can make with the stem pair. Similarly, an *avalanche* is caused by too much *snow*. In choices (A), (C), and (E), the first word is not caused by too much of the second word. Choice (D) contains a pair of synonyms.

3. **(C)** Cause and Effect *Moderate*
"CARELESSNESS can lead to an ACCIDENT" is the best sentence you can make with the stem pair. Similarly, a *disagreement* may lead to an *argument*. The word pairs in choices (A) and (E) contain synonyms. Choices (B) and (D) contain pairs of antonyms. Unfamiliar vocabulary may include the following: *quandary* is a dilemma or *predicament*; *dissonance* refers to clashing musical sounds; *languor* means "listlessness"; *hindrance* and *deterrent* both refer to obstacles.

4. **(A)** Cause and Effect *Difficult*
"A SEICHE is caused by an EARTHQUAKE" is the best sentence you can make with this stem pair. In the same manner, *heat* is caused by *fire*. In choices (B) and (D), the first word does not cause the second word. Choice (C) contains a pair of synonyms, and the words in Choice (E) are antonyms. Unfamiliar vocabulary may include the following: *melancholy*, which means "sad"; *disorientation*, which refers to confusion; and *volatility*, which means "a lack of stability."

10. Lack

Lack analogies follow two basic forms: NOUN : NOUN or ADJECTIVE : NOUN. In NOUN : NOUN lack analogies, one noun describes something that the other noun, by definition, lacks:

DROUGHT : WATER ::

- (A)   gully : river
- (B)   tornado : wind
- (C)   plague : health
- (D)   store : goods
- (E)   vestibule : hangars

The correct answer is **(C)**. A DROUGHT involves a lack of WATER, just as a **plague** involves a lack of **health.**

    In ADJECTIVE : NOUN lack analogies, the adjective describes a state of being, and the noun describes what is lacking in order to make that state of being a reality. ADJECTIVE : NOUN lack analogies are usually a little harder than NOUN : NOUN lack analogies because the ADJECTIVE : NOUN versions tend to use somewhat harder vocabulary:

LISTLESS : ENERGY ::

- (A)   devout : prayer
- (B)   frigid : warmth
- (C)   potent : power
- (D)   distant : location
- (E)   somber : gravity

The correct answer is **(B).** To be LISTLESS is to lack ENERGY, just as to be **frigid** is to lack **warmth.**

Lack

1.   SOBER : INTOXICATION ::

- (A)   vociferous : noise
- (B)   tenuousness : stillness
- (C)   fractious : irritability
- (D)   stoic : emotion
- (E)   nebulous : shapelessness

2.   UNBRIDLED : CONTROL ::

- (A)   difficult : complication
- (B)   typical : indistinction
- (C)   asymmetric : irregular
- (D)   voluble : talkativeness
- (E)   vapid : excitement

3.   NOVICE : EXPERTISE ::

- (A)   ostentation : modesty
- (B)   haughtiness : pride
- (C)   deference : obsequiousness
- (D)   authority : proficiency
- (E)   grandioseness : pretentiousness

4.   PERFIDIOUS : FAITH ::

(A)   inflexible : constriction
(B)   introverted : reclusiveness
(C)   prudent : recklessness
(D)   identical : uniformity
(E)   frivolous : thoughtlessness

Answers and Explanations

1.   **(D)** Lack   *Easy*

"Someone who is SOBER lacks INTOXICATION" is the best sentence you can develop from this stem pair. Likewise, someone who is *stoic* lacks *emotion*. You should be able to eliminate choices (A), (C), and (E), because in each of these word pairs, the second word is not caused by a lack of the first word. The words in choice (B) do not have a clear or necessary relationship. Unfamiliar vocabulary may include these words: *vociferous,* or noisy, *fractious,* or irritable, and *nebulous,* or vague.

2.   **(E)** Lack   *Easy*

By definition, to be UNBRIDLED is to lack CONTROL. Similarly, to be *vapid* is to lack *excitement*. The word pairs in all of the other choices are such that the first word does not indicate a lack of the second word. In choices (C) and (D), the first words describes a condition characterized by the second word.

3.   **(A)** Lack   *Moderate*

"To be a NOVICE is to lack EXPERTISE" is the best sentence that you can develop form from using this stem pair. Likewise, to have *ostentation* is to lack *modesty*. The word pairs in all of the other choices are such that if someone is were described with the first word in the pair, he or she does would not lack the second word.

4.   **(C)** Lack   *Moderate*

By definition, to be PERFIDIOUS is to lack FAITH. Similarly, to be *prudent* is to lack *recklessness*. The word pair in choice (A) maintains no clear or meaningful relationship, and choices (B), (D), and (E) show a characteristic of the first word, not a lack of it.

11. Characteristic Use

In this type of analogy, one word is a person or thing and the other is what that person or thing uses. Characteristic use analogies are always NOUN : NOUN. Often one of the nouns is a tool used by the other, such as CAMERA : PHOTOGRAPHER. These analogies are usually either easy or moderately difficult.

PALETTE : PAINTER ::

- (A) trial : jury
- (B) barber : scissors
- (C) sandwich : restaurant
- (D) saddle : jockey
- (E) tapestry : weaver

The correct answer is **(D).** A PAINTER uses a PALETTE as part of his job, just as a **jockey** uses a **saddle** as part of his job. (Note that *barber : scissors* is a trick, since its order is flipped.)

Characteristic Use

1.   TRUSS : TIE ::

- (A) rostrum : aim
- (B) gun : shoot
- (C) sedative : enliven
- (D) fence : eliminate
- (E) stimulant : tranquilize

2.   LANCET : PUNCTURE ::

- (A) invasion : tackle
- (B) furnace : cool
- (C) shield : expose
- (D) oven : bake
- (E) quota : appraise

3.   MAGNIFIER : ENLARGE ::
- (A) curb : promote

- (B) union : separate
- (C) oracle : suppress
- (D) muscle : sequester
- (E) pannier : carry

4.   PANTOGRAPH : COPY ::

- (A) demand : revolutionize
- (B) monitor : overlook
- (C) parole : release
- (D) sachet : proliferate
- (E) samaritin : disregard

Answers and Explanations

1.   **(B)**   Characteristic Use   *Easy*

"A TRUSS is used to TIE something" is the best sentence that you can make from this stem pair. In the same way, a *gun* is used to *shoot* something. You can eliminate choices

(A) and (D), as these word pairs have no meaningful relationship. Choices (C) and (E) have pairs of words that incorporate opposite uses. Unfamiliar words may include *rostrum*, which is a stage for public speaking.

2.   **(D)**   Characteristic Use   *Easy*
"A LANCET is used to PUNCTURE" is the best sentence that you can make from this stem pair. In the same way, an *oven* is used to *bake*. In choices (A) and (E), the word pairs have no meaningful relationships. Choices (B) and (C) are pairs of opposite characteristic uses.

3.   **(E)**   Characteristic Use   *Moderate*
"A MAGNIFIER is used to ENLARGE something" is the best sentence that you can make from this stem pair. In the same way, a *pannier*, or large basket, is used to *carry* something. The word pairs in (A) and (D) have no meaningful relationship. Choices (B) and (C) demonstrate word pairs with opposite characteristic uses. Unfamiliar vocabulary may include *oracle*, which means "a source of divine knowledge as in ancient Greece," and *sequester*, which means "to set apart or seclude."

4.   **(C)**   Characteristic Use   *Moderate*
"A PANTOGRAPH is used to COPY something" is the best sentence that you can make from this stem pair. In the same way, *parole* used to *release* something. The words in choices (A) and (D) have no meaningful relationship. Choices (B) and (E) demonstrate word pairs with opposite characteristic uses. Unfamiliar vocabulary may include *sachet*, which is a small bag of scent used to perfume clothes; *proliferate*, which makes means "to grow rapidly"; and *samaritin*, or one who is ready and generous to help those in distress.

12. Other

About ⅙ of the analogies you will encounter on practice SATs—and on the real thing—will not fit into any of the 11 categories we have defined. If you come upon an analogy that doesn't seem to fit, don't worry. The process you should follow is exactly the same. Create a sentence that defines the relationship between the stem words, and then apply that sentence to the answer choices.

Analogy Tricks the SAT Likes to Pull

The SAT embeds certain tricks in its analogy questions to trip up the careless and to lure the confused. Such tricks are most common among difficult questions, which can be particularly troublesome since tricks work most effectively when you are already a little confused. All of the tricks used by ETS on analogy questions are designed to make a wrong answer look like the right one. When you have little time and desperately want to find the right answer, those "attractive" wrong answers become very enticing.

If you know the tricks are lurking out there, you will be much less likely to fall into their diabolical clutches. Plus, if you learn to identify an answer choice as a trick, you can use that knowledge to eliminate it. After all, if an answer choice is a trick, it can't be the right answer.

Bogus Associations

One kind of SAT analogy trickery involves the use of an answer pair in which one of the words is somehow associated with one of the words in the stem pair. Take a look at the example:

BANDAGE : BLOOD ::

(A)   cable : bridge
(B)   cast : injury
(C)   fort : army
(D)   dam : river
(E)   pacemaker : heart

The correct answer for this question is **(D) dam : river,** since a dam stops the flow of a river in the same way that a BANDAGE stops the flow of BLOOD. However, let's say you didn't immediately see the answer and had to scour through the answer choices. BANDAGE : BLOOD conjurse images of pain and injury, as does the answer choice *cast : injury.* Because the words in this answer pair are related to those in the stem pair, you might be tempted to think it is the correct answer. Don't be. The relation between *cast* and *injury* is very different from that between BANDAGE and BLOOD. (In fact, the relation between a cast and an injury isn't clear; an injury is too general a term to have any real relation to a cast, which is used to immobilize broken bones but is unrelated to injuries like burns.)

To avoid the SAT trap of bogus associations, you should make sure to focus on the relation between the words in the analogies rather than on the words themselves. Also, when you see a word in an answer pair that is similar or closely associated with a word in the stem pair, be suspicious. Now that you are aware that this type of trap exists on the SAT, you should be able to avoid it.

Analogies

Flipped Answers

As discussed earlier in this section, word order is extremely important in analogies. EYE : VISION cannot be related to HEARING : EAR because the two relations are flipped. The SAT will sometimes give you questions with the answers flipped, such as:

PALETTE : PAINTER ::

(A)   trial : jury
(B)   barber : scissors
(C)   sandwich : restaurant
(D)   saddle : jockey
(E)   tapestry : weaver

In this example, a barber uses scissors for his job, just as a PAINTER uses his PALETTE, but the order of the two word pairs is reversed. *Barber : scissors* cannot be the answer. (The correct answer is **saddle : jockey**). When you pick an answer, be sure that its words are in the same order as those in the stem pair. You might want to touch each word with your pencil when you insert it into your sentence to remind you to check for the correct word order.

When Vocabulary Is Difficult

On harder analogies, you will often come across difficult vocabulary, some of which you might not know. So how can you possibly form a sentence to relate two words you don't know? And if you can't form a sentence, how can you even try to answer the question?

There are a few strategies to help you come to an answer if you don't know the vocabulary of one or even both words in the stem pair. Using these strategies may occasionally enable you to come to a single answer. More likely, the strategies will help you to eliminate two or three of the answer pairs, putting you in a good position to guess.

If You Don't Know One of the Stem Words

If you can't form a relational sentence because you don't know one of the stem words in an analogy, you obviously won't be able to identify an answer immediately. However, that doesn't mean all is lost. Remember, because SAT questions are multiple-choice, the answer is always right there in front of you. So if you can't pick it out of the crowd, perhaps you can eliminate the crowd around it.

There's a handy two-step method that will help you to eliminate incorrect analogy answer choices.

1.Go through the answer pairs and try to make defining sentences. Often, the words in an answer pair will not be very well related. If that is the case, you can eliminate that answer pair. Stem words always have a strong relation to each other, so the words in the correct answer pair will too. Here's the strategy in action:

???????? : GOVERNMENT ::

(A)   leader : office
(B)   claimant : throne
(C)   soldier : platoon
(D)   attorney : trial
(E)   boss : business

Answer choices (B), (C), (D), and (E) all have fairly good relations. A *claimant* desires to ascend to the *throne*, a *soldier* is a member of a *platoon*, an *attorney* works at a *trial*, and a *boss* heads a *business*. However, *leader : office* does not have a very good relation—a leader might work in an office, but he or she certainly doesn't have to. Therefore, you can eliminate (A) as a possible answer. Now you're down to four choices, shifting the odds in your favor.

2.Find the relation for each answer pair, and see if the word you know in the stem pair can possibly fit. We'll use the same example we did before. Remember, (A) has already been eliminated. In (B), a *claimant* desires to ascend to the *throne*. Can you imagine the unknown word means "someone who wants to ascend to government"? Seems unlikely, so you can eliminate (B). In (C), a *soldier* is a member of a *platoon*. Could the unknown word mean "member of a government"? Possibly. Keep it. In (D), an *attorney* works at a *trial*. Is there a name for a person who "works in government"? Seems likely, though you might notice that an attorney working at a trial is not quite the same thing as a bureaucrat working in a government. This relation is possible, but it's not as good as (C). If guessing, you probably shouldn't choose this one. In (E), a boss heads a business. Could the word mean "head of the government"? Possibly. Keep this one too.

The Results of the Process

After employing the two-step process, we were able to eliminate two answer pairs. Further, while we weren't willing to entirely eliminate (D), we did have the sense that it wasn't as good as the other two we kept. So we have to guess between (C) and (E), which leaves our odds for getting the question right at 50 percent. Not bad for an analogy in which we didn't even know the meaning of one of the words.

If You Don't Know Either of the Stem Words

If you don't know either of the stem words in an analogy, you can still look through the answers to see if any of the pairs has a bad internal relation. If you can eliminate even one possibility this way, it's in your favor to guess. If you can't eliminate any, you should move on to another question.

Analogies Unit Test - 30 questions

1. COWARDLY : BRAVERY ::

    (A) elated : joy
    (B) obstinate : flexibility
    (C) serene : patience
    (D) courageous : boldness
    (E) frightful : tenacity

2. REVILE : DISLIKE ::

    (A) hate : despise
    (B) feel : touch
    (C) want : like
    (D) adore : admire
    (E) expect : await

3. ARMORY : WEAPONS ::

    (A) shield : swords
    (B) barn : horses
    (C) cage : lions
    (D) shelf : books
    (E) wardrobe : clothing

4. REPUBLIC : REPRESENTATIVE ::

    (A) democracy : judicial
    (B) senate : legislative
    (C) dictatorship : autocratic
    (D) presidency : secretarial
    (E) admiral : naval

5. SYRUP : SWEETENER ::

    (A) vinegar : acid
    (B) sugar : granule
    (C) salt : pepper
    (D) oil : lubricant
    (E) water : liquid

6. PLANE : FLAT ::

    (A) line : straight
    (B) earth : cloudy
    (C) helicopter : vertical
    (D) ship : large
    (E) sky : clear

7.   RADIUS : ARM ::

     (A)   scapula : neck
     (B)   diameter : circle
     (C)   angle : degree
     (D)   ankle : wrist
     (E)   fibula : leg

8.   SCHOOL : FISH ::

     (A)   hamster : wheels
     (B)   cattle : herd
     (C)   sheep : flock
     (D)   club : members
     (E)   armada : soldiers

9.   PEAK : MOUNTAIN ::

     (A)   roof : building
     (B)   hood : car
     (C)   trunk : tree
     (D)   pedal : bicycle
     (E)   base : statue

10. ODOMETER : DISTANCE ::

     (A)   kilometer : miles
     (B)   barometer : depth
     (C)   thermometer : fever
     (D)   chronometer : time
     (E)   altimeter : range

11. LANTERN : ILLUMINATE ::

     (A)   water : wash
     (B)   parasol : shade
     (C)   decanter : drink
     (D)   radio : entertain
     (E)   pencil : illustrate

12. KLEPTOMANIAC : STEAL ::

     (A)   chatterbox : talk
     (B)   stockbroker : deceive
     (C)   murderer : slay
     (D)   athlete : compete
     (E)   attorney : prosecute

13. INVADER : TRESPASS ::

     (A)   traitor : explain
     (B)   colonel : obey
     (C)   physicist : create
     (D)   chauffeur : drive
     (E)   journalist : assign

Analogies

14. WEAK : STRENGTH ::

(A) happy : joy
(B) calm : patience
(C) foolish : wisdom
(D) penitent : remorse
(E) sad : tragedy

15. INGENUE : SOPHISTICATION ::

(A) anarchist : perfection
(B) atheist : faith
(C) stagehand : believability
(D) musician : artistry
(E) surgeon : wit

16. TAILOR : SEW ::

(A) waiter : cook
(B) pharmacist : argue
(C) artist : paint
(D) director : act
(E) carpenter : build

17. MICROSCOPE : MAGNIFY ::

(A) invention : patent
(B) electron : reduce
(C) billboard : advertise
(D) microphone : speak
(E) instrument : record

18. LINEN : FABRIC ::

(A) cotton : wool
(B) wood : metal
(C) shell : egg
(D) steel : alloy
(E) iron : clothing

19. BREEZE : WIND ::

(A) storm : hurricane
(B) drizzle : rain
(C) ice : air
(D) shelter : umbrella
(E) ocean : water

20. FOG : VISIBILITY ::

(A) caution : danger
(B) light : clarity
(C) sound : deafness
(D) noise : music
(E) patience : balance

21. COLD : SHIVER ::

    (A)   rain : soak
    (B)   ice : freeze
    (C)   flood : swim
    (D)   heat : perspire
    (E)   milk : thirsty

22. METEORITE : PLANET ::

    (A)   crater : surface
    (B)   asteroid : comet
    (C)   quasar : supernova
    (D)   constellation : cluster
    (E)   rocket : moon

23. INKLING : INDICATION ::

    (A)   crash : collision
    (B)   tap : knock
    (C)   echo : tunnel
    (D)   bend : fold
    (E)   crime : punishment

24. SCALE : NOTE ::

    (A)   weight : gram
    (B)   length : distance
    (C)   collection : coin
    (D)   ship : sail
    (E)   spectrum : color

25. PARABOLA : CURVE ::

    (A)   triangle : pyramid
    (B)   rectangle : polygon
    (C)   tetrahedron : square
    (D)   graph : equation
    (E)   isotope : circle

26. DISHONEST : TRUTHFUL ::

    (A)   greedy : selfish
    (B)   abrasive : rough
    (C)   loud : noisy
    (D)   slender : stout
    (E)   mad : angry

27. CONSCIENTIOUS : SCRUPLES ::

    (A)   methodical : details
    (B)   observant : eyes
    (C)   anxious : worries
    (D)   frightening : scars
    (E)   small : teeth

28.   SPLASH : WAVES ::

   (A)   acorn : oaks
   (B)   promise : obligations
   (C)   garbage : pollution
   (D)   iron : rust
   (E)   pet : companionship

29.   SPARROW : BIRD ::

   (A)   cat : lion
   (B)   reptile : lizard
   (C)   salamander : frog
   (D)   fish : trout
   (E)   cobra : snake

30.   ARCHIVE : RECORDS ::

   (A)   box : jewelry
   (B)   garage : yachts
   (C)   safe : valuables
   (D)   refrigerator : fruit
   (E)   books : bookshelf

Answers and Explanations

1.   **(B)**   Lack   *Moderate*

"To be COWARDLY is to lack BRAVERY" is the best sentence that you can make
with this stem pair. Similarly, to be *obstinate*, or stubborn, is to lack *flexibility*. In each
pair for choices (A), (C), and (D), the first word describes someone who has, rather
than lacks, the trait described by the second word. The words in choice (E) do not have
a clear and necessary relationship.

2.   **(D)**   Relative Size and Degree   *Easy*

"To REVILE something is to DISLIKE it intensely" is the best sentence that you can
make for this stem pair. Similarly, to *adore* something is to *admire* it intensely. You
should be able to eliminate choices (A), (B), and (E), because each of those responses
offers pairs of synonyms rather than pairs that vary in degree. Choice (C) should be
eliminated, because to *want* something is not necessarily to *like* it.

3.   **(E)**   Function/Purpose   *Moderate*

"By definition, an ARMORY is a place where WEAPONS are stored" is the best sentence that you can make with this stem pair. Similarly, by definition, a *wardrobe* is a
place where *clothing* is stored. Choice (A) counts on yourcounts on the fact that you
will confusing confuse the word *armory* with *armor*; while there is a relationship

between *shield* and *swords*, it is not the same relationship as the words in the stem pair. (B), (C), and (D) seem to be plausible choices, but they can be eliminated, because a *barn*, *cage*, and *shelf* are not, by definition, places where *horses*, *lions*, and *books* are stored or housed.

4. **(C)** Attribute   *Difficult*
The best sentence for this stem pair is "A REPUBLIC is a REPRESENTATIVE form of government." Similarly, a *dictatorship* is an *autocratic* form of government. None of the other choices fits this sentence. The pairs of words in choices (A) and (D) do not have a good internal relationships. Choice (B) offers a pair of related words in the sense that a *senate* is a *legislative* branch of government, but this is not the same relationship as the one between the words in the stem pair. Choice (E) also offers a pair of related words, but these words also do not share the same type of relationship as the stem pair.

5. **(D)** Descriptive Pair   *Difficult*
The best sentence for this stem pair can take the form of "_____ is a viscous, or thick, _____." Thus, SYRUP is a viscous SWEETNER, and *oil* is a viscous *lubricant*. A simpler sentence in the form of "_____ is a type of _____" will not work well because it does not eliminate choices (A) and (E). *Sugar* often comes in the form of *granules*, but the relationship does not parallel that of the stem pair, so you should eliminate choice (B), while and choice (C) offers a pair that does not really share a good internal relationship.

6. **(A)** Attribute   *Easy*
The best sentence for this stem pair is "A PLANE is FLAT." Similarly, a *line* is *straight*. The relationships here are geometrical; technically, there is no such thing as a curved *plane* or a crooked *line*. Once you realize that *plane* does not refer to airplane, you should be able to eliminate choices (C) and (D). *Sky* and *earth* both have spatial dimensions and may seem related to *plane* in a geometrical sense, but neither word is necessarily has a relationrelated to the words *cloudy* and *clear*, so you would eliminate choices (B) and (E).

7. **(E)** Characteristic Location   *Moderate*
The best sentence for this stem pair is "The RADIUS is a bone found in the ARM." Similarly, the *fibula* is a bone found in the *leg*. Eliminate choice (A), because the *scapula* is the shoulder blade, which is not in the *neck*. Similarly, eliminate choice (D), because the *ankle* has no direct relation to the *wrist*. Choices (B) and (C) should be eliminated, because they have nothing to do with bones or bodies. Note that a sentence in the form of "_____ is part of the _____" may not be an effective way of solving this analogy, because it could leave too many choices. One may argue, for

example, that a *diameter* is part of a *circle*, or that a *degree* is part of an *angle* (though a *degree* is more accurately a unit of measure for an *angle*).

8. **(D)** Part/Whole   *Easy*
The best sentence for this stem pair is "A SCHOOL is a group of FISH," just as a *club* is a group of *members*. Eliminate (A), because there is no necessary relationship between *hamster* and *wheels*. Eliminate (B) even though a *herd* can be a group of *cattle*, because the relationship is the reverse of the stem pair; in other words, a *cattle* is not a group of *herds*. Similarly, eliminate (C), because a *sheep* is not a group of flocks. Eliminate (E), because an *armada* is a group of warships, not *soldiers*.

9. **(A)** Part/Whole   *Easy*
The best sentence for this stem pair is "The PEAK is the highest part of a MOUNTAIN." Similarly, the *roof* is the highest part of a *building*. None of the other pairs will fit in this sentence. Note that if you simply use a sentence of the form "The _____ is part of a _____," you will not be able to eliminate any of the choices.

10. **(D)** Characteristic Use   *Difficult*
The best sentence for this stem pair is "An ODOMETER measures DISTANCE." Similarly, a *chronometer* measures *time*. You can eliminate (A), because a *kilometer* is a unit of distance, just as *miles* are units of distance; in other words, the relationship between the words of this pair is nothing like the relationship in the stem pair. You can eliminate choices (B), (C), and (E), because the first word of each pair measures something other than the second word in the same pair. A *barometer* measures pressure, not *depth*; a *thermometer* measures temperature, not *fever*; and an *altimeter* measures altitude, not *range*.

11. **(B)** Function/purpose   *Difficult*
The best sentence for this stem pair is "The function of a LANTERN is to ILLUMINATE." Similarly, the function of a *parasol* is to *shade*. You can eliminate the other choices, because there is no similar relationship between the pairs of words. Eliminate (A), because while *water* can be used to *wash*, it has no specific purpose. Eliminate (B), because the purpose of a *decanter* is to separate sediment from a liquid. Eliminate (D) and (E), because although a *radio* can be used to *entertain* and a *pencil* can be used to *illustrate*, they may also have other functions, such as to inform and to write, respectively.

12. **(A)** Characteristic Action   *Difficult*
The best sentence for this stem pair is "A KLEPTOMANIAC is someone who STEALS compulsively." Similarly, a *chatterbox* is someone who *talks* compulsively. None of the other choices link persons to compulsive actions. Eliminate (B), because a

stockbroker is not someone who, by definition, *deceives*. Eliminate (C) and (D), because a *murderer* does not necessarily *slay* compulsively, and an *athlete* does not *compete* compulsively. Eliminate (E), because an *attorney* does not necessarily *prosecute*.

13. **(D)** Characteristic Action   *Moderate*
The best sentence for this stem pair is "An INVADER is someone who TRESPASSES," since trespassing is what makes an invader an invader. Similarly, a *chauffeur* is someone who *drives*. A *colonel* may very well *obey* a superior officer, but obedience is not what makes him or her a colonel, so you may eliminate (B). You may also eliminate (C) and (E), because the word pairs in these choices don't do not have obvious relationships.

14. **(C)** Lack   *Easy*
The best sentence for this stem pair is "To be WEAK is to lack STRENGTH." Similarly, to be *foolish* is to lack *wisdom*. None of the other choices offers a similarly related pair of words.

15. **(B)** Lack   *Difficult*
An *ingenue* is someone who is naive. The best sentence for this stem pair is "An INGENUE is someone who lacks SOPHISTICATION." Similarly, an *atheist* is someone who lacks *faith*. A *musician* may or may not lack *artistry*; therefore, while these two words may possibly be linked, it's it is not clear what their relationship would be, so eliminate choice (D). Eliminate the other choices, because there are also no clear relationships between any of these word pairs.

16. **(E)** Characteristic Action   *Easy*
The best sentence for this stem pair can be "A TAILOR'S job is to SEW." Similarly, a *carpenter's* job is to *build*. Eliminate choices (A) and (B), because it is not a *waiter's* job to *cook*, and it is not a *pharmacist's* job to *argue*. An *artist* may *paint*, but may also use another means of expression, such as sculpture, so eliminate choice (C). A *director* may also *act*, but acting is not his or her job, so eliminate choice (D).

17. **(C)** Function/Purpose   *Moderate*
The best sentence for this stem pair is "The purpose of a MICROSCOPE is to MAGNIFY." Similarly, the purpose of a *billboard* is to *advertise*. Eliminate choice (A), because while an *invention* can be *patented*, *inventions* all have different purposes. You can eliminate (B), because there is no internal relationship between *electron* and *reduce*. Eliminate (D), because the purpose of a *microphone* is to amplify sound, not to *speak*. Eliminate (E), because *instrument* can refer to a musical instrument or to a tool, neither of which necessarily has the function of *recording*.

Analogies

18. **(D)** Type   *Moderate*

The best sentence for this stem pair is "LINEN is a type of FABRIC." Similarly, *steel* is a type of *alloy*, which is a substance composed of a metal and something else -- either other metals or nonmetals. You can eliminate the other four choices, because their word pairs do not have clear internal relationships.

19. **(B)** Relative Size and Degree   *Easy*

The best sentence for this stem pair is "A BREEZE is a light WIND." Similarly, a *drizzle* is a light *rain*. Eliminate choice (A); even though a *storm* may sometimes be considered of lesser degree than a *hurricane*, it doesn't does not really make sense to describe a storm as "light." Eliminate (C), because there is no obvious relationship between *ice* and *air*. Also, eliminate choices (D) and (E); while we can say that one kind of *shelter* is an *umbrella*, and that an *ocean* is a large body of *water*, but these word pairs do not have relationships similar to that of the stem pair.

20. **(A)** Cause and Effect   *Moderate*

The best sentence for this stem pair is "FOG reduces VISIBILITY." Similarly, *caution* reduces *danger*. Eliminate choice (B) because the word pair has a relationship opposite that of the stem pair: *light* usually increases *clarity*. Choices (C) and (D) offer word pairs that all relate to sound, but there is no necessary and direct relationship between *sound* and *deafness* or between *noise* and *music*. Eliminate (E), because there is no relationship between *patience* and *balance*.

21. **(D)** Cause and Effect   *Easy*

The best sentence for this stem pair is "COLD makes people SHIVER." Similarly, *heat* makes people *perspire*, or sweat. Although (B) may seem like an attractive choice, you should eliminate it, because while *ice* can make people cold, it usually does not literally make people *freeze*. Eliminate choice (C), because a *flood* does not necessarily make people *swim*, and eliminate (E), because milk does not make people *thirsty*.

22. **(A)** Characteristic Location   *Difficult*

A *meteorite* is a meteor that has landed on a planet. The best sentence for this stem pair is "A METEOR is found on a PLANET." Similarly, a *crater* is found on a *surface*. Although all of the other choices have words that relate to astronomy, there are no necessary internal relationships among these individual pairs, so choices (B), (C), (D) and (E) can be eliminated.

23. **(B)** Relative Size and Degree   *Moderate*

The best sentence for this stem pair can be "An INKLING is a faint INDICATION." Similarly, a *tap* is a faint *knock*. Eliminate choice (A), because there is no clear degree of difference between the words of the pair. Eliminate choices (C), (D) and (E), because the word relationships in these three pairs are not the same as that of the stem pair.

24. **(E)** Part/Whole *Difficult*

In this stem pair the word *scale* refers to the musical scale, so the best sentence that you could come up with may be "A SCALE is made up of different NOTES." Similarly, a *spectrum* is made up of different *colors*. You can eliminate the choices (A), (B), and (D), because it does not make sense to make up similar sentences with these word pairs. A *weight* is not made up of *grams*, a *length* is not made up of *distances*, and a *ship* is not made up of *sails*. Eliminate (C), because it gives a relation that is too specific. A *collection* can be made up of *coins*, but it can also be made up of any number of other items, such as stamps, or cars.

25. **(B)** Type *Difficult*

The best sentence for this stem pair is "A PARABOLA is a type of CURVE." Similarly, a *rectangle* is a type of *polygon*. You should eliminate choices (A) and (D); although the word pairs seem to have relationships because a *triangle* forms some of the faces of a *pyramid* and a *graph* can be of an *equation*, the relationships are not similar to the one in the stem pair. Eliminate choices (C) and (E), because there is no clear relationship between *tetrahedron* and *square* or between *isotope* and *circle*.

26. **(D)** Descriptive Pair *Easy*

The best sentence for this stem pair is "A DISHONEST person is not TRUTHFUL." Similarly, a *slender* person is not *stout*. You can eliminate the other four choices, because their word pairs all have relationships that are opposite to the relationship in the stem pair.

27. **(C)** Descriptive Pair *Difficult*

The best sentence for this stem pair is "A CONSCIENTIOUS person has SCRUPLES." Similarly, an *anxious* person has *worries*. None of the other choices offers a similar relationship. Eliminate (A), because a *methodical* person would pay attention to *details* rather than has have details. Eliminate choices (B), (D), and (E), because persons who are *observant*, *frightening*, *or small*, may or may not have *eyes*, *scars*, or *teeth*; there is no inherent relationship between the words of each pair.

28. **(B)** Cause and Effect *Moderate*

The best sentence for this stem pair is "A SPLASH creates WAVES." Similarly, a *promise* creates *obligations*. Although an oak can grow from an acorn, you can eliminate choice (A), because it wouldn't would not makes sense to say that an *acorn* creates *oaks*. Garbage can be the same as pollution, but *garbage* does not necessarily create *pollution* (unless, perhaps, it is burned, but the sentence for the stem pair does not make an allowance for burning), so eliminate choice (C). Similarly, *iron* can *rust*, but iron does not create rust, and a *pet* can offer *companionship*, but a pet does not create companionship, so eliminate choices (D) and (E).

29. **(E)** Type   *Easy*
The best sentence for this stem pair is "A SPARROW is a kind of BIRD." Similarly, a *cobra* is a type of *snake*. None of the other choices has have a similar relationship. Choices (A), (B), and (D) offer word pairs with relationships opposite to that of the stem pair. A *cat* is not a kind of *lion*, a *reptile* is not a kind of *lizard*, and a *fish* is not a kind of *trout*; and since only the reverse of all three could be considered accurate, you can eliminate these choices. Eliminate choice (C), because there is no clear relationship between *salamander* and *frog*.

30. **(C)** Characteristic Use   *Moderate*
The best sentence for this stem pair is "An ARCHIVE is used to store RECORDS." Similarly, a *safe* is used to store *valuables*. A *box* may well store *jewelry*, but it can store any number of other things, so eliminate choice (A), because it is too specific. Eliminate choice (D) for the same reason, since a *refrigerator* can store any number of foods besides *fruit*. Eliminate choice (B), because a *garage* is where one might find cars rather than *yachts*, and eliminate choice (E), because it offers a word relationship opposite to that of the stem pair: a *bookshelf* is a place for storing *books*, not the other way around.

Reading Comprehension

Of THE 78 QUESTIONS IN THE VERBAL half of the SAT, 40 are reading comprehension. That's more than half. In other words, to do well on the verbal SAT, you have to do well on reading comprehension.

Regrettably, studying for reading comprehension is not as easy as preparing for the other verbal sections. Reading comprehension questions don't come in one basic form, and there aren't always tricks for eliminating answers (though you will often be able to eliminate an answer choice). The best way to study for the reading comprehension section is to read newspapers, magazines, or books, and to question yourself about what you read, both while you do it and after you've finished. Through this sort of practice, you can build up your ability to read and understand quickly.

Location of Reading Comprehension

The SAT includes four sets of reading comprehension passages and questions. One of these four sets is actually a dual passage, involving two passages and subsequent questions. Of the four, two are located at the end of one of the 30-minute verbal sections, one will be at the end of the other 30-minute verbal section, and one will take up the entire final 15-minute verbal section. Usually the dual passage will be found in the 15-minute verbal section, but that is not always the case.

Order of Difficulty

Reading comprehension questions are organized by what part of the passage they test, not by difficulty. The early questions on each passage test the early portions of the passage; the later ones test the end of it. This organizational pattern provides no clue for determining question difficulty within each passage. In an analogy group, you can determine the difficulty of a question based on its location. However, in reading comprehension groups, you can make those decisions only after you've looked at the questions. Since the goal is to answer as many questions as possible, you may want to skip those that immediately strike you as difficult. Of course, how many questions you want to skip depends on your target score. Even so, you should be aware of how the unique organizational scheme for reading comprehension affects your strategy for answering these questions.

Reading Comprehension Instructions

Here are the instructions for reading comprehension, as they appear on the SAT.

> Each passage below is followed by questions based on its content. Answer the questions following each passage on the basis of what is stated or implied in that passage and in any introductory material that may be provided.

Have you read them? Read them again. Do you understand them? Will you remember them tomorrow? Good. Let's move on.

Format and Structure

Reading comprehension sections follow a fairly standard format. Preceding each passage is an italicized introductory blurb that offers some contextual information. *Read this introduction.* Knowing the context it provides will help you understand the passage. Below the introduction is the passage, which can range from 450 to 900 words. The four reading passages on each SAT generally fit into one of the following categories:

- Science

- Art

- Literary criticism

- History or historical criticism

- Fiction or nonfiction narrative

Some passages might overlap categories, as when an artist provides a narrative about his or her experience with art. A few passages might not fit into any of these categories well. There will be at least one science and one narrative passage on every SAT.

Anywhere from 5 to 13 questions accompany each passage. These questions test your comprehension of general themes, points, or tone; your ability to comprehend and breakdown arguments; your ability to interpret implied and explicit information; and your understanding of vocabulary words in context. We cover each of these types of questions later in this section. In addition to the types of questions mentioned above, dual passages include questions that ask you to relate the two passages.

To simplify a bit, reading comprehension questions ask about two things: general understanding and specific information. Questions about general understanding focus on themes, tone, and techniques of writing. Questions on specific information will pinpoint a specific section in the passage and then ask about the meaning of some implied or explicit information in that section, or the meaning of a specific word in context. It is important to note that the questions that ask for specific information will tell you where that information is located. We'll explain how this should affect your reading strategy in the aptly named "Strategic Approaches" section, below.

Of the four reading comprehension passages, one will usually be around 500 words long with 5 questions, one around 700 words with 10 questions , and two around 900 words with 12 or 13 questions. The dual passage will be one of the 900-word passages.

Strategic Approaches

To do well on reading comprehension, you must learn to find the proper balance between time spent reading the passage and time spent answering the questions. There's no use laboring over the passage and making sure you understand everything if you run out of time before getting to the questions. Similarly, there's no use flying through the passage and understanding nothing, since that will obviously make it difficult to answer the questions.

In the following paragraphs, we will provide some strategies to help you balance your time between reading the passages and answering the questions. These strategies will certainly help, but to put your time and effort to best use, you must also practice and learn how quickly you can read without sacrificing understanding. Some test preparation companies promote the use of speed-reading techniques, but in our opinion, these techniques are dubious and often don't result in a very good understanding of the material you read.

Knowing that reading comprehension questions will test your understanding of both general and specific information probably makes you think that when you read the passage, you'll have to spend time focusing on the big themes and the small details.

But that's not really true. A single passage contains one general tone and one general theme, and it will have a particular point. That same passage will have numerous pieces of specific information. At most, you will have to answer 13 questions about a passage, and while those 13 might be able to cover most of the general themes, there's simply no way they can test *all* of the specific information. The strategy we propose for approaching reading comprehension passages will minimize wasted time and effort. It will allow you to get a general sense of the passage and a contextual understanding that will make answering questions about specific information that much easier.

Passage First, Questions After

In this method, you read the passage first and pay no attention to the questions until after you've finished reading. You should read the passage quickly and lightly. Do not dwell on details, but make sure you get a general understanding of what is going on in the passage. Pay active attention to what's going on, but don't get bogged down trying to completely assimilate every fact. This doesn't mean you should ignore the core of every paragraph and focus only on the topic sentence. It means that you should read the passage and see the lay of the land. You should read so that you understand the themes of the passage and the reason the passage was written.

The specific facts are a part of the author's effort to achieve his or her goals, but as you read, you should be more concerned with the cumulative effect of the specific facts than with the specific facts themselves. The only time you should slow down and go back is if you lose the flow of the passage and end up lost. Read the passage with an awareness of the general questions the SAT might ask you. What is the author's goal in writing the passage? What are the tone, themes, and major points? When you finish a passage, you should be able to answer these questions and also have a sense of the passage's structure and of where things lie within it.

When you finish the passage, go to the questions. You should be able to answer general questions without needing to look at the passage. Questions on specific information will indicate the lines in the passage to which they refer. Before going back to the paragraph, articulate to yourself exactly what the question is asking, but don't look at the answers (this will help you avoid being influenced by "trick" answers). Then go to the specified area in the passage and read a few lines before and after it to get a sense of the context. Come up with your own answer to the question, then go back and find the answer that best matches yours.

The Merits of the Passage-First Strategy

Some test-prep courses or books advise you to skim over the questions before reading the passage so you know what to look for. In theory it sounds like a good idea, but in the end we think it will just make your life confusing. Holding 13 questions in your head isn't easy, and some are bound to get mixed up. Also, to answer the specific questions swarming in your head you would have to concentrate on the small facts of the passage to make sure you don't miss anything. That concentration is likely to limit your speed, lessen your understanding of the passage as a whole, and perhaps even affect your memory of the questions you skimmed. It's more effective to take a top-down approach and understand the passage as a whole before trying to fill in the specific blanks, questions by question.

Concentration Strategies for Reading Comprehension

Many students have trouble with reading comprehension passages because they find it hard to maintain focus for the entire passage. To combat the devastating loss-of-focus disease, we've provided some practical advice.

Paragraph-by-Paragraph Analysis

If you have a tendency to drift, to suddenly realize that you have read a hundred words but have no idea what they said, you could take a brief moment—and we mean brief—and think about each paragraph once you've finished. Think about what the paragraph said, what it was about, and how it fit into the overall passage. By stopping after each paragraph, you give yourself a structure that will help you concentrate and better understand what's happening in the passage.

Underline and Circle

Another way to help you focus and remember things when you have to go back to the passage is to underline or circle key arguments, sentences, and facts—anything relating to general themes and ideas, the main idea of each paragraph, or other aspects of the passage that strike you as important. This will reinforce what you read and give you a sort of map for when you go back to the passage to answer specific questions.

Special Strategy for Dual Passages

Dual passages are exactly what their name implies: two passages that deal with the same subject. Because of the way the passages and the questions that follow them are organized, however, your approach to them should be different.

As you look at the dual passage section, you will first see a single introductory blurb that puts both passages into context. The two passages follow the blurb, one after the other. The two passages might differ in length relative to each other, but together they will take up 80–100 lines. Either 12 or 13 questions accompany the dual passages. As with the questions for single passages, dual-passage questions are organized according to line number. Those questions dealing with passage 1 will therefore

Reading Comprehension

be first, followed by the questions asking about passage 2. The last few questions will ask you to relate the two passages.

When you come to the dual passage, read the introductory paragraph and passage 1, using the techniques outlined earlier. After you've finished passage 1, go to the questions, starting with the first. Answer the questions that ask about passage 1, skipping and marking for later those that seem as if they'll take too much time. When you reach the first question about passage 2, go back and read passage two. Ask yourself while you're reading how this second passage relates to the first. Does it agree? Disagree? Does it do both at different times? Mark places where the second passage seems to most intersect with the first, whether in disagreement or agreement. After reading passage 2, return to the questions and begin answering where you left off. Eventually you'll reach the questions that relate the two passages. By this point, you'll not only have read both passages, you'll also have a better understanding of each because of the questions you've already answered.

Types of Reading Passages

As we said earlier, the reading passages on the SAT usually fit into one of five categories: science, art, literary criticism, history or historical criticism, and fiction or nonfiction narrative. Every SAT has at least one passage on science and one narrative. The other two passages on each test can come from any of the five categories. On rare occasions, ETS chooses a passage that doesn't really fit into any of the five categories. If that happens on a test you're taking, don't worry—these passages don't test any skills that are different from those tested by the five categories with which you will soon be familiar.

We can give you some idea about the content you can expect within each passage type and what kinds of questions are usually asked about each. Note, however, that when we say that the questions about a certain type of passage *usually* focus on one thing, we are not saying that you'll *never* be asked anything else about that type of passage. For example, though the questions about fiction or nonfiction narratives often focus on the writer's technique, that doesn't mean that you can't be asked about the writer's intentions.

Science Passages

Science passages range from discussions or debates about science to descriptions of historical scientific events. Students tend to be a little frightened by these passages simply because they cover science, and students think that they have to do a lot of studying to understand science and scientific topics. Do not be intimidated by these passages. No SAT passage will ever require advanced scientific knowledge. The scientific claims these passages make are always general. For example, one thesis in a scientific passage might be "genetics affect decisions about where people build their cities." In those instances when the test wants you to understand scientific arguments, the actual science will be fairly simple. If the passage uses a technical term, it will define that term for you, so don't panic when you see a word or words you don't immediately recognize. Look at the surrounding sentences, and find the term's explanation.

There may be some passages that do discuss more advanced science, but in those instances the passages will focus on the history of a discovery rather than on the science behind the discovery. In these passages, the science is rather unimportant compared to the history or the argument that the writer is making about the history. Questions about science passages will focus on how well you understand the arguments that have been made, on specific information, and on your ability to comprehend words in context. There will be at least one science passage on every SAT.

Passage 1 - SCIENCE

The following passage discusses Sir Isaac Newton's three laws of motions.

When we think of the most illustrious physical scientists in history, Newton may be only one of several who come to mind. Aristotle, Pythagoras, Copernicus, Galileo, Kepler, Schrödinger, Einstein, Heisenberg, Planck, Bohr, and Hawking would certainly all be members of this elite club. But if we had to pick a short list, the names would be cut to
5   about two—Newton and Einstein.

Newton's *Principia Mathematica* is generally considered the most important work in the history of physical science. Newton's laws of motion, which he advances in *Principia Mathematica,* describe and predict the actions of all forces and bodies. In this regard, Newton's work dwarfs the greatest discoveries made by virtually any physicist since. Many
10   modern physicists have attained greatness by making findings in extremely specific, often arcane fields of study. But Newton was the first to comprehend such a large chunk of the cosmic plan. What's more, he also developed the complicated mathematical frameworks that prove his theories.

Newton's findings center on three laws, each of which can be summarized in a single
15   statement. Newton's first law states that a body remains at rest, or moves in a straight line at a constant speed, unless acted upon by an outside force. The implications of this law are crucial. All movement is caused by the application of certain forces. Therefore, we can express the movement of a body by the forces that act upon it. Objects don't have energy within themselves. If a ball stops rolling, then some force made it stop—it can't have simply
20   "run out of steam" or lost some sort of internal energy. The ball stops because the force of friction (the floor rubbing against the ball) overtakes the force of the original push a person might have given the ball. The only way to keep the ball moving at the same speed is to continue to push the ball at that speed.

Newton's second law states that the net outside force on an object equals the mass of the
25   object times its acceleration. The greater the force, the more the object accelerates. The larger the mass of an object, the more force is needed to make the object move faster (or move at all, if the object begins at rest). This law is easy to picture: it's easier to throw a baseball than a bowling ball. Also, the harder a ball is thrown, the faster it goes. As intuitive as this may seem to us today, the mathematical implications of the theory are profound. For one, it

30   helpedNewton to determine the exact force of gravity on Earth, which is essential for
      predicting the motions of all universal bodies (except those of small particles, which are
      governed by the laws of quantum mechanics).

           Newton's third law: "Whenever one body exerts a force on a second body, the second body
      exerts an equal and opposite force on the first body." More succinctly, for every action there is
35   an equal and opposite reaction. When you push against a wall, the wall exerts an equal force
      back against your palms. The third law led to a fourth, which is known as Newton's universal
      law of gravitation: "Two bodies attract each other with a force that is directly proportional to
      the mass of each body and inversely proportional to the square of the distance between
      them." This law is perhaps the most important, for it tells us that *everything* in the universe
40   exerts a force on everything else. The sun exerts an attractive gravitational force on the
      Earth, which keeps us in orbit. But the Earth also exerts an attractive force (though a
      significantly smaller one) on the sun. You exert a force on the person sitting next to you, and
      they exert one back on you.

           Newton's laws of motion and his universal law of gravitation allow us to understand and
45   predict virtually every action in our known universe, from the movement of a ball being hit
      by a bat to the movement of galaxies. In this sense, Newton's contribution remains essential
      to our understanding of the universe. Newton's laws are also the template Einstein used to
      develop his theories of relativity, which might be imagined as extensions of Newton's laws.

           Now, the goal of many scientists is to formulate an integrative "theory of
50   everything" that unifies all other theories in physical science. Any theory of everything will
      be indebted to Newton's theory—or will evolve out of his theory. His laws describe what we
      might call all "practical" events, those that we encounter and observe in everyday life, both
      on Earth and beyond. Today, we still rely on Newton's laws in every field of engineering or
      design, whether it be for making spaceships faster or cars safer, buildings more structurally
55   sound, or sports equipment more effective. But this kind of summary of the uses of Newton's
      laws is only an understatement. They describe our every action, both those we can see and
      those that are too small—or too vast—for us to perceive.

1.   The primary purpose of this passage is to

      (A)   provide a synopsis of Newton's *Principia Mathematica*
      (B)   discuss scientists' efforts to formulate a unifying "theory of everything"
      (C)   inform the reader of Newton's enduring importance in physical science
      (D)   dismiss Newton's accomplishments as outdated
      (E)   compare Newton with Einstein

2.   The tone of the passage can best be described as

      (A)   eulogizing
      (B)   pedantic
      (C)   informational
      (D)   florid
      (E)   spare

3.   The author states all of the following about Newton EXCEPT:

      (A)   Newton's laws allow us to understand the actions of forces and bodies
      (B)   Newton's theories influenced Einstein
      (C)   Newton developed mathematical frameworks that prove his theories
      (D)   Newton developed the theory of relativity
      (E)   Newton calculated the exact force of gravity on Earth.

4.   The paragraphs that summarize Newton's laws are meant to

    (A)   point out flaws in Newton's discoveries
    (B)   provide the mathematical proofs behind Newton's discoveries
    (C)   explain Newton's discoveries in the context of other scientists' discoveries
    (D)   fill in the reader on the fundamentals of Newton's discoveries
    (E)   draw broad parallels between the fields of physics and astronomy

5.   As it is used in line 11, the word "arcane" most closely means

    (A)   obscure
    (B)   fascinating
    (C)   influential
    (D)   technical
    (E)   uninteresting

6.   In line 13, what is the meaning of the word "frameworks"?

    (A)   Branches
    (B)   Concepts
    (C)   Outlines
    (D)   Borders
    (E)   Instructions

7.   Which example does the author use to illustrate Newton's third law?

    (A)   A person pushing against a wall
    (B)   A bat hitting a ball
    (C)   A ball rolling across a surface
    (D)   The sun's gravitational force keeping the Earth in orbit
    (E)   Two people sitting next to each other

8.   As it appears in line 49, the word "integrative" means

    (A)   groundbreaking
    (B)   difficult
    (C)   superlative
    (D)   mathematical
    (E)   uniting

9.   The discussion of scientists' efforts toward a "theory of everything" is meant to

    (A)   demonstrate how much physical science has changed since Newton's time
    (B)   imply that Newton's discoveries do not compare to current discoveries
    (C)   dismiss these scientists' efforts as futile
    (D)   show how Newton's discoveries influence physical science even today
    (E)   convey how difficult it will be to formulate such a "theory of everything"

10.   Which of the following titles best summarizes the passage?

    (A)   Newton's Laws
    (B)   Newton and Einstein
    (C)   Newton's Contributions to Physical Science
    (D)   Gravity and Relativity
    (E)   Newton and His Contemporaries

Reading Comprehension

Answers and Explanations - Science

1. **(C)** Main Theme or Idea   *Moderate*
The focus of the passage is on Newton, so you can quickly eliminate choice (B); although the passage does mention the idea of a "theory of everything," such a theory is not the passage's main focus. Although the writer does summarize Newton's laws, no complete summary of *Principia Mathematica* is provided, so eliminate (A). By no means does the writer dismiss Newton's accomplishments, so eliminate (D). Finally, in choice (E), although the writer does link Newton and Einstein in several ways, a comparison of the two scientists is not the focus of the passage. The correct answer is (C).

2. **(C)** Author's Attitude or Tone   *Moderate*
(C) is the only appropriate answer choice. The passage does not mourn Newton's passing, so (A) is inappropriate. (B) does not work because the passage does not dwell on insignificant trivia or details. The prose of the passage is neither excessively flowery, (D), nor excessively pared down, (E). Rather, it is meant to provide information, (C).

3. **(D)** Specific Information   *Easy*
Throughout the passage, the author explains Newton's achievements and influence. However, it was Einstein rather than Newton who developed the theory of relativity, so answer (D) is correct. Although Einstein drew on Newton's discoveries in developing the theory of relativity, the theory did not arise for several hundred years after Newton's time.

4. **(D)** Author's Technique   *Moderate*
Eliminate (A) because the author does not attempt to refute Newton's laws. Choice (B) is incorrect because the author does not provide any mathematical background during the course of these paragraphs. Likewise, the author does not provide a broader context of other scientists' discoveries but instead focuses solely on Newton's laws, so (C) is not correct. Finally, eliminate (E) because although the author does mention several astronomical applications of Newton's theories, the passage does not draw broader parallels between the fields of physics and astronomy. The correct answer is (D)—the paragraphs on Newton's laws are meant to convey, in simple form, Newton's fundamental discoveries to readers who might not already be familiar with them.

5. **(A)** Words in Context   *Moderate*
You may not know that "arcane" means "mysterious or obscure," but you should be able to figure out its rough meaning from the context of the paragraph. The passage

says that many other scientists' great discoveries have been in specific fields that have not had as wide-ranging an impact as Newton's discoveries. From this sentence, you should realize that arcane means something that is not well known or wide-ranging. The best answer is (A), "obscure."

6. **(B)** Words in Context   *Moderate*

"Frameworks" means conceptual structures or ideas, so the best answer is choice (B), *concepts.* Choices (A) and (D) clearly do not fit into the sentence and can be eliminated. Choice (C), *outlines,* is too vague and does not fit the meaning of the sentence as well. Choice (E), *instructions,* implies that Newton drew up instructions for preexisting mathematical concepts when in fact he came up with the concepts himself.

7. **(A)** Specific Information   *Easy*

The author states Newton's third law, paraphrases it, and then gives an example similar to (A), a person pushing against a wall and the wall exerting a force back on the person's palms. Although the author does use all the other examples to illustrate different aspects of Newton's laws, choice (A) is the only one associated with Newton's third law.

8. **(E)** Words in Context   *Moderate*

The author writes that scientists hope to discover a theory "that unifies all other theories in physical science," which implies that "integrative" means "unifying." Choice (E) is the best answer to this question, for "uniting" it is the word with meaning closest to "unifying." Although choices (A), (B), and (D) likely are all words that might be used to describe the new theory, they do not fit the context of the sentence as well as (E), "uniting."

9. **(D)** Understanding Themes and Arguments   *Moderate*

The author states that "Any theory of everything will be indebted to Newton's theory—or will evolve out of his theory." With this context, it becomes clear that the best answer is (D), for the author is showing how Newton's discoveries endure in the present day. Choices (B) and (C) are dismissive and can be eliminated immediately. Although (E) is correct in implying that the formulation of a "theory of everything" will likely be difficult, it is not the main reason that the author includes this discussion in the passage.

10. **(C)** Main Theme, Idea, or Point   *Moderate*

Since the focus of this passage is Newton himself, you can eliminate choice (D). Choice (A) is misleading because the passage does not dwell solely on Newton's laws but also on the broader context of his accomplishments. Likewise, (B) does not work because the passage does not focus exclusively on the relationship between Newton's and Einstein's discoveries. Eliminate (E) because the passage does not discuss Newton's contemporaries—the scientists working along with him at the time—in any depth. The most appropriate answer is (C), which conveys the fact that the passage is a broad discussion of Newton's enduring contributions to physical science.

Fiction or Nonfiction Narratives

The content of fiction or nonfiction narratives is not so easy to pinpoint. Often a narrative will focus on a description of a particular person. You will have to intuit information from that description. Sometimes the narratives describe a coming-of-age anecdote or an important experience. As you read these narratives, you should think about why the author is choosing to write what he or she is writing. Why does the writer choose the metaphors used in the passage? What is the tone? Why are some details explored and others barely acknowledged? The writers of these narratives make artistic choices to mold an overall sense of their stories. Pay attention to these aspects of the passage as you read. The questions will likely ask you about them.

The questions for fiction or nonfiction narratives tend to cover quite a bit, with emphasis on words in context, understanding arguments or points, the writer's technique, and both implied and explicit information.

Passage 2 - NARRATIVE

The following excerpt is taken from a short story about a married couple in Dublin after the husband bites off a small piece of his tongue when he is drunk.

She was an active, practical woman of middle age. Not long before she had celebrated her silver wedding and renewed her intimacy with her husband by waltzing with him to Mr. Power's accompaniment. In her days of courtship, Mr. Kernan had seemed to her a not ungallant figure: and she still hurried to the chapel door whenever a wedding was
5   reported and, seeing the bridal pair, recalled with vivid pleasure how she had passed out of the Star of the Sea Church in Sandymount, leaning on the arm of a jovial well-fed man, who was dressed smartly in a frock-coat and lavender trousers and carried a silk hat gracefully balanced upon his other arm. After three weeks she had found a wife's life irksome and, later on, when she was beginning to find it unbearable, she had become a
10   mother. The part of mother presented to her no insuperable difficulties and for twenty-five years she had kept house shrewdly for her husband. Her two eldest sons were launched. One was in a draper's shop in Glasgow and the other was clerk to a tea-merchant in Belfast. They were good sons, wrote regularly and sometimes sent home money. The other children were still at school.
15   Mr. Kernan sent a letter to his office next day and remained in bed. She made beef-tea for him and scolded him roundly. She accepted his frequent drunkenness as part of the climate, healed him dutifully whenever he was sick and always tried to make him eat a breakfast. There were worse husbands. He had never been violent since the boys had grown up, and she knew that he would walk to the end of Thomas Street and back again to book

20   even a small order.

Two nights after, his friends came to see him. She brought them up to his bedroom, the
air of which was impregnated with a personal odor, and gave them chairs at the
fire. Mr. Kernan's tongue, the occasional stinging pain of which had made him
somewhat irritable during the day, became more polite. He sat propped up in the bed by
25   pillows and the little color in his puffy cheeks made them resemble warm cinders. He
apologized to his guests for the disorder of the room, but at the same time looked at them a
little proudly, with a veteran's pride.

He was quite unconscious that he was the victim of a plot which his friends, Mr.
Cunningham, Mr. M'Coy and Mr. Power had disclosed to Mrs. Kernan in the parlor. The idea
30   had been Mr. Power's, but its development was entrusted to Mr. Cunningham. Mr. Kernan
came of Protestant stock and, though he had been converted to the Catholic faith at the time
of his marriage, he had not been in the pale of the Church for twenty years. He was fond,
moreover, of giving side-thrusts at Catholicism.

When the plot had been disclosed to her, Mrs. Kernan had said:
35   "I leave it all in your hands, Mr. Cunningham."

After a quarter of a century of married life, she had very few illusions left. Religion for
her was a habit, and she suspected that a man of her husband's age would not change greatly
before death. She was tempted to see a curious appropriateness in his accident and, but that
she did not wish to seem bloody-minded, would have told the gentlemen that Mr. Kernan's
40   tongue would not suffer by being shortened. However, Mr. Cunningham was a capable man;
and religion was religion. The scheme might do good and, at least, it could do no harm. Her
beliefs were not extravagant. She believed steadily in the Sacred Heart as the most
generally useful of all Catholic devotions and approved of the sacraments. Her faith was
bounded by her kitchen, but, if she was put to it, she could believe also in the banshee and in
45   the Holy Ghost.

1.   It can be inferred that Mrs. Kernan "still hurried to the chapel door whenever a wedding was
reported" (lines 4–5) because

(A)   she knows people who are attending the weddings
(B)   the weddings remind her of her own wedding, which she remembers fondly
(C)   she yearns for romance, which her marriage to Mr. Kernan lacks
(D)   watching weddings helps her overcome her boredom now that her sons are grown
(E)   she is curious to see what the bride is wearing

2.   In relation to the first paragraph, the first sentence of the second paragraph (line 15) serves to

(A)   move away from the character description of the first paragraph and advance the action
of the story
(B)   build on the description in the first paragraph of Mrs. Kernan's sons
(C)   enhance the reader's understanding of Mrs. Kernan's character
(D)   offer a description of Mrs. Kernan that contrasts with the description given in the first
paragraph
(E)   provide a specific example of the generalizations made in the first paragraph

3. The second paragraph suggests that the Kernans' marriage is characterized primarily by

    (A)   Mr. Kernan's violence against his wife

    (B)   Mrs. Kernan's patience with her husband

    (C)   Mr. Kernan's fondness for his wife's beef-tea

    (D)   Mrs. Kernan's irritation with her husband's frequent drunkenness

    (E)   Mr. Kernan's willingness to go to the store for his wife

4. Which of the following best captures the meaning of the word "impregnated" in line 22?

    (A)   marked by

    (B)   fertilized

    (C)   saturated

    (D)   replaced

    (E)   oppressed

5. The reference to Mr. Kernan's tongue in lines 23–24 is used to describe both his actual tongue and

    (A)   the kind of language he uses

    (B)   his physical appearance

    (C)   the gestures he makes

    (D)   warm cinders

    (E)   his personal odor

6. The word "stock" in line 31 most nearly means

    (A)   birth

    (B)   structure

    (C)   framework

    (D)   faith

    (E)   lineage

7. In the passage, Mr. Kernan is characterized as

    (A)   foolish and excessive

    (B)   sensible and intelligent

    (C)   stubborn and unreasonable

    (D)   proud of his accomplishments

    (E)   irreverent but generally considerate

8. It can be inferred from the fourth paragraph (lines 28–33) that the goal of the friends' plot is to

    (A)   turn Mr. Kernan into a better husband

    (B)   cure Mr. Kernan of his alcohol abuse

    (C)   make Mr. Kernan a good, practicing Catholic

    (D)   go to Thomas Street for Mrs. Kernan while her husband recovers

    (E)   donate money and furniture to the Kernans

9. The last paragraph suggests that Mrs. Kernan's belief in religion is

    (A)   practical but faithful

    (B)   fervently pious

    (C)   nonexistent

    (D)   superficial

    (E)   marked by skepticism

Reading Comprehension

10.   Throughout the passage, the primary focus is on

    (A)   Mr. Kernan's recovery

    (B)   the relationship between Mr. Kernan and his friends

    (C)   the practice of Catholicism

    (D)   Mrs. Kernan's attitudes toward her marriage and religion

    (E)   the plot hatched against Mr. Kernan

Answers and Explanations - Narrative

1. **(B)** Implied Information   *Moderate*

The key to answering this question is to read past the quoted material. The sentence says, "she still hurried to the chapel door whenever a wedding was reported and, seeing the bridal pair, recalled with vivid pleasure how she had passed out of the Star of Sea Church in Sandymount, leaning on the arm of a jovial well-fed man, who was dressed smartly in a frock-coat and lavender trousers and carried a silk hat gracefully balanced upon his other arm." The second part of the sentence describes Mrs. Kernan's memory of her own wedding, and it says that she recalls her wedding "with vivid pleasure." This sentence suggests that nostalgia for her own wedding is one of the reasons why Mrs. Kernan watches other people's weddings, so the best answer to this question is (B). You can also arrive at this answer through elimination. The passage does not say that Mrs. Kernan knows people at the wedding, so you can rule out (A). It never implies that she yearns for romance, so you can rule out choice (C). Finally, the passage does not talk about her boredom or her curiosity, so you can rule out (D) and (E).

2. **(A)** Structure and Technique   *Easy*

The first paragraph focuses on giving a character description of Mrs. Kernan. The second paragraph begins with the sentence, "Mr. Kernan sent a letter to his office next day and remained in bed." This sentence represents a shift away from the character description of the first paragraph, and it describes an action in the plot. The best answer to this question is (A).

3. **(B)** Implied Information   *Moderate*

This question asks you to make a general characterization based on the description given in the second paragraph of the Kernans' relationship. While the paragraph does mention violence, the narrator notes that Mr. Kernan "had never been violent since the boys had grown up," so choice (A) is wrong. You can rule out choice (C) because the passage never implies that Mr. Kernan likes the beef-tea that his wife makes for him, and you can rule out choice (D) since the passage never says that Mrs. Kernan was irritated by her husband's drunkenness. While choice (E) seems to be a true statement (the paragraph says that "he would walk to the end of Thomas Street and back again to book even a small order"), his willingness to go there doesn't adequately characterize their relationship. The best answer is choice (B). The third sentence indicates that (B) is the right answer: "She accepted his frequent drunkenness as part of the climate, healed him dutifully whenever he was sick and always tried to make him eat a breakfast." Words like "accepted" and "dutifully" suggest Mrs. Kernan's patient resignation to her life and duties.

4.   **(C)** Words in Context   *Easy*
In the context of this sentence, the word "impregnated" means "filled or saturated," so the correct answer to this question is choice (C). If you can't identify the answer, you can improve your chances of guessing correctly by first eliminating obviously wrong answers. The best method of elimination is to substitute the answer choices into the sentence for "impregnated." If you use this method, you should see that *fertilized, replaced,* and *oppressed* don't make sense in the context of the sentence, so you can rule out choices (B), (D), and (E).

5.   **(A)** Structure and Technique   *Moderate*
In the sentence "Mr. Kernan's tongue, the occasional stinging pain of which had made him somewhat irritable during the day, became more polite," the tongue describes both the actual organ in Mr. Kernan's mouth and the language he uses. The correct answer to this question is (A).

6.   **(E)** Words in Context   *Moderate*
As its used in this passage, "stock" means "lineage" or "family," so the correct answer is (E). If you don't know the definition of "stock," you can narrow down the answer choices through elimination. Since neither *framework* or *structure* makes sense in the context of the sentence, you can rule out choices (B) and (C), leaving you with a one in three chance of guessing the correct answer.

7.   **(E)** Implied Information   *Easy*
Nothing in the passage suggests that Mr. Kernan has any of the characteristics given in choices (A), (B), or (C), so you can rule out those answer choices. Although Mr. Kernan appears to be proud of his injury at the end of the third paragraph, the passage does not suggest that he is proud in general of his accomplishments. The correct answer is choice (E). The narrator of the passage describes Mr. Kernan's verbal lack of respect for Catholicism, and Mrs. Kernan thinks that her husband's "tongue would not suffer by being shortened" (in other words, he talks too quickly and too rashly), so you can characterize him as "irreverent," or "lacking proper respect or seriousness." The passage also implies that Mr. Kernan is " considerate" when it describes his willingness to run errands for his wife.

8.   **(C)**   Implied Information   *Difficult*

The fourth paragraph begins by saying that Mr. Kernan is the victim of his friends'
plot. Since the rest of the paragraph is devoted primarily to Mr. Kernan's religious
background and his attitude toward Catholicism, you can reasonably infer that the
friends' plot has to do with religion, so (C) seems like a likely answer. You can confirm
that (C) is the right answer by eliminating the other answer choices. Since the passage
never mentions making Mr. Kernan a better husband, you can rule out choice (A). There is
no mention of Mr. Kernan's drinking after the second paragraph, so you can also rule out
choice (B). Choice (D) tries to lure you off track by mentioning Thomas Street, an unrelated but specific piece of information from the passage. There is no mention of donating
money or furniture to the Kernans, so you can eliminate choice (E).

9.   **(A)**   Understanding Themes and Arguments   *Moderate*

Since the last paragraph describes Mrs. Kernan's belief in religion, you can immediately eliminate choice (C), which says that her belief in religion does not exist. The sentence "Her beliefs were not extravagant" should help you eliminate choice (B), which
says that Mrs. Kernan is *fervently pious,* or "intensely religious and devoted to wor-
ship." The paragraph never says or implies that Mrs. Kernan is superficial in her religious belief or skeptical of Catholicism, so you can rule out choices (D) and (E).
Choice (A) is the best answer because the paragraph describes her as faithful ("if she
was put to it, she could believe also in the banshee and the Holy Ghost") and practical
("Her beliefs were not extravagant").

10.   **(D)**   Main Theme, Idea, or Point   *Difficult*

The main focus of this passage is Mrs. Kernan. Even though the passage contains a
couple of paragraphs that describe Mr. Kernan, the narrator tends to describe him
from the point of view of his wife. Since the passage opens with a discussion of Mrs.
Kernan's views about marriage and ends with a discussion of her views about religion,
the best answer to this question is (D).

History Passages

The history passages either contain a passage taken from history—such as a historical
address about an event or situation in society—or will be a passage in which a historian
writes about and interprets history. In either case, these passages usually contain a lot
of argumentation, with the use of examples or facts as support. Often, the writer will
refer to other writers or thinkers, either to agree with or to refute what the other writer
has said.

Questions about history passages focus on your ability to understand the arguments being made, your understanding of specific and implied information, and, to some extent, your comprehension of words in context.

Passage 5 - Dual Passage, History

The following passages discuss the reign of the nineteenth-century British monarch Queen Victoria after the death of her husband, Prince Albert, to whom she was devoted. Passage 1 is a biographical account of the Queen's mourning period written in the late twentieth century. Passage 2 is a biographical account of the mourning period written in the early twentieth century.

Passage 1

Perhaps the most significant turning point in Queen Victoria's life was the death of her husband, Prince Albert, in December 1861. His death sent Victoria into a deep depression, and she stayed in seclusion for many years, rarely appearing in public. She mourned him by wearing black for the remaining forty years of her life.

5 Albert's death came suddenly. In November 1861, he contracted typhoid fever. He lay sick in bed for several weeks, finally succumbing to the disease on December 14. He was only forty-two years old. Victoria was devastated. She wrote to her daughter Victoria shortly afterwards: "How I, who leant on him for all and everything—without whom I did nothing, moved not a finger, arranged not a print or photograph, didn't put on a gown or bonnet

10 if he didn't approve it shall go on, to live, to move, to help myself in difficult moments?"

The Queen turned mourning into the chief concern of her existence the next several years. The Prince's rooms in their residences were maintained exactly as he had them when he was alive. Her servants were instructed to bring hot water into his dressing room every day as they had formerly done for his morning shave. She had statues made of him, displayed

15 mementos of his around the royal palaces, and spent most of her time secluded in Windsor Castle or in Balmoral up in Scotland, where she had formerly spent so many happy times with her husband.

After the first year, her mourning came to be viewed by many in Britain as obsessive, and public unease arose about the Queen's state of mind and the state of the monarchy generally.

20 This unease was aggravated by Victoria's refusal to appear in public except on the rarest occasions. She made her first public appearance only on October 13, 1863, and then only to unveil a statue of Albert at Aberdeen, Scotland. She appeared publicly in London on June 21, 1864, riding out through the streets in an open carriage. She did not personally appear to open Parliament until the 1866 session, and then only reluctantly.

25 During Victoria's years of mourning and seclusion she reformed the British Army. By 1870, Victoria abolished the Army's patronage system, which had allowed offices to be purchased and granted as gifts. The Army Regulation Bill, which was designed to bring about reforms, was rejected in the House of Lords in 1870, and the changes only came about by royal warrant from the Queen. Victoria approved of restricting royal power in the military,

30 as the reform included the subordination of the role of Commander-in-Chief—a royal appointee, Victoria's cousin, the Duke of Cambridge—to below that of the Secretary of State. She was reluctant to go ahead with these reforms, but judged it the right thing to do despite her personal inclinations to support royal patronage.

Passage 2

The death of the her husband Albert, the Prince Consort, was the central turning-point in the history of Queen Victoria. She herself felt that her true life had ceased with her husband's, and that the remainder of her days upon earth was of a twilight nature—an epilogue to a drama that was done.

5 With appalling suddenness Victoria had exchanged the serene radiance of happiness for the utter darkness of woe. In the first dreadful moments those about her had feared that she might lose her reason, but the iron strain within her held firm, and in the intervals between the intense paroxysms of grief it was observed that the Queen was calm. She remembered, too, that Albert had always disapproved of exaggerated manifestations of feeling, and her

10 one remaining desire was to do nothing but what he would have wished.

Yet there were moments when her royal anguish would brook no restraints. One day she sent for the Duchess of Sutherland, and, leading her to the Prince's room, fell prostrate before his clothes in a flood of weeping, while she adjured the Duchess to tell her whether the beauty of Albert's character had ever been surpassed. At other times a feeling akin to

15 indignation swept over her. "The poor fatherless baby of eight months," she wrote to the King of the Belgians, "is now the utterly heartbroken and crushed widow of forty-two! My LIFE as a HAPPY one is ENDED! The world is gone for ME! . . . Oh! to be cut off in the prime of life— to see our pure, happy, quiet, domestic life, which ALONE enabled me to bear my MUCH disliked position, CUT OFF at forty-two—when I HAD hoped with such instinctive certainty

20 that God never WOULD part us, and would let us grow old together (though HE always talked of the shortness of life)—is TOO AWFUL, too cruel!" The tone of outraged Majesty seems to be discernible. Did she wonder in her heart of hearts how the Deity could have dared?

Though the violence of her perturbations gradually subsided, her cheerfulness did not

25 return. For months, for years, she continued in settled gloom. Her life became one of almost complete seclusion. Arrayed in thickest crepe, she passed dolefully from Windsor to Osborne, from Osborne to Balmoral. Rarely visiting the capital, refusing to take any part in the ceremonies of state, shutting herself off from the slightest intercourse with society, she became almost as unknown to her subjects as some potentate of the East. They might

30 murmur, but they did not understand. What had she to do with empty shows and vain enjoyments? No! She was absorbed by very different preoccupations. She was the devoted guardian of a sacred trust. Her place was in the inmost shrine of the house of mourning. That, and that only was her glorious, her terrible duty. For terrible indeed it was. As the years passed her depression seemed to deepen and her loneliness to grow more intense. "I am

35 on a dreary sad pinnacle of solitary grandeur," she said. Again and again she felt that she could bear her situation no longer—that she would sink under the strain.

1. The quotation in lines 8–10 suggests that Victoria mourned her husband's death primarily because

(A) he had managed all of her affairs
(B) he had played an integral part in every aspect of her life
(C) she would not be able to have more children
(D) he had died at an unexpectedly young age
(E) he could no longer advise her on political matters

2.   According to Passage 1, Victoria did all of the following to mourn her husband EXCEPT

(A)   keep everything as it had been before his death
(B)   display his mementos around her palaces
(C)   erect statues of him
(D)   appear publicly to open Parliament
(E)   wear black for the remainder of her life

3.   The tone of Passage 1 can best be described as

(A)   informal
(B)   comic
(C)   academic
(D)   passionate
(E)   satirical

4.   Which of the following titles best summarizes Passage 1?

(A)   The Power of the Prince Consort: Prince Albert's Influence on Queen Victoria
(B)   The Fruitful Marriage of Queen Victoria and Prince Albert
(C)   Queen Victoria and the Victorians
(D)   The Legacy of Queen Victoria
(E)   The Reign of Queen Victoria during her Mourning Period

5.   The comparisons of Victoria's mourning to twilight and to an epilogue in lines 3–4 serve to

(A)   illustrate how Victoria considered her life to be a stage drama
(B)   indicate that the most prominent period of Victoria's reign was her mourning period
(C)   underscore Victoria's feeling that the main part of her life was her marriage to Albert
(D)   describe how Victoria's mourning took place mostly in the evenings
(E)   detract from the seriousness and intensity of her feelings after Albert died

6.   The sentence "No!" in line 31 represents

(A)   the author's objection to the statement
(B)   the reader's response to the passage
(C)   a meaningless interjection
(D)   the imagined response of Victoria
(E)   the public's outcry against the mourning period

7.   In line 11, "brook" most nearly means

(A)   tolerate
(B)   stream
(C)   punish
(D)   advocate
(E)   refuse

8.   The word "adjured" is used in line 13 to mean

(A)   forbade
(B)   allowed
(C)   asked
(D)   commanded
(E)   reprimanded

9.   With which of the following statements would the authors of the passages most likely agree?

    (A)   Victoria's obsessive mourning harmed the state of the country.

    (B)   Albert was not worthy of such diligent mourning from his wife.

    (C)   The public was wrong to criticize Victoria for her long mourning period.

    (D)   Victoria accomplished a great deal of political reform during her mourning period.

    (E)   Albert's death was the most catastrophic event in Victoria's life.

10.   The main difference between the two descriptions of Victoria's mourning period is that

    (A)   Passage 1 focuses on the political implications of the mourning period, while Passage 2 focuses on its social implications

    (B)   Passage 1 puts more emphasis on Victoria's actions during her mourning period than Passage 2 does

    (C)   Passage 1 is more interested in Victoria's emotional reaction to Albert's death than Passage 2 is

    (D)   Passage 1 praises Victoria's behavior, while Passage 2 condemns her behavior

    (E)   Passage 1 is less interested in giving a factual account of the mourning period than Passage 2 is

Answers and Explanations – Dual Passage, History

1.   **(B)**   Understanding Themes and Arguments   *Moderate*
When answering this question, you should reread the quotation to which the question refers: "How I, who leant on him for all and everything—without whom I did nothing, moved not a finger, arranged not a print or photograph, didn't put on a gown or bonnet if he didn't approve it shall go on, to live, to move, to help myself in difficult moments?" Victoria says that she relied on Albert "for all and everything;" in other words, he played an important role in every aspect of her life. Her chief cause for grief, according to this quotation, is that she has lost someone integral to her life, so choice (B) is the best answer to this question.

2.   **(D)**   Specific Information   *Easy*
This question asks you to figure out what Victoria did NOT do to mourn her husband, so make sure you don't identify something that she did do. If you go back to the passage, particularly to the third paragraph, you will see that Victoria did all of the answer choices but appear publicly to open Parliament. The author states in the fourth paragraph that Victoria "did not personally appear to open Parliament until the 1866 session, and then only reluctantly." Although Victoria did eventually open Parliament, this gesture was not part of her mourning for Albert, so choice (D) is the correct answer to this question.

3. **(C)** Author's Attitude or Tone   *Easy*

Passage 1 is a pretty neutral examination of Victoria's mourning period, so the best answer to this question is choice (C). If you feel uncertain about this answer, you can try eliminating the other answer choices first. The passage is neither informal nor comic nor satirical, although these descriptions could apply to Passage 2, so you can rule out choices (A), (B), and (E). The author of Passage 1 never betrays any extreme emotion, so you can rule out choice (D), thus leaving you with the correct answer, (C).

4. **(E)** Main Theme, Idea, or Point   *Easy*

In order to answer this question, try to identify the main focus of this passage. The passage describes Victoria's reign after the death of her husband, so the best title for the passage is choice (E). You can confirm this answer by eliminating the other answer choices. Choice (A) puts too much emphasis on Prince Albert. Choice (B) focuses on the period of Victoria and Albert's marriage, although the passage never actually describes what their marriage was like. Choice (C) focuses on Victoria and the Victorians, but the Victorian public is mentioned only once in the passage. Choice (D) describes Victoria's legacy, but the passage focuses on Victoria's life, not on what Victoria left to future generations.

5. **(C)** Understanding Themes and Arguments   *Difficult*

The author compares Victoria's mourning period to the twilight of the day and the epilogue of a drama. The twilight is the end of the day, and the epilogue is what comes after a drama, or play, is finished. These comparisons emphasize that Victoria's life with Albert represented the main part of her life, or her "true life," so choice (C) is the best answer to this question. You can rule out the other answer choices to double-check this answer. The passage never implies that Victoria thought her life was a stage drama, so choice (A) is wrong. Since twilight is dwarfed by the day and since an epilogue is dwarfed by a play, choice (B) is wrong, because it says that the mourning period is the most prominent part of Victoria's life. Choice (D) incorrectly takes the comparison too literally, and finally, there is no evidence for choice (E) in the passage.

6. **(D)** Structure and Technique   *Difficult*

If you refer back to the passage, you can immediately rule out choices (B) and (E) because neither the reader nor the public is mentioned in this part of the passage. You can also rule out choice (C) since the interjection is not meaningless. In order to answer the question, you need to decide whether the interjection "No!" represents the author's or Victoria's response. Although the author does not make it explicit, in this part of the passage he is trying to portray Victoria's thoughts as she would have thought them. Thoughts such as "she was the devoted guardian of a sacred trust" do not necessarily represent the author's view, but they do represent Victoria's view of herself. The interjection "No!" is how the author imagines Victoria would respond to the implication that she is affected by "empty shows and vain enjoyments," so choice (D) is the best answer to this question.

7. **(A)** Words in Context   *Moderate*
As it is used in this context, "brook" means "tolerate," so choice (A) is the correct answer. If you don't know the meaning of brook, you can answer this question through elimination. You can immediately rule out choice (B) because it does not make sense in the context of the sentence: "stream" is a noun, while you're looking for a verb. You can substitute the remaining answer choices into the sentence for "brook" to see whether they make sense. Since the paragraph describes how Victoria brooked her restraint and showed much emotion, you can infer that "brook" has a positive meaning, and you can rule out words with negative meanings, such as choices (C) and (E). By eliminating these answer choices, you increase your chances of guessing correctly to one in two.

8. **(D)** Words in Context   *Moderate*
The definition of "abjured" is "commanded," so the correct answer to this question is (D). If you don't know this definition, try eliminating the other answer choices to improve your odds of guessing correctly. The best way to eliminate is to substitute the other answer choices into the original sentence and see which ones do not make sense in context. Neither choice (A) nor choice (E) makes sense in the context of the sentence, so you can rule them out. Choice (B) seems unlikely because you can infer from the passage that Victoria instigates most of the conversations praising her husband. Although both choices (C) and (D) make sense in the context of the sentence, (D) is a more likely answer because in her position as queen, Victoria would most likely command her subjects to do something than simply ask them to do something.

9. **(E)** Main Theme, Idea, or Point   *Moderate*
This question asks you to identify a point on which the authors of the two passages would agree. If you read the first sentences of each passage, you will see that both authors consider the death of Albert to be the main "turning point" in Victoria's life, and each passage goes on to describe Victoria's depression after her husband's death. Based on this, you can infer that both author's consider her husband's death to be the most catastrophic event in her life, so choice (E) is the best answer to this question. You can also answer this question by ruling out the other answer choices. Neither of the authors implies that Victoria's mourning harmed her country, and neither of the passages implies that Albert was unworthy of her mourning, so choices (A) and (B) are wrong. Although the passages mention that the public grew tired of Victoria's mourning, neither one explicitly criticizes her on this point, so you can rule out choice (C).

Only Passage 1 mentions a piece of political reform passed during the mourning period; Passage 2 focuses exclusively on Victoria's feelings, so choice (D) is wrong.

10. **(B)**   Main Theme, Idea, or Point   *Difficult*
While the passages are very similar, there is a subtle difference in approach to the subject matter. Passage 1, which is more academic in tone than Passage 2, focuses slightly more than Passage 2 on Victoria's actions during her mourning period. For example, it discusses Victoria's efforts to keep the memory of her husband alive; it describes how she withdrew from the public eye; and it describes a piece of reform that she passed during this period. The second passage, by contrast, focuses on Victoria's emotional state after her husband's death. Thus choice (B) is the best answer to this question.

Literary Criticism Passages

Like the history passages, literary-criticism articles are also quite heavy on argument. In these passages, a critic or writer discusses a particular book or writer, a literary movement or trend, or some literary idea. As you read these passages, you should make sure that you understand the arguments the writer is making about the subject in question. You probably don't have to worry very much about the subject itself. For example, if the passage is on *Robinson Crusoe*, you will see questions such as, "How does the writer of the passage feel about Crusoe's religious conversion?" You will *not* see questions like, "At what point in the book does Robinson Crusoe begin to dedicate himself completely to God?"

Questions following literary-criticism passages focus mostly on your ability to understand the arguments being made and your comprehension of words in context.

Passage 3 – Literary Criticism

The following passage was written by a literary critic about the use of shoes in Flannery O'Connor's short stories and novels.

Despite the growing mass of criticism on Flannery O'Connor, a single recurring detail in her fiction has either escaped the notice of most critics or been deemed unworthy of their attention: the shoe. But in her work, O'Connor draws the reader's attention to shoes so often that they should not be ignored. With the exception of "Greenleaf" and "The Comforts of
5   Home," all of O'Connor's fiction contains shoe imagery, and shoes assume meanings beyond their pedestrian function. In fact, O'Connor's characters are often inseparable from the shoes they wear.

In O'Connor's fiction, shoes are a means of identifying social class and signaling the personalities of her characters. In "Revelation," the protagonist, Mrs. Turpin, looks around
10   the waiting room in her doctor's office and classifies its occupants by the types of shoes they wear. A well-dressed lady wears red and gray suede shoes that match her dress; an ugly, bookish girl wears thick Girl Scout shoes (a type of shoe that appears often in O'Connor's writing); a trashy woman wears flimsy bedroom slippers made of black straw threaded with

15 gold braids. Mrs. Turpin herself wears "her good black patent leather pumps," a sign of respectability. This method of classification occurs again in "Everything that Rises Must Converge." In this story, riders on a bus are identified primarily by their shoes. One of the women on the bus is given no name or description other than "the owner of the red and white canvas sandals."

O'Connor further develops the notion that the shoe is connected to a person's identity in
20 *Wise Blood*. In this novel, Enoch buries all of his clothes before donning an ape suit and relinquishing his human identity. He then discovers that he is still wearing his shoes. To complete his transformation into an animal, he removes his shoes and flings them aside.

Other characters in O'Connor's stories have a harder time discarding their identities than Enoch does. In "A Late Encounter with the Enemy," Sally Poker Sash remembers
25 attending the premiere of *Gone with the Wind* in Atlanta with her grandfather, a very old and cantankerous man and a former Confederate general. The prestige of attending the event swells Sally's sense of self-importance, but her pride is dashed when, standing on the stage next to her grandfather, she realizes that she is wearing her old pair of brown Girl Scout Oxfords underneath her evening gown instead of the silver slippers she planned to
30 wear. Despite Sally's efforts to remake her appearance for the evening, her unsophisticated, clumsy shoes betray her true self.

Sally's shoes also warn the reader about the precarious perch upon which pride and vanity are built. Sally's realization that she is wearing the brown shoes recalls the traditional literary metaphor of the peacock. Clergymen used the peacock to represent the
35 folly of pride, vanity, and materialism. The first notable use of the peacock metaphor occurred in the fourteenth century in *Piers Plowman*. In this poem, the peacock represents vanity. The bird proudly displays its magnificent tail, but when it looks down and notices its ugly feet, it becomes crestfallen: a reminder that vanity is a weakness. The peacock's feet are analogous to Sally's shoes. Despite the grand occasion and her beautiful dress,
40 Sally lets vanity get the better of her and destroy her evening.

Sally's vanity has more dire consequences later in the story. At her graduation ceremony from teacher's college, she wants to show off by having her grandfather appear on stage with her. By having him participate in the graduation ceremony, she hopes to show everyone that she has descended from an important family and thus that she is someone far above average.
45 The stress and the heat of the day prove too much for the old man, and when he is pushed on stage in his wheel chair, Sally Poker Sash sees that he has died in order to serve her vanity.

1. The primary purpose of this passage is to

(A) explain why critics should examine the use of shoe imagery in O'Connor's writings
(B) summarize the use of shoe imagery in "A Late Encounter with the Enemy" and "Everything that Rises Must Converge"
(C) list and describe the most important mentions of shoes in O'Connor's short stories and novels
(D) praise O'Connor for her subtle use of shoe imagery and the peacock metaphor
(E) examine some of the ways in which O'Connor uses shoe imagery in her writing

2.   The author's attitude toward critics who fail to recognize the importance of shoes in O'Connor's work can best be described as one of

   (A)   surprised pleasure
   (B)   mild annoyance
   (C)   strong disagreement
   (D)   disbelief
   (E)   unbridled anger

3.   According to the second paragraph, what does Mrs. Turpin notice in "Revelation"?

   (A)   The shoes worn by people in the doctor's waiting room
   (B)   The occupations of people in the doctor's waiting room
   (C)   The clothing worn by people in the doctor's waiting room
   (D)   The shoes worn by people on the bus
   (E)   The clothing worn by people on the bus

4.   Which of the following does the author give as a difference between Enoch and Sally Poker Sash?

   (A)   Enoch does not experience the same kind of disappointment that Sally does.
   (B)   Enoch is able to shed his identity, while Sally is not.
   (C)   Enoch treats his grandfather poorly, while Sally does not.
   (D)   Enoch does not want to impress other people, while Sally does.
   (E)   Enoch wants to be an animal, while Sally wants to be a beautiful woman.

5.   Which of the following statements best describes the way in which the third paragraph in the passage is related to the second?

   (A)   The third paragraph refutes the claims made in the second paragraph.
   (B)   The third paragraph makes a generalization based on the statements in the second paragraph.
   (C)   The third paragraph extends the arguments made in the second paragraph to their logical limit.
   (D)   The third paragraph adds further evidence to the argument made in the second paragraph.
   (E)   The third paragraph is not related to the second paragraph.

6..   What do lines 26–31 suggest about the nature of people who wear Girl Scout shoes?

   (A)   They are old and worn.
   (B)   They are unsophisticated.
   (C)   They are not interested in dressing up.
   (D)   They are smart and practical.
   (E)   They are ugly and bookish.

7.   According to the passage, the peacock in *Piers Plowman* represents

   (A)   shoes
   (B)   human feet
   (C)   beauty
   (D)   sorrow
   (E)   vanity

Reading Comprehension

8.   According to the passage, Sally Poker Sash is a character in

    (A)   "Greenleaf"
    (B)   "The Comforts of Home"
    (C)   "A Late Encounter with the Enemy"
    (D)   "Revelation"
    (E)   *Wise Blood*

9.   Which of the following best captures the meaning of "analogous to" as used in line 39?

    (A)   different from
    (B)   the opposite of
    (C)   unrelated to
    (D)   similar to
    (E)   the same as

10.   What does the author's description of Sally Poker Sash imply about Sally's relationship with her grandfather?

    (A)   He dotes on her and always gives in to her demands.
    (B)   He blames her for the embarrassing moments they have on stage.
    (C)   She is ashamed of him and does not speak to him.
    (D)   She is proud of his accomplishments and takes care of him.
    (E)   She treats him like a trophy and uses him to show off.

Answers and Explanations - Literary Criticism

1.   **(E)**   Main Theme, Idea, or Point   *Moderate*

The author's main purpose in writing the passage is to examine ways in which O'Connor uses shoe imagery in her writings, so the correct answer is (E). Although the author states that critics rarely address shoes in O'Connor's writings, the author never explicitly argues why addressing the issue of shoes is important, so choice (A) is wrong. Choice (B) is the wrong answer because the passage focuses on works besides "A Late Encounter with the Enemy" and "Everything that Rises Must Converge." Also, the word "summarizes" in (B) suggests that the author's discussion of shoe imagery in "A Late Encounter" and "Everything that Rises" covers every use of shoe imagery in those stories, but the author never makes that implication in the passage. You can eliminate choice (C) because the author never suggests that the shoe imagery discussed in the passage is the most important shoe imagery in O'Connor's works, and you can eliminate choice (D) because the author never explicitly praises O'Connor.

2.   **(C)**   Author's Attitude or Tone   *Moderate*

The passage opens with a statement that critics have tended to dismiss or ignore the issue of shoes in O'Connor's fiction. The author then disagrees with these critics by writing: "But in her work O'Connor draws the reader's attention to shoes so often that they should not be ignored." Since you know the author's reaction to these critics is negative, you can eliminate choice (A), "surprised pleasure." You can also eliminate choices (B), "mild annoyance," and (D), "disbelief," since the author expresses neither annoyance nor astonishment. Choosing between (C), "strong disagreement," and (E), "unbridled anger," is a matter of distinguishing the degree to which the author reacts against the critics. Since the author's response is measured rather than passionate, (C) is the best answer to this question.

3.   **(A)** Specific Information   *Easy*

In order to answer this question, you simply need to go back to the second paragraph, where the author describes how Mrs. Turpin observes the shoes worn by people in the doctor's waiting room. Choice (A) is the right answer to this question. Be careful to read carefully because in the same paragraph, the author describes how characters on the bus in "Everything that Rises Must Converge" are described by their shoes. If you don't read carefully, you may be tempted to choose (D).

4.   **(B)** Specific Information   *Moderate*

Answering this question can be a little bit tricky, since you need to choose a difference that the author gives (in other words, directly states) rather than implies. You may think, for example, that you can infer choices (D) and (E) from the passage, but those answers are wrong because they are never explicitly stated in the passage. The only difference the author gives between Enoch and Sally is choice (B). The author states this difference at the beginning of the fourth paragraph: "Other of her characters have a harder time discarding their identities than Enoch does." Then the author gives Sally an example of one of those characters.

5.   **(D)** Structure and Technique   *Difficult*

Before you try to answer this question, you should go back to the passage and quickly glance over the second and third paragraphs. Because the paragraphs are related to each other, you should immediately eliminate choice (E). You can also rule out choice (A), because the third paragraph does not refute anything stated in the second, and choice (B), because the third paragraph does not make a generalization (instead, it focuses on a specific example). Be wary of answer choices that use extreme phrases like "extend to their logical limits." While the third paragraph arguably does extend an argument made in the second paragraph, the argument made in the third paragraph does not reach a "logical limit." Choice (D) is the best answer to this question. The third paragraph develops the argument made in the second paragraph by adding another example to support the argument that O'Connor draws a connection between a person's shoes and his identity.

6.   **(B)**   Implied Information   *Difficult*

In lines 26–31, the author describes Sally's disappointment when she notices she is still wearing her Girl Scout shoes. The author writes: "Despite Sally's efforts to remake her appearance for the evening, her unsophisticated, clumsy shoes betray her true self." These lines suggest that Sally tries to make herself look elegant in the evening dress but that she fails because her shoes reveal how unsophisticated she really is. Choice (B) is the best answer to this question. You may be tempted to pick choice (E) because "ugly" and "bookish" are words attached to the girl in "Revelation" who also wears Girl Scout shoes, but because the question does not refer you to the second paragraph, (E) is the wrong answer to this question.

7.   **(E)**   Specific Information   *Easy*

To answer this easy specific-information question, you should go back to the fifth paragraph, where the author discusses the peacock metaphor. The author writes: "The first notable use of the peacock metaphor occurred in the fourteenth century in *Piers Plowman*. In this poem, the peacock represents vanity." Reading the last sentence, you should see that choice (E) is the correct answer to this question.

8.   **(C)**   Specific Information   *Easy*

This is a straightforward specific information question. If you don't remember what story Sally is in, you should go back to the fourth paragraph where she is mentioned for the first time. The second sentence of that paragraph is: "In 'A Late Encounter with the Enemy,' Sally Poker Sash remembers attending the premiere of *Gone with the Wind* in Atlanta with her grandfather." Choice (C) is the correct answer.

9.   **(D)**   Words in Context   *Moderate*

"Analogous to" means "similar to." If you don't know this definition, though, you can figure out the meaning of "analogous" from the context in which it's used. At the end of the fifth paragraph, the author writes that "the peacock's feet are analogous to Sally's shoes." The author then says that Sally lets vanity get the better of her, just as vanity got the better of the peacock when it realized that it had ugly feet. From these lines, you should be able to see that the peacock's feet and Sally's shoes are similar. Since you're looking for a word that suggests similarity, you can eliminate (A), (B), and (C), all of which suggest difference. Choice (D) is a better answer than choice (E) because "the same as" is too strong a statement to describe the comparison made between the peacock's feet and Sally's shoes.

10.   **(E)**   Implied Information   *Moderate*

The passage focuses on one aspect of Sally's relationship with her grandfather: how she uses him to show off. The author states: "By having him participate in the graduation ceremony, she hopes to show everyone that she has descended from an important family and that she is someone far above average." The correct answer to this question is (E). Although Sally is clearly proud of her grandfather (otherwise she wouldn't want to show him off), choice (D) is wrong because she does not take good care of him. In fact, her callous treatment of her grandfather at her graduation results in his death: "The stress and the heat of the day prove too much for the old man, and when he is pushed on stage in his wheel chair, Sally Poker Sash sees that he has died in order to serve her vanity."

Art Passages

Art passages discuss specific pieces of art (painting, architecture, or music) or particular artists. The passages might involve the artist speaking about his or her own work, the artist speaking about his field in general, a critic discussing a specific work or artist, or a description of some controversy in the art world. Like history and literary-criticism passages, art passages are often centered on arguments, since they are often about interpreting or explaining the subject they address.

Questions on art passages focus on your ability to understand arguments, specific information, and words in context.

Passage 4 - ART

The following passage is an account of Pablo Picasso's art from 1906 to 1909.

Pablo Picasso soaked in all the experimental energy of the Parisian art scene and, inspired by other artists—especially Cézanne, and also the "primitive" art of Africa and the Pacific—Picasso began to create for himself a radically new style. In the summer of 1906, vacationing in a Catalan village, Picasso began carving wooden sculptures. In these works,
5 Picasso was driven to a simplification of form by both the technical properties of the wood he worked with and by the compelling memory of the prehistoric Spanish sculpture he had seen in the Louvre. His experience in wood-carving led to changes in his painting; his portrait of Gertrude Stein—in which he so radically simplified her face that it became the image of a chiseled mask—marks a crucial shift in his painting. He stopped painting what he saw and
10 started painting what he thought.

At the beginning of 1907, Picasso began a painting, "Les Demoiselles d'Avignon" ("The Young Women of Avignon"), which would become arguably the most important of the century. The painting began as a narrative brothel scene, with five prostitutes and two men. But the painting metamorphosed as he worked on it; Picasso painted over the clients, leaving the
15 five women to gaze out at the viewer, their faces terrifyingly bold and solicitous. The features of the three women to the left were inspired by the prehistoric sculpture that had interested Picasso the previous summer; those of the two to the right were based on the masks that he saw in the African and Oceanic collections in a museum in Paris. Picasso was deeply impressed by what he saw in these collections, and they were to be one of his primary
20 influences for the next several years.

Art historians once classified this phase of Picasso's work as his "Negro Period." French

imperialism in Africa and the Pacific was at its high point, and gunboats and trading
steamers brought back ritual carvings and masks as curiosities. While the African carvings,
which Picasso owned, had a kind of dignified aloofness, he, like other Europeans of his time,
25   viewed Africa as the symbol of savagery. Unlike most Europeans, however, Picasso saw this
savagery as a source of vitality and renewal that he wanted to incorporate in his painting.
His interpretation of African art, in these mask-like faces, was based on this idea of African
savagery; his brush-strokes are hacking, impetuous, and violent.

        "Les Demoiselles" was so shockingly new that Gertrude Stein called it "a veritable
30   cataclysm." She meant this, of course, as a compliment. Not only did this painting
later become a turning point duly remarked upon in every history of modern art, but Picasso
felt at the time that his whole understanding of painting was revised in the course of this
canvas' creation.

        In 1907, Picasso met Georges Braque, another young painter deeply interested in
35   Cézanne. Braque and Picasso worked together closely; Braque later said they were "roped
together like mountaineers" as they explored a new approach to organizing pictorial space.
While Picasso had cleared the ground with "Les Demoiselles," Cubism was a joint
construction, to the extent that sometimes Picasso and Braque could not tell their work
apart. Afterwards, describing Braque's role in Cubism's later evolution, Picasso called him
40   "just a wife," simultaneously dismissing both his colleague and women. But Braque's
integral role in Cubism's initial invention cannot be disputed.

        During the summer of 1908 Braque went to L'Estaque, in southern France, where his
idol Cézanne had painted before him. The way in which Cubism attempted to see all
angles at once, to paint an analysis of a form instead of its appearance, is illustrated by
45   comparison of Braque's painting "Houses at L'Estaque" with a photograph of the view that
Braque was painting. In the painting, scale and perspective are gone; forms are simplified
into blocks. There is no distinction between foreground and background; the shapes of the
painting seem to be stacked on top of each other.

        The influence of Braque and Cézanne is clear in Picasso's paintings from the summer of
50   1909, which he spent in Horta de Ebro. Braque and Picasso had extended Cézanne's method
landscape painting to the point where a view became an almost monochromatic field of
faceted form. This method led to paintings that were almost indecipherable combinations of
fragmented facets in grays and browns. Kahnweiler was later to name this stage of Picasso
and Braque's work Analytical Cubism, because it was based on an analytical description of
55   objects. Describing this period, Kahnweiler wrote, "The great step has been made. Picasso
has exploded homogenous form." Indeed, Cubism was an explosion; not only did Cubist
paintings resemble the shrapnel of their ostensible subjects, but the intent was a kind of
joyous destruction of the tradition of Western painting and the result was a revolution in art
history.

1.   According to the passage, the prehistoric Spanish sculpture Picasso saw at the Louvre inspired him
        to

        (A)   paint "Les Demoiselles d'Avignon"
        (B)   channel the savagery of African art into his painting
        (C)   explode homogeneous form
        (D)   explore Cubism with Georges Braque
        (E)   simplify the forms in his wooden sculptures

2.   The word "metamorphosed" in line 14 most nearly means

(A)   stalled
(B)   grew worse
(C)   developed
(D)   became larger
(E)   transformed

3.   The "Negro Period" referred to in the third paragraph most likely derived its name from

(A)   the period of French rule in Africa and the Pacific
(B)   the collections which influenced Picasso at a museum in Paris
(C)   the inspiration Picasso took from African and Pacific art
(D)   the dress of the women depicted in "Les Demoiselles d'Avignon"
(E)   Gertrude Stein's reaction to Picasso's new style of painting

4.   The author most likely includes the sentence "She meant this, of course, as a compliment" in line 30 because the author wants to

(A)   second Stein's praise of Picasso
(B)   refute allegations that Stein's comment was mean-spirited
(C)   chastise Stein for using abstruse language
(D)   eliminate any ambiguity about Stein's comment
(E)   praise Stein for her astute observations

5.   The main purpose of the fifth paragraph is to

(A)   emphasize the role that Braque played in the evolution of Cubism
(B)   reveal Picasso as a selfish attention-seeker
(C)   credit Braque with the creation of Cubism
(D)   suggest that some paintings now attributed to Picasso were actually created by Braque
(E)   disparage Braque's role in the development of Cubism

6.   The author refers to a comparison between Braque's painting and the photograph in lines 43–48 in order to

(A)   help the reader identify the content of the painting
(B)   emphasize the way the painting distorts conventional ways of seeing
(C)   demonstrate another link between Picasso and Braque
(D)   show how the painting epitomizes the endeavors of Cubism
(E)   underscore the differences between Braque's style of painting and Cézanne's

7.   The author would most likely agree that Picasso's remark that Braque was "just a wife" (line 40) is

(A)   an accurate assessment of the relationship
(B)   an attempt to steal fame from Braque
(C)   unfair and sexist
(D)   ironic
(E)   integral to understanding Picasso and Braque's relationship

8.   According to the passage, how did Picasso's artistic style change during his "Negro Period"?

   (A)   He moved away from painting representations of reality to painting representations of his ideas and thoughts.

   (B)   He started working with wood sculpture instead of paint.

   (C)   He depicted more complex forms in his art, gradually moving away from the simplification that had marked his earlier works.

   (D)   He stopped producing European art and worked exclusively to create African and Pacific art.

   (E)   He began to copy the Cubist style pioneered by Braque and Cézanne.

9.   The main purpose of this passage is to

   (A)   provide a biographical sketch of Picasso's life

   (B)   examine the influence of Picasso's friends on his work

   (C)   describe two stages of Picasso's artistic career

   (D)   explain the significance of "Les Demoiselles d'Avignon" to modern art

   (E)   argue that Braque deserves more credit than he receives for developing Cubism

10.   It can be inferred from the passage that the importance of "Les Demoiselles d'Avignon" to twentieth-century art is that

   (A)   it merged the business of French imperialism with the creation of art

   (B)   it represented an acceptance of African and Pacific art in European cultural spheres

   (C)   it shocked the public by explicitly depicting prostitutes in a brothel

   (D)   its success made Picasso a famous, well-regarded painter

   (E)   it marked a major stylistic change in Picasso's art and in art in general

Answers and Explanations - Art

1.   **(E)**   Specific Information   *Easy*
The answer to this question is in the first paragraph, which states, "Picasso was driven to a simplification of form by both the technical properties of the wood he worked with and by the compelling memory of the prehistoric Spanish sculpture he had seen in the Louvre." Using this sentence, you can identify the correct answer: (E).

2.   **(E)**   Words in Context   *Easy*
If you don't know the definition of "metamorphosed," you can answer this question using contextual clues. The sentence says, "the painting metamorphosed as he worked on it; Picasso painted over the clients, leaving the five women to gave out at the viewer." Since the second part of the sentence describes a drastic change that Picasso made to the painting, you can infer that "metamorphosed" means "changed." Of the answers, choice (E), "transformed," is closest in meaning to "changed."

3.   **(C)**   Implied Information   *Easy*

The last sentence of the second paragraph says that the African and Oceanic collections Picasso saw at a museum "were to be one of his primary influences for the next several years." Directly following this sentence, the next paragraph begins: "Art historians once classified this phase of Picasso's work as his 'Negro Period.'" These sentences suggest that this period derived its name from the inspiration Picasso took from African and Pacific art, so (C) is the best answer. While you may be tempted to choose (B), you should remember that it was not the art itself that gave this period its name, but Picasso's use of the art.

4.   **(D)**   Structure and Technique   *Moderate*

This question asks you to identify the function of the sentence "She meant this, of course, as a compliment." The word "this" refers to Stein's comment quoted in the first sentence of the fourth paragraph: "'Les Demoiselles' was so shockingly new that Gertrude Stein called it 'a veritable cataclysm.'" The word "cataclysm" means "a moment of violent upheaval, demolition, and change," and depending on the context, it can have negative connotations. Since some people could interpret Stein's comment as a criticism of Picasso's art rather than as praise, the author of the passage is trying to explain Stein's comment and to remove any sense of ambiguity or uncertainty that Stein's comment could raise. The correct answer is (D).

5.   **(A)**   Main Idea, Point, or Theme   *Moderate*

This question asks you to identify the author's intended point in the fifth paragraph. The paragraph focuses on Braque and Picasso's Cubist endeavors. The author writes that "Braque and Picasso worked closely" and that "Cubism was a joint construction." The last sentence of the paragraph states that "Braque's integral role in Cubism's initial invention cannot be disputed." These sentences indicate that the author is arguing that Cubism was a joint effort by Braque and Picasso, despite Picasso's later claims that Braque was "just a wife." The correct answer is (A); the author is trying to emphasize that importance of Braque's involvement in Cubism without trying to overstate Braque's role.

6.   **(B)**   Understanding Themes and Arguments   *Difficult*

The purpose of the author's comparison is to contrast the views of the painter and the photographic lens. The photograph ostensibly shows a normal view of the houses, in contrast to the view depicted by the painting, in which all angles are seen at once, perspective and scale disappear, and no distinction is made between foreground and background. Choice (B), which says that the comparison shows how the painting distorts conventional ways of seeing, is correct. Although the comparison points to the style of the painting, the comparison does not show that the style is specifically Cubist, so don't be tempted by choice (D).

Reading Comprehension

7.   **(C)**   Author's Attitude or Tone   *Moderate*
Although the author makes no explicit criticism of the remark, she points out how the remark is doubly insulting to Braque and women: "Picasso called him 'just a wife,' simultaneously dismissing both his colleague and women." The author makes it clear that (A) cannot be true by emphasizing the role Braque played in the evolution of Cubism. (B) is never implied in the passage, nor is (D). Choice (E) tries to trick you by using a word ("integral") from later in the paragraph, but the author of the never implies that Picasso's statement is important to understanding his relationship with Braque. The correct answer is (B) because Picasso's statement unfairly diminishes Braque's involvement in Cubism and makes a sexist assumption about being a wife.

8.   **(A)**   Specific Information   *Moderate*
Answering this question is a little tricky because the answer is in the first paragraph but the phrase "Negro Period" isn't mentioned until the third paragraph. You learn in the third paragraph that the period described in the beginning of the passage (the first four paragraphs) is called the "Negro Period" by art historians. In the first paragraph, the author states that during this period, Picasso "stopped painting what he saw and started painting what he thought." This sentence sums up how Picasso's artistic style changed during this period. Using this sentence, you can pick (A) as the best answer to the question. You can also try eliminating the other answer choices. You can immediately rule out choice (B) because according to this passage, Picasso does not stop painting in order to work exclusively with wood sculpture. You can also eliminate choice (C) since the passage focuses on how Picasso's style increasingly focused on simplified forms, the opposite of complex forms. You know that (D) is wrong because Picasso was only inspired by African art; he did not stop producing European art in order to create African art. Finally, you can rule out choice (E) since Cubism belongs to the stylistic period that follows the "Negro Period."

9.   **(C)**   Main Idea, Theme, or Point   *Easy*
While this passage touches on a number of issues—including events in Picasso's life, the influence of his friends, and the importance of "Les Demoiselles d'Avignon"—the main object of the passage is to describe two stages—the periods of primitivism and Analytical Cubism—in Picasso's art.

10.   **(E)**   Understanding Themes and Arguments   *Moderate*
The passage suggests that the significance of this painting to twentieth-century art arises from its newness—particularly its newness of style and execution. Of the answer choices, (E) is the best answer to the question. The painting marked a new style and a new understanding of art not only for Picasso but also, through Picasso's influence, for art in general.

Types of Reading Comprehension Questions

ETS has created eight basic types of questions to test reading comprehension skills.

1. Main Theme, Idea, or Point

2. Author's Attitude or Tone

3. Specific Information

4. Implied Information

5. Understanding Themes and Arguments

6. Structure and Technique

7. Understanding Words in context

8. Relating Two Passages

Below, we describe each of these eight question types and provide examples of each. The examples should familiarize you with the most common ways that ETS phrases its questions, and get you thinking about what sort of understanding each question tests.

1. Main Theme, Idea, or Point Questions

Main theme, idea, or point questions—which we'll call main idea questions—test your understanding of the entire passage. The questions do not provide line numbers or specific quotations to focus your search. Instead, they ask broad questions that focus on the passage's primary issues. It is unlikely that you'll see more than three main idea questions for a given passage. Often, though not always, main idea questions will be among the first few you encounter.

Main idea questions come in a variety of forms. Below are examples of the most common ones. We include answer choices with each example to give you a better idea of what the question will look like. You shouldn't be able to answer these questions, since you haven't seen the reading passage on which they are based. Don't worry about that. Just study the questions and figure out what they're asking and how you would have to read the unknown passage from which they came to answer them. If while reading the passage you remain alert to the sorts of general questions that the SAT is likely to ask, you probably won't have to go back to the passage to answer such questions when you encounter them, thereby saving valuable time.

Example

The primary purpose of the passage is to

(A)   describe the day to day life of inmates in American insane asylums in the early twentieth century

(B)   raise concerns about the inhumane treatment of the clinically insane in America today

(C)   prompt psychiatrists to be more diligent when they diagnose someone as insane

(D)   examine the benefits and detriments of the insane asylum to those it is meant to treat

(E)   demand an alternative method of housing and treating the insane

2. Author's Attitude or Tone Questions

This type of question tests whether you understand how the author views the subject about which he or she writes. Attitude and tone questions will ask you for a description of the author's feelings about the subject. As you read these kinds of passages, think to yourself about whether the argument the writer is making seems to support or attack his subject. Also pay attention to the language the author uses, which will help you to determine tone.

As you will see in the examples, the differences between the answer choices are sometimes slight. For example, you might have to choose between "anger" and "disapproval." Both of these words imply that the author has negative sentiments about what the passage is discussing, so to answer this question correctly you have to determine the intensity of the author's negative perspective. Is the author enraged, mildly disturbed, or strongly disapproving? If you have one answer choice that describes the author as feeling positive about his subject and one as feeling negative, then you know one must be wrong. If you are unable to figure out the definitive answer to this type of question, you may still have a good chance of eliminating some answers so that you can guess.

Examples

The passage as a whole suggests that the author disagrees with his parents about

(A)   the wisdom of moving from their homeland to the United States

(B)   his parents' unwavering belief in the benefits of American capitalism

(C)   his parents' decision to wear traditional clothes on the cultural holidays of their homeland

(D)   the importance of maintaining a connection with their roots

(E)   his parents' adoption of Christmas as a special holiday though they did not celebrate it in their own country

Which of the following titles best summarizes the passage?

(A)   Lost Land: the Tragedy of Native Americans
(B)   Native Americans and Oral History
(C)   The Importance of Oral History in Contemporary Native American Literature
(D)   The Cultural Legacy of Native American Creation Myths
(E)   Coping with Loss: The Native American Effort to Reappropriate Land Through Literature

The author's attitude toward those who believe that better technology is the only measure of progress is one of

(A)   disgust
(B)   amazement
(C)   amusement
(D)   agreement
(E)   disbelief

In this question, if you know that the author's attitude toward these people is not negative, you can immediately throw out (A) *disgust* as a possible answer, and possibly also (E) *disbelief*.

The tone of the passage might best be described as

(A)   gently mocking
(B)   bitterly angry
(C)   emphatically approving
(D)   cautiously ambivalent
(E)   powerfully optimistic

In this example, the negative answer choices (A) and (B) are direct opposites of the positive (C) and (E). You should definitely be able to eliminate at least two choices simply by determining whether the passage's tone is positive or negative.

3. Specific Information Questions

Questions on specific information ask you to find precisely that: specific information. The questions will indicate a section of the passage, usually through the use of line numbers, and ask a question about the information presented within that specific area. The specific information that these questions ask about varies widely, making it difficult to provide you with representative examples covering all possible forms. However, we will provide you with a few sample questions to help you get a feel for the type of information these questions are after.

Examples

Lines 15–18 suggest that the attempted restoration of the paintings actually served to reveal

(A)   that the supposed originals were forgeries
(B)   the impressive skill of medieval artists
(C)   some of the techniques, hitherto unknown, employed by medieval painters
(D)   that the paintings were themselves restorations of earlier works
(E)   that modern, polluted air contains chemicals that react with medieval paints, dramatically dulling them

The author claims which of the following about the "fops" (line 65)?

(A)   They were more concerned about personal glory than justice.
(B)   They were an important part of the political structure of the royal courts.
(C)   Their relations were dependent on their success at the royal court.
(D)   They cared only about luxury and influence and were willing to stoop to political fawning of all kinds to achieve their goals.
(E)   They were excellent equestrians.

The claim that "everyone is always wrong" (line 78) is presented by the passage as the opinion of

(A)   Jacques
(B)   Robertson
(C)   Crane
(D)   Minstrel
(E)   Kramer

Because these questions test specific information, you can only eliminate an answer if you know that the information it states is wrong. Sometimes you might be able to eliminate an answer simply because it seems rather flimsy. In the case of the first question, it seems unlikely that a restoration of a painting would suddenly illuminate the great skill of medieval painters, so (B) seems weak as an answer choice. Otherwise, there is no easy strategy for eliminating answers. However, because the answer choices state facts, you should be able to compare what they say with the facts discussed in the indicated section of the passage.

4. Implied Information Questions

Questions on implied information are quite similar in form to those on specific information. Just as in specific information questions, these questions will identify and inquire about a particular section of the passage. However, whereas specific information questions ask about concrete information contained in the text, implied information questions ask about the less obvious information contained "between the lines" of the text. Often, you will be able to identify these questions through the use of words such as "inferred," "implied," "indicated," or "suggested."

Examples

The author's use of the phrase "irreconcilable tragedy" (line 18) in reference to the bombing of Hiroshima suggests that

(A)   the devastating effects of the bombing cannot be lessened even if the reasons or the bombing were noble
(B)   there are many different interpretations of why the US dropped the bomb
(C)   the US dropped the bomb on Hiroshima for the wrong reasons
(D)   the dropping of the bomb was justified if you consider the historical context
(E)   the dropping of the bomb changed the world

In the context of the passage, lines 80–82 imply that the author

(A)   saw himself as the embodiment of a mythical savior
(B)   believed that only he could lead his people to independence
(C)   felt burdened by his birthright
(D)   hated the inequality created by the caste system
(E)   never wanted to be involved in politics

It can be inferred that "early architects" (line 47) did their work with little concern for

(A)   aesthetic values
(B)   structural integrity
(C)   geography
(D)   materials
(E)   functionality

Each of these examples asks you to discern information that is vital to the passage but that is not offered outright. As you might imagine, questions on implied information are therefore fairly uncommon in science passages, in which the author's main goal is to be clear and specific. But in passages where the author tries to create a picture or portrait of something, information is often implied, since a straight retelling of facts can be boring.

As with questions on specific information, there is no distinct strategy to help you answer question choices. Some answer choices might simply seem weak to you, but that is a gut instinct more than a strategy. Your best bet is to go back to the passage and see how each answer fits with what the passage says.

5. Understanding Themes and Arguments Questions

These questions test your ability to look at particular lines in the text and identify the underlying assumptions. Alternatively, you might look at these questions as testing your ability to understand how particular lines fit into the larger arguments or themes in the passage. Argument questions are very common, so it pays to be ready for them. Because these questions are so dependent on passages, they vary widely. We will provide you with a number of examples to give you a sense of the types of issues these questions tend to address. Be aware that these examples give a glimpse rather than an exhaustive survey of this type of question.

Examples

The discussion of sculpture (lines 51–57) illuminates the author's assumption that

(A)   sculpture in the classical period is far superior to modern sculpture
(B)   good sculpture must involve the human form
(C)   sculpture is superior to painting as an art form
(D)   the best sculptors often move into sculpture from another field
(E)   modern sculpture places too little emphasis on the craft of building

Which of the following most clearly expresses what the author means by claiming to be "adept at the smaller forms of communication" (lines 33–34)?

(A)   He is capable of adapting to whatever situation in which he finds himself.
(B)   He speaks eloquently and concisely.
(C)   He can intuit others' thoughts by observing their body language.
(D)   He likes to engage in deep conversations.
(E)   He is shy with his feelings.

The comment by the shopkeeper in lines 79–81 serves primarily to

(A)   illustrate the extent to which the town loves football
(B)   indicate how Coach Lombardi's lessons on the football field also helped his players become terrific businessmen
(C)   demonstrate the affection the players felt for Coach Lombardi
(D)   describe how football can be seen as a metaphor for the United States
(E)   explain how Coach Lombardi's success helped save football in the United States

Each of these examples asks you to look at information within the context of the passage and synthesize it into some paraphrased form that allows you to answer the question. The ability to paraphrase is an important skill in reading comprehension—the better you are at paraphrasing, the better you will be at answering these questions.

6. Structure and Technique Questions

Technique questions test your understanding of the nuts and bolts of writing. These questions will ask about how everything from parenthetical statements to full paragraphs function in the passage. These questions might also ask you about the overall structure of the passage.

As you should be able to see from these three examples, structure and technique questions ask about the function of very small units in the paragraph, such as a single word or simple parenthetical statement, as well as larger units, such as the relation between entire paragraphs. Again, other than going back to look at the passage as you answer, there are no easy strategies for eliminating answers. The best way to study for this type of question—and for most reading comprehension questions—is to read widely, question yourself about what you read, and take a lot of practice tests to get the hang of it.

Explanations

In what way is the second paragraph related to the first?

- (A)   It provides examples to support the claims made in the first paragraph.
- (B)   It focuses the broad claims of the first paragraph.
- (C)   It uses the information in the first paragraph.
- (D)   It refutes the statements made in the first paragraph.
- (E)   It extends the arguments made in the first paragraph to their logical limit.

The parenthetical statement in lines 31–32 serves to

- (A)   provide support for the author's earlier arguments through citation of other authorities
- (B)   allow the author to comment critically on his own theories
- (C)   distance the author from the controversial claims made by hi contemporaries
- (D)   undercut all disagreeing theories
- (E)   tell an amusing anecdote

The author uses the word "cacophonous" (line 54) to

- (A)   describe the confusion apparent in scientific debate
- (B)   illustrate the excitement created by new discoveries
- (C)   describe the rancor that can emerge between scientists promoting competing theories
- (D)   indicate the chaos that emerges when science proves insufficient
- (E)   emphasize the view that science cannot answer every question

7. Words-in-Context Questions

Words-in-context questions follow a very standard form. These questions will provide you with a line number and a word or short phrase in quotes and ask you about the meaning of that word in the context of the passage.

The majority of words-in-context questions look like this:

The word "content" (line 34) most nearly means

- (A)   destitute
- (B)   satisfied
- (C)   subject
- (D)   matter
- (E)   technical

Unlike most other reading comprehension questions, you can approach these questions in a strategic way that will—at the very least—help you eliminate choices. When you see a words-in-context question, before looking at the answer choices, go to the line number of the passage indicated by the question. Then, turn the question into a sentence completion. Read the sentence that contains the word on which you're being tested, but ignore the word itself. Come up with a different word or phrase to fill that space. Once you have your synonym in mind, go back to the question and compare your synonym to the answers. When you've found a match, you have your answer. In effect, you are building a sort of synonym bridge between the word in the passage and the correct word in the answer choices.

Using this bridge-building method is important because it can help you avoid the tricks embedded in the answer choices. Often, the answer choices will include words that are correct secondary meanings of the tested word. For instance, in the example above, *satisfied* and *subject* are both correct meanings of the word *content*. Remember that these questions are testing the word *in context*. By going back to the passage and approaching the sentence as if it were a sentence completion, you can take the context into account and make sure that you aren't distracted by tricky answer choices. Also, by approaching the question as a sentence completion, you can use the sentence completion strategies you already know for eliminating answer choices even if you cannot come up with a definite answer.

Some words in context questions take different forms. The two most common are:

> Which of the following best captures the meaning of the word "traitorous" in line 65?

> The phrase "subliminal influence" (line 18) refers to

These modified forms should not affect your strategy for tackling the question. Be aware, however, that the answers may be phrases rather than words.

8. Questions Relating Two Passages

The final questions for the dual passage test your ability to understand the passages in relation to each other. The three most common types of question are:

Relating Main Ideas. Which statement best describes a disparity between the two passages?

Relating Arguments. How would the author of passage 2 react to the concept of "responsibilities of brotherhood" (line 65) described in passage 1?

Relating Specific Information. Which piece of information in passage 2 provides the best support for the "value of friendship and cooperation" (line 80) referred to in passage 1?

While thinking about these questions, you can often uncover a clue to the answers by thinking of the general relation between the passages. For example, if you know the passages disagree completely, you can use that knowledge to assume that the author of passage 2 will feel negatively about the "illicit codes of honor" described in passage 1.

Sample Passage and Questions

In the following pages, we provide an entire sample passage and accompanying questions with explanations. Use the passage and questions to focus your strategies for reading comprehension. The type of question is identified at the end of each explanation.

The following passage discusses the scientific life of Galileo Galilei in reference to the political, religious, artistic, and scientific movements of the age

Galileo Galilei was born in 1564 into a Europe wracked by cultural ferment and religious divisions. The popes of the Roman Catholic Church, powerful in their roles as both religious and secular leaders, had proven vulnerable to the worldly and decadent spirit of the age, and their personal immorality brought the reputation of the papacy to historic lows. In 1517,
5 Martin Luther, a former monk, attacked Catholicism for having become too worldly and politically corrupt and for obscuring the fundamentals of Christianity with pagan elements. His reforming zeal, which appealed to a notion of an original, "purified" Christianity, set in motion the Protestant Reformation and split European Christianity in two. In response, Roman Catholicism steeled itself for battle and launched the Counter-Reformation, which
10 emphasized orthodoxy and fidelity to the true Church.

The Counter-Reformation reinvigorated the Church and, to some extent, eliminated its excesses. Unfortunately, the Counter-Reformation also contributed to the decline of the Italian Renaissance, a revival of arts and letters that sought to recover and rework the classical art and philosophy of ancient Greece and Rome. The popes had once been great
15 patrons of Renaissance arts and sciences, but the Counter-Reformation put an end to the Church's liberality and leniency in these areas. Further, the Church's new emphasis on religious orthodoxy would soon clash with the emerging scientific revolution.

Galileo, with his study of astronomy, found himself at the center of this clash. Conservative astronomers of Galileo's time, working without telescopes, ascribed without
20 deviation to the ancient theory of geocentricity. This theory of astronomy held that the earth ("geo," as in "geography" or "geology") lay at the center of the solar system, orbited by both the sun and the other planets. Indeed, to the casual observer, it seemed common sense that since the sun "rose" in the morning and "set" at night, it must have circled around the earth. Ancient authorities like Aristotle and the Roman astronomer Ptolemy had championed this
25 viewpoint, and the notion also coincided with the Catholic Church's view of the universe, which placed mankind, God's principal creation, at the center of the cosmos. Buttressed by common sense, the ancient philosophers, and the Church, the geocentric model of the universe seemed secure in its authority.

The Ptolemaic theory, however, was not impervious to attack. In the 16th century,
30 astronomers strained to make modern observations fit Ptolemy's geocentric model of the universe. Increasingly complex mathematical systems were necessary to reconcile these new observations with Ptolemy's system of interlocking orbits. Nicholas Copernicus, a Polish astronomer, openly questioned the Ptolemaic system and proposed a heliocentric system in which the planets—including earth— orbited the sun ("helios"). This more mathematically
35 satisfying way of arranging the solar system did not attract many supporters at first, since the available data did not yet support a wholesale abandonment of Ptolemy's system. By the end of the 16th century, however, astronomers like Johannes Kepler (1571–1630) had also begun to embrace Copernicus's theory.

Once Galileo began to observe the heavens through his telescope, the fate of the
40 Ptolemaic system was sealed. But so too was Galileo's fate. The Catholic Church, desperately

trying to hold the Protestant heresy at bay, could not accept a scientific assault on its own theories of the universe. The pressures of the age set in motion a historic confrontation between religion and science, one which would culminate in 1633 when the Church put Galileo on trial, forced him to recant his stated and published scientific beliefs, and put him
45   under permanent house arrest.

Sample Questions

1.   The term "ferment" in line 1 most closely means

    (A)   alienation
    (B)   turmoil
    (C)   consolidation of social institutions
    (D)   anachronisms in the Church
    (E)   stagnation

2.   Which of the following was *not* a reason for Martin Luther's attack on the Catholic Church (lines 4–6)?

    (A)   pagan elements in its practices
    (B)   the amorality of its leadership
    (C)   its excessive attention to piety
    (D)   its corruption and worldliness
    (E)   the political involvement of the popes

3.   According to this passage, the Catholic Church started the Counter-Reformation primarily to

    (A)   fight scientific heresy
    (B)   clean out its own ranks
    (C)   reinvigorate artists and intellectuals
    (D)   elect a new pope
    (E)   counter Protestant challenges

4.   Which of the following is *not* part of the meaning of the term "conservative" in line 19?

    (A)   reverent of ancient thinkers
    (B)   old-fashioned
    (C)   religiously orthodox
    (D)   technologically limited
    (E)   simple-minded

5.   The development of the heliocentric model of the solar system, as discussed in this passage, suggests that observations of the natural world

    (A)   are often dependent on technology
    (B)   are never to be trusted
    (C)   should fit with common sense
    (D)   can always be explained mathematically
    (E)   can only be made by scientists

Reading Comprehension

6. Which of the following best states the underlying theme of the passage?

    (A)   Science always conflicts with religion.
    (B)   Science is vulnerable to outside social forces.
    (C)   Ideally, scientific theories should reinforce religious doctrine.
    (D)   Science operates in a vacuum.
    (E)   Advanced technology is the only route to good scientific theories.

Answers and Explanations

1. **(B)**

To answer this word-in-context question, you should first go back to the specified line and read the sentence in which the word is contained and the surrounding sentences. In this case, the sentence refers to "cultural ferment and religious divisions," and the following sentences go on to describe a Europe in the midst of religious and political strife. The word "ferment," therefore, must describe this division and strife. *Turmoil* is the only word to come close to filling this need. Try substituting the answer choices into the passage if you are unsure.

2. **(C)**

This specific information question is a little tricky, since it asks you which of the answer choices did *not* cause Martin Luther's attack. If you missed that *not*, then you very well might have looked at the first answer choice, seen that it caused Martin Luther's attack on the Catholic Church, and chosen that as the correct answer. So be careful when reading the question.

To answer this question correctly, you must simply go back to the indicated area and read. Since this is a *not* question, all of the wrong answers must be stated as reasons for Martin Luther's hatred of the church in the text. So the best way to go about answering this question is to eliminate answers until you're left with one. The indicated lines clearly state that Luther hated what he saw as the church's worldliness and corruption. That throws out answer choice (D). It also throws out answer choices (B) and (E), since those are both aspects of the Church's corruption and worldliness. The text also clearly states that Luther felt the Church was incorporating pagan instruments, so you can throw out answer (B). That leaves you with (C), the right answer.

3. **(E)**

This question tests whether you can follow the flow of argument within the text. More specifically, it tests your ability to differentiate between the causes and effects of the Counter-Reformation. Answers (A), (B), and (C) refer to effects of the Counter-Reformation. Answer (D) has absolutely no basis in the text. Only answer choice (E) refers to the cause of the Counter-Reformation as defined by the passage.

4. **(E)**

Most of the answers to this words in context question can be eliminated by carefully rereading the section of the passage that contains the word "conservative." This section explains that "conservative" astronomers were technologically limited (they worked without telescopes), relied on ancient authorities, and did not challenge common beliefs—this lets us eliminate answers (A), (B), (C), and (D). The passage does not, however, suggest that these individuals were of limited intelligence, so (E) is the best answer to this question.

5. **(A)**

This question tests your general understanding of the passage. You shouldn't have to go back to the passage to answer the question. This question gives you a good gauge of whether you understood enough during your read-through. This question also teaches an important lesson. The right answer on reading comprehension questions will almost never be absolute or all-encompassing answers such as "Science can only be proven mathematically." If you see an answer choice that includes the words always, only, never, or any other word that implies a definitive statement lasting through all eternity, beware. For this question, you can throw out all the absolute answers: (B), (D), and (E). Answer (C) is not mentioned anywhere in the text, so (A) is the right answer.

6. **(B)**

This question also tests your general understanding of the passage. Once again, you'll see some absolute statements within the answer choices ("science always conflicts with religion") that should immediately make you suspicious. With some thought you should be able to eliminate answers (A) and (E). Also, nowhere does the passage espouse the idea that science should only reinforce religion, so you can knock out (C). Answer (D) is proven wrong by the example of Galileo, so you can throw that out also, leaving you with the right answer, (B).

SAT Verbal
Practice Test 1

SAT VERBAL PRACTICE TEST ANSWER SHEET

VERBAL SECTION 1	VERBAL SECTION 2	VERBAL SECTION 3
1. Ⓐ Ⓑ Ⓒ Ⓓ Ⓔ	1. Ⓐ Ⓑ Ⓒ Ⓓ Ⓔ	1. Ⓐ Ⓑ Ⓒ Ⓓ Ⓔ
2. Ⓐ Ⓑ Ⓒ Ⓓ Ⓔ	2. Ⓐ Ⓑ Ⓒ Ⓓ Ⓔ	2. Ⓐ Ⓑ Ⓒ Ⓓ Ⓔ
3. Ⓐ Ⓑ Ⓒ Ⓓ Ⓔ	3. Ⓐ Ⓑ Ⓒ Ⓓ Ⓔ	3. Ⓐ Ⓑ Ⓒ Ⓓ Ⓔ
4. Ⓐ Ⓑ Ⓒ Ⓓ Ⓔ	4. Ⓐ Ⓑ Ⓒ Ⓓ Ⓔ	4. Ⓐ Ⓑ Ⓒ Ⓓ Ⓔ
5. Ⓐ Ⓑ Ⓒ Ⓓ Ⓔ	5. Ⓐ Ⓑ Ⓒ Ⓓ Ⓔ	5. Ⓐ Ⓑ Ⓒ Ⓓ Ⓔ
6. Ⓐ Ⓑ Ⓒ Ⓓ Ⓔ	6. Ⓐ Ⓑ Ⓒ Ⓓ Ⓔ	6. Ⓐ Ⓑ Ⓒ Ⓓ Ⓔ
7. Ⓐ Ⓑ Ⓒ Ⓓ Ⓔ	7. Ⓐ Ⓑ Ⓒ Ⓓ Ⓔ	7. Ⓐ Ⓑ Ⓒ Ⓓ Ⓔ
8. Ⓐ Ⓑ Ⓒ Ⓓ Ⓔ	8. Ⓐ Ⓑ Ⓒ Ⓓ Ⓔ	8. Ⓐ Ⓑ Ⓒ Ⓓ Ⓔ
9. Ⓐ Ⓑ Ⓒ Ⓓ Ⓔ	9. Ⓐ Ⓑ Ⓒ Ⓓ Ⓔ	9. Ⓐ Ⓑ Ⓒ Ⓓ Ⓔ
10. Ⓐ Ⓑ Ⓒ Ⓓ Ⓔ	10. Ⓐ Ⓑ Ⓒ Ⓓ Ⓔ	10. Ⓐ Ⓑ Ⓒ Ⓓ Ⓔ
11. Ⓐ Ⓑ Ⓒ Ⓓ Ⓔ	11. Ⓐ Ⓑ Ⓒ Ⓓ Ⓔ	11. Ⓐ Ⓑ Ⓒ Ⓓ Ⓔ
12. Ⓐ Ⓑ Ⓒ Ⓓ Ⓔ	12. Ⓐ Ⓑ Ⓒ Ⓓ Ⓔ	12. Ⓐ Ⓑ Ⓒ Ⓓ Ⓔ
13. Ⓐ Ⓑ Ⓒ Ⓓ Ⓔ	13. Ⓐ Ⓑ Ⓒ Ⓓ Ⓔ	13. Ⓐ Ⓑ Ⓒ Ⓓ Ⓔ
14. Ⓐ Ⓑ Ⓒ Ⓓ Ⓔ	14. Ⓐ Ⓑ Ⓒ Ⓓ Ⓔ	
15. Ⓐ Ⓑ Ⓒ Ⓓ Ⓔ	15. Ⓐ Ⓑ Ⓒ Ⓓ Ⓔ	
16. Ⓐ Ⓑ Ⓒ Ⓓ Ⓔ	16. Ⓐ Ⓑ Ⓒ Ⓓ Ⓔ	
17. Ⓐ Ⓑ Ⓒ Ⓓ Ⓔ	17. Ⓐ Ⓑ Ⓒ Ⓓ Ⓔ	
18. Ⓐ Ⓑ Ⓒ Ⓓ Ⓔ	18. Ⓐ Ⓑ Ⓒ Ⓓ Ⓔ	
19. Ⓐ Ⓑ Ⓒ Ⓓ Ⓔ	19. Ⓐ Ⓑ Ⓒ Ⓓ Ⓔ	
20. Ⓐ Ⓑ Ⓒ Ⓓ Ⓔ	20. Ⓐ Ⓑ Ⓒ Ⓓ Ⓔ	
21. Ⓐ Ⓑ Ⓒ Ⓓ Ⓔ	21. Ⓐ Ⓑ Ⓒ Ⓓ Ⓔ	
22. Ⓐ Ⓑ Ⓒ Ⓓ Ⓔ	22. Ⓐ Ⓑ Ⓒ Ⓓ Ⓔ	
23. Ⓐ Ⓑ Ⓒ Ⓓ Ⓔ	23. Ⓐ Ⓑ Ⓒ Ⓓ Ⓔ	
24. Ⓐ Ⓑ Ⓒ Ⓓ Ⓔ	24. Ⓐ Ⓑ Ⓒ Ⓓ Ⓔ	
25. Ⓐ Ⓑ Ⓒ Ⓓ Ⓔ	25. Ⓐ Ⓑ Ⓒ Ⓓ Ⓔ	
26. Ⓐ Ⓑ Ⓒ Ⓓ Ⓔ	26. Ⓐ Ⓑ Ⓒ Ⓓ Ⓔ	
27. Ⓐ Ⓑ Ⓒ Ⓓ Ⓔ	27. Ⓐ Ⓑ Ⓒ Ⓓ Ⓔ	
28. Ⓐ Ⓑ Ⓒ Ⓓ Ⓔ	28. Ⓐ Ⓑ Ⓒ Ⓓ Ⓔ	
29. Ⓐ Ⓑ Ⓒ Ⓓ Ⓔ	29. Ⓐ Ⓑ Ⓒ Ⓓ Ⓔ	
30. Ⓐ Ⓑ Ⓒ Ⓓ Ⓔ	30. Ⓐ Ⓑ Ⓒ Ⓓ Ⓔ	
31. Ⓐ Ⓑ Ⓒ Ⓓ Ⓔ	31. Ⓐ Ⓑ Ⓒ Ⓓ Ⓔ	
32. Ⓐ Ⓑ Ⓒ Ⓓ Ⓔ	32. Ⓐ Ⓑ Ⓒ Ⓓ Ⓔ	
33. Ⓐ Ⓑ Ⓒ Ⓓ Ⓔ	33. Ⓐ Ⓑ Ⓒ Ⓓ Ⓔ	
34. Ⓐ Ⓑ Ⓒ Ⓓ Ⓔ	34. Ⓐ Ⓑ Ⓒ Ⓓ Ⓔ	
35. Ⓐ Ⓑ Ⓒ Ⓓ Ⓔ	35. Ⓐ Ⓑ Ⓒ Ⓓ Ⓔ	

SAT TEST

Time—30 Minutes
30 Questions

For each question in this section, select the best answer from among the choices given and fill in the corresponding oval on the answer sheet.

Each sentence below has one or two blanks, each blank indicating that something has been omitted. Beneath the sentence are five words or sets of words labeled A through E. Choose the word or set of words that, when inserted in the sentence, <u>best</u> fits the meaning of the sentence as a whole.

Example:
Medieval kingdoms did not become constitutional republics overnight; on the contrary, the change was ----.

(A) unpopular
(B) unexpected
(C) advantageous
(D) sufficient
(E) gradual

1. Covering her face with her hands as he told her the bad news, Laura seemed ----.

   (A) nonchalant
   (B) distraught
   (C) ecstatic
   (D) poised
   (E) exuberant

2. Allie was unable to stop her husband's embarrassing behavior, and the ---- expression on her face showed her disapproval.

   (A) aloof
   (B) animated
   (C) confident
   (D) mortified
   (E) cheerful

3. Benjamin Franklin, well known as a man who came from ---- beginnings as the son of a poor candle maker, was himself a lover of the ---- crowd of upper-class France.

   (A) meager…cosmopolitan
   (B) effulgent…enigmatic
   (C) grandiose…frugal
   (D) destitute…servile
   (E) sublime…impoverished

4. Andrea has lost many friends as a result of her ---- sense of humor.

   (A) accessible
   (B) acerbic
   (C) hardy
   (D) sanguine
   (E) whimsical

5. Aretha Franklin is often hailed as a lyrical force in soul music; her vocals are heartfelt and ----.

   (A) vapid
   (B) contrite
   (C) vacuous
   (D) strident
   (E) evocative

GO ON TO THE NEXT PAGE

6. Although the speaker's comments about the country seemed ----, underlying these statements was a(n) ---- intent to begin a revolution in the small nation.

   (A) insipid...adept
   (B) innocuous...insidious
   (C) emollient...eloquent
   (D) banal...affable
   (E) amicable...conciliatory

7. Although scholars have dismissed a number of Sigmund Freud's hypotheses as ----, many believe that his theory linking ancient Greek literature with universal human experiences is a(n) ---- one.

   (A) fallacious...specious
   (B) astute...ingenious
   (C) perceptive...adroit
   (D) sagacious...perspicacious
   (E) spurious...shrewd

8. Ellie seemed like the ---- businesswoman; she wore a three-piece suit to work each day, stayed late at work every night, and brokered power deals even during her leisure time.

   (A) archetypal
   (B) slovenly
   (C) animated
   (D) bellicose
   (E) pompous

9. Niccolò Machiavelli, a writer known for his work *The Prince*, instructed rulers of nations that ---- fear in one's citizens is more desirable than garnering their love.

   (A) bolstering
   (B) inculcating
   (C) annihilating
   (D) eschewing
   (E) proffering

GO ON TO THE NEXT PAGE

Each question below consists of a related pair of words or phrases, followed by five pairs of words or phrases labeled A through E. Select the pair that best expresses a relationship similar to that expressed in the original pair.

Example:
CRUMB : BREAD ::

(A) ounce : unit
(B) splinter : wood
(C) water : bucket
(D) twine : rope
(E) cream : butter

10.   ABBREVIATION : SHORTEN ::

(A)   link : separate
(B)   silhouette : outline
(C)   demonstration : conceal
(D)   procedure : diverge
(E)   ruler : measure

11.   INSTRUCTION : DIRECT ::

(A)   conflict : predict
(B)   agitation : pacify
(C)   announcement : inform
(D)   tribute : propagate
(E)   citation : pardon

12.   PARISHIONERS : CONGREGATION ::

(A)   musicians : instrument
(B)   keys : lock
(C)   pillars : column
(D)   speakers : audience
(E)   players : team

13.   TRUNK : TREE ::

(A)   seat : chair
(B)   mask : disguise
(C)   injunction : law
(D)   lawn : preservation
(E)   scale : weight

14.   HEDONIST : PLEASURE ::

(A)   demagogue : innocence
(B)   irritant : mollification
(C)   mediator : reconciliation
(D)   mendicant : affluence
(E)   idyll : profit

15.   PROFESSOR : TEACH ::

(A)   feminist : engender
(B)   illusionist : deceive
(C)   epicure : starve
(D)   eccentric : forestall
(E)   expatriate : battle

GO ON TO THE NEXT PAGE

SAT TEST

The passage below is followed by questions based on its content. Answer the questions on the basis of what is <u>stated</u> or <u>implied</u> in the passage and in any introductory material that may be provided.

Questions 16–20 are based on the following passage.

The following passage discusses government paper shortages in the United States during the 1940s.

Shortage of printing paper were a major problem for the United States Government Printing Office (GPO) during World War II. The GPO's paper requirements accounted for as much as 60 percent of U.S. paper mill capacity for some grades of paper
5 and an overall average of some 40 percent for all types of paper. The GPO enjoyed no priority over other paper consumers during the war and therefore was forced to compete with commercial printers and other federal departments for the limited supply that was available.
10 Shipments of wood pulp from Scandinavian countries—the principal suppliers of this commodity—were cut off in 1939 when war broke out in Europe. As early as July 1941, the Office of Production Management (later renamed the War Production Board) warned of an impending shortage of all types of paper.
15 Newsprint supplies were especially hard-hit by slower-than-normal Canadian production, transportation difficulties, and severe winter weather in the northern United States.

Another factor that limited the production of paper was the competition of war industries for essential ingredients. The
20 cellulose fibers that were used to make pulp—essential to paper-making—were also used to process smokeless powder. Because chlorine, used as a paper bleach, was requisitioned for war uses, printing paper during the war became dull gray and peppered with specks.
25 One of the first printing problems during the war arose in connection with the printing of ration stamps. Ration stamps were coupons issued to the American public that were required for wartime purchases of rationed commodities such as gasoline and sugar. Ration program planners realized that these stamps
30 in effect were the currency of the realm during the war and must be printed so as to render them difficult to duplicate by counterfeiters. Printing alone could not accomplish this, so planners had to devise a paper characterized by peculiarities that counterfeiters could not detect. Perfecting and patenting
35 such paper was the task of Office chemists, who devised built-in safety features that were completely hidden and changed from time to time to further baffle counterfeiters.

The paper shortages extended past the end of the war. During the war, the War Production Board could, under their
40 war powers, commandeer paper stocks for the Office. But when these war agencies had served their purpose, the GPO lost its procuring power. Paper inventories remained dangerously low, and the situation required some positive action so that the Office could carry on with its duties.

16. The primary purpose of this passage is to:

   (A) describe the activities of the Government Printing Office during the 1940s
   (B) discuss the causes of the limited paper supplies during World War II
   (C) pay tribute to the United States Government Printing Office
   (D) provide a comprehensive discussion of the paper industry in the United States
   (E) promote a discussion of the need for recycling paper

17. Which of the following best summarizes the underlying theme of the passage?

   (A) A lack of paper can bring governments to a standstill.
   (B) Producing mass quantities of paper requires an enormous amount of raw materials.
   (C) Producing standard supplies during times of war is a complex task.
   (D) Special chemicals are required for the production of high-quality paper.
   (E) The Government Printing Office made its own paper.

18. In line 21, the phrase "currency of the realm" suggests tha ration stamps:

   (A) were a form of royal stamps
   (B) became objects of the realm
   (C) were a current form of artwork
   (D) were going to be used as passports
   (E) were essentially used as money during the war

GO ON TO THE NEXT PAGE

19. In lines 24–26, the writer states, "Perfecting and patenting such paper was the task of Office chemists, who devised built-in safety features that were completely hidden and changed from time to time to further baffle counterfeiters." This statement implies that:

    (A) special paper was a luxury
    (B) only the government could make unique paper
    (C) the government expected people to attempt to counterfeit ration stamps
    (D) counterfeiting was accepted due to the economy
    (E) printing is an art

20. In lines 27–28, the word "commandeer" means:

    (A) require
    (B) identify
    (C) borrow
    (D) seize
    (E) accept

GO ON TO THE NEXT PAGE

Questions 21–30 are based on the following passage.

The following passage describes the raising of a Civil War era gunboat and the objects the gunboat contained.

For almost a century, the *U.S.S. Cairo* lay quietly beneath the swift, muddy waters of the Yazoo River. In that one hundred years, the vessel gradually was submerged in silt, mud, tree branches, and underwater vegetation until only the pilothouse

5 was visible. The *Cairo* did not sink out of memory, though. In the summer of 1962, historians from the Vicksburg National Military Park, joined by The New England Naval and Maritime Museum and local scuba divers, began a thirty-day survey to determine the condition of the *Cairo*'s structure in order to see if

10 it might be possible to raise the ship. Every beam and structural support they tested was sound.

The great adventure got underway on August 3, 1964, when divers began the painstaking process of slowly see-sawing cables beneath the hull. It took almost three months to get

15 seven cables wedged in place, but by October 17, the workers on the project were ready to commence the raising operation. Four derricks with a total lifting capacity of 1,000 tons pitted their strength against the dead weight of the massive ironclad gunboat, but even their combined power could not lift her out of

20 the water. The thick iron armor, waterlogged timbers, and mud-filled holds were too much.

Bowed but not beaten, the engineers on the project developed a new strategy. A giant barge was towed to the scene and sunk. On October 29, the derricks tugged on the old vessel

25 once more, but rather than lifting the *Cairo* out of the water, they instead wanted to get the boat on top of the sunken barge. The engineers felt they could raise both together without difficulty. Again, the cables strained, and the hulk moved, but with a sickening noise, two of the cables cut deeply into the

30 wooden hull. All hope of raising the boat intact was gone.

Now it was a question of saving as much of the historic vessel as possible. The professionals decided to cut the *Cairo* into three sections: bow, midship, and stern. On December 12, 1964, the last piece of the gunboat was raised from the water,

35 102 years after it had sunk.

Even in fragments, the *Cairo* proved a gold mine of information. It was, in fact, a century-old time capsule loaded with everyday objects of naval life, ranging from kitchen utensils to medical supplies. The discoveries provided a much

40 more detailed vision of life on the ship than anyone could previously have imagined. For instance, evidence from the *Cairo* shows that the sailors ate in messes of about fourteen men, and that each mess had a special chest to hold its gear: tin plates, cups, spoons, glass condiment bottles, scrub brushes, a washtub,

45 and an earthenware jug of molasses. Every man took care of his own utensils and scratched his name or initials on each piece, indicating that even those who could not write at least could make an identifying mark. The discovery of a rolling pin suggested that fare on the ship sometimes included biscuits and

50 pastry, a fact not previously known. The vessel itself also offered new information, as researchers discovered that some parts of the ship had not been built according to the original specifications. Museum models and drawings across the country had to be reworked, old concepts changed, and new features

55 added.

Although the effort to raise the *Cairo* in one piece failed, the historic objects salvaged from the *Cairo* brought the period to life. As for the *Cairo* itself, after resting for about a dozen years at the Ingalls Shipyard in Pascagoula, Mississippi, it was

60 returned to Vicksburg in 1977 under the custody of the National Park Service. Following extensive research, restoration of the ironclad's remains was completed in 1984, and the boat was placed on exhibit at Vicksburg National Military Park. A large selection of the artifacts removedfrom the gunboat is on display

65 at the Cairo Museum in the park.

21. The primary purpose of the passage is to

(A) explain the necessity of salvaging shipwrecks
(B) describe the influence of water currents on salvage operations
(C) discuss the history of gunboats during the Civil War
(D) reevaluate commonly-held views about life during the Civil War
(E) describe how the *Cairo* was raised and what was found onboard the wreck

22. The tone of the passage can be best described as

(A) informed
(B) critical
(C) skeptical
(D) dramatic
(E) reverent

23. According to the first paragraph of the passage, the New England Naval and Maritime Museum conducted a survey in order to

(A) ascertain whether local opinion supported the raising of the *Cairo*
(B) study the water currents in the Yahoo river
(C) determine whether the *Cairo* was in good enough condition to be raised
(D) research the best methods of raising the *Cairo* out of the river
(E) understand how historians have described and depicted the *Cairo*

GO ON TO THE NEXT PAGE

24. In line 8, the word "sound" most nearly means

   (A) undamaged
   (B) noise
   (C) decayed
   (D) rotten
   (E) healthy

25. The author's use of the phrase "great adventure" (line 9) implies that salvaging the *Cairo* was

   (A) an unnecessary risk
   (B) an exploration of a new frontier
   (C) an exciting project
   (D) a foolish enterprise
   (E) an unrealistic goal

26. In the third paragraph, the author suggests that the *Cairo* could not be lifted intact because

   (A) two of the seven cables snapped during the second attempt to lift the *Cairo*
   (B) the barge that the engineers planned to use had sunk into the riverbed
   (C) the river was moving too swiftly
   (D) the engineers decided that the *Cairo* was structurally unsound
   (E) the *Cairo* was damaged during the second attempt to raise it

27. In lines 22–23, the author implies that cutting the gunboat into sections in order to raise it out of the water was

   (A) only one of many options for salvaging the boat
   (B) the best method for salvaging the boat
   (C) ultimately the only way the boat could be raised out of the river
   (D) a good option under the project's time constraints
   (E) a sign of poor judgment

28. Which of the following most clearly expresses what the author means by stating that "museum models and drawings across the country had to be reworked, old concepts changed, and new features added" (line 37–38)?

   (A) All historical models are incorrect.
   (B) Every discovery will result in the rewriting of museum literature.
   (C) Earlier models and drawings of the *Cairo* were done sloppily.
   (D) The discovery of new information can result in a revision of history.
   (E) Computer modeling is useful for drawing accurate models of boats.

29. All of the following were objects discovered on the *Cairo* EXCEPT:

   (A) a washtub
   (B) tin plates
   (C) a rolling pin
   (D) biscuits
   (E) eating utensils

30. The word "artifacts" (line 44) refers to

   (A) plastic objects
   (B) recovered items
   (C) the body of the boat
   (D) works of art
   (E) models of items found on the *Cairo*

GO ON TO THE NEXT PAGE

SAT TEST

Time—30 Minutes
30 Questions

For each question in this section, select the best answer from among the choices given and fill in the corresponding oval on the answer sheet.

Each sentence below has one or two blanks, each blank indicating that something has been omitted. Beneath the sentence are five words or sets of words labeled A through E. Choose the word or set of words that, when inserted in the sentence, <u>best</u> fits the meaning of the sentence as a whole.

Example:

    Medieval kingdoms did not become constitutional republics overnight; on the contrary, the change was ----.

    (A) unpopular
    (B) unexpected
    (C) advantageous
    (D) sufficient
    (E) gradual

---

1. In Greek mythology, Narcissus was a(n) ---- boy who could never love anyone but himself; because of his ---- , he was cursed to stare at his own reflection until he died of starvation.

    (A) amiable...amity
    (B) insipid...fecundity
    (C) cavalier...egotism
    (D) benevolent...churlishness
    (E) contemptuous...gullibility

2. The gymnast has a(n) ---- task, for he must perform movements that require considerable strength while ---- maintaining grace and fluidity.

    (A) formidable...simultaneously
    (B) facile...nevertheless
    (C) onerous...triumphantly
    (D) serendipitous...carefully
    (E) arduous...eminently

3. Rita jumped as Mark approached; she was obviously ---- by his appearance.

    (A) coerced
    (B) denigrated
    (C) flabbergasted
    (D) accosted
    (E) lambasted

4. John's red face proved his ---- reaction to Anna's rude comment.

    (A) amenable
    (B) erudite
    (C) magnanimous
    (D) incensed
    (E) placid

5. Alan's coworkers have great respect for him because of his ---- during the crisis.

    (A) ire
    (B) audacity
    (C) reverence
    (D) fortitude
    (E) belligerence

6. Popular rappers such as Eminem are making their fortune by showing great ---- in their talents; many are talented movie stars and stage actors as well as musicians.

    (A) stagnancy
    (B) rigidity
    (C) fluidity
    (D) multiformity
    (E) invariability

GO ON TO THE NEXT PAGE

7. George Washington Carver, an African-American scientist, is most famous for his ---- inventions using the peanut; he created hundreds of ---- ways to use this type of nut.

    (A)   mundane...advantageous

    (B)   ingenious...propitious

    (C)   superficial...irrelevant

    (D)   grandiose...practicable

    (E)   prodigious...inconsequential

8. A triptych is a three-panel painting; this elaborate method was often used during the medieval period to ---- the details of a(n) ---- narrative, such as the creation of the world.

    (A)   illuminate...prominent

    (B)   obfuscate...illusive

    (C)   eliminate...obscure

    (D)   divulge...obtuse

    (E)   invalidate...meticulous

9. Henry David Thoreau, a nineteenth-century American philosopher, thought that the ---- beliefs of a noble man should be ---- in his dealings with an errant government.

    (A)   meritorious...paramount

    (B)   callous...lenient

    (C)   venerable...ambiguous

    (D)   divergent...flippant

    (E)   effulgent...enmeshed

10. The teacher's ---- demeanor led many students to believe that she never had any fun outside of class.

    (A)   sanguine

    (B)   melancholic

    (C)   obsequious

    (D)   jocund

    (E)   obdurate

GO ON TO THE NEXT PAGE

Each question below consists of a related pair of words or phrases, followed by five pairs of words or phrases labeled A through E. Select the pair that best expresses a relationship similar to that expressed in the original pair.

Example:
CRUMB : BREAD ::

(A) ounce : unit
(B) splinter : wood
(C) water : bucket
(D) twine : rope
(E) cream : butter   Ⓐ ● Ⓒ Ⓓ Ⓔ

11. BURN : INCINERATE ::

(A) aspire : succeed
(B) inveigh : decry
(C) depart : malinger
(D) qualify : equivocate
(E) destroy : obliterate

12. HILARIOUS : COMICAL ::

(A) depleted : exhausted
(B) repugnant : unpleasant
(C) somber : grave
(D) empathetic : impetuous
(E) disloyal : transient

13. SOFA : FURNITURE ::

(A) ruby : gemstone
(B) bridge : water
(C) obstacle : success
(D) truck : garage
(E) convention : tradition

14. JET : AIRCRAFT ::

(A) desk : office
(B) keys : typewriter
(C) beaver : dam
(D) television : media
(E) joyfulness : exuberance

15. MONEY : BANK ::

(A) tree : leaf
(B) glove : hand
(C) mountain : valley
(D) gravity : atmosphere
(E) food : pantry

16. SCOUNDREL : DISREPUTABLE ::

(A) aesthetician : beautiful
(B) cad : sensitive
(C) glutton : greedy
(D) egotist : elusive
(E) vicar : analytical

17. MEMBRANE : IMPERMEABLE ::

(A) fortress : impregnable
(B) cell : nucleus
(C) liquid : frozen
(D) solid : opaque
(E) border : guarded

18. EXHAUSTIVE : RESEARCH ::

(A) demented : decayed
(B) accurate : fact
(C) imprecise : calculation
(D) comprehensive : analysis
(E) weary : fatigue

19. TWLIGHT : DARKNESS ::

(A) problem : solution
(B) adolescence : adulthood
(C) illness : death
(D) boredom : excitement
(E) wound : healing

20. WATER : HYDRATION ::

(A) temperature : condensation
(B) sadness : bereavement
(C) literacy : reading
(D) sheath : covering
(E) inconsistency : hiatus

GO ON TO THE NEXT PAGE

21. INTRACTABLE : FLEXIBILITY ::

   (A) voluble : amicability
   (B) amorphous : shape
   (C) truculent : aggression
   (D) garrulous : loquaciousness
   (E) salient : prominence

22. MOROSE : HAPPINESS ::

   (A) equipoise : equilibrium
   (B) desultory: direction
   (C) adamant : torpor
   (D) multifarious : diversity
   (E) persistent : tenacity

23. CATECHISM : INSTRUCT ::

   (A) effigy : ameliorate
   (B) deterrent : foment
   (C) lubricant : abrade
   (D) diatribe : denounce
   (E) brush : upbraid

GO ON TO THE NEXT PAGE

SAT TEST

The passage below is followed by questions based on its content. Answer the questions on the basis of what is <u>stated</u> or <u>implied</u> in the passage and in any introductory material that may be provided.

Questions 24–35 are based on the following passage.

The following passage provides a general description and history of forests in the eastern region the United States.

The hardwood forests of the northeastern United States are unique. In sheer sylvan beauty, they are unsurpassed. However, the eastern forests are not all identical. The northernmost forests are in the transition forest zone that lies between the
5   boreal forests—the cold and slow-growing forests, such as those of Canada—and the deciduous forests of warmer climates. The transition zone is about 150 miles wide, extending from Minnesota to New England. In this zone, the conifer species of the boreal forest mixes with the hardy deciduous species. The
10 zone is filled with a system of large lakes, but in New England, the forests extend to high elevations and even to the summits of mountains and ridges. In the transition zone, the dominant tree is the sugar maple, which can crowd out spruce, fir, pine, and hemlock. The sugar maple usually associates with such
15 deciduous trees as yellow birch, poplars, and basswoods.

From the Great Lakes to the southern portion of the eastern region is the deciduous forest zone. These forests once completely covered the Northeast with a veritable explosionof species—well over one hundred. The sugar maple no longer
20 dominates but mixes withpoplar, sycamore, sweetgum, oak, and yellow birch.

All of the eastern region is in the temperate climatic zone. The length of the growingseason ranges from 210 days per year along the Atlantic seaboard to 90 days per year in thefar north,
25 where the Hiawatha, Green Mountain, and White Mountain National Forests arelocated. The plant hardiness zones range from northern Minnesota, where the temperaturesdrop as low as –50 degrees Fahrenheit, to the relatively balmy zone of Maryland and Southern Illinois, where the average minimum
30 temperatures range from 0–10 degrees Fahrenheit. Naturally, the climates of the higher elevations of the Appalachians and Adirondacks call for hardier plants. Overall, the region has a humid climate. Precipitation in the region is less in the northwest and greater in the east and highlands.

35 The far northern highland forests of the region are home to many insect-eating birds, the most common of which are yellow-bellied and olive-sided flycatchers, tree swallows, and warblers. The mammals in these areas are shy, nocturnal creatures such as the river otter, porcupine, muskrat, bobcat, and beaver. The
40 largest mammal is the moose; also seen are lynx, snowshoe hares, black bears, gray wolves, and caribou. Throughout the Great Lakes and New England forests, where the food chain depends largely on seeds and leaves, gray squirrels flourish in the deciduous forests, and red squirrels flourish in the

45 coniferous woods. Grosbeaks, finches, buntings, towhees, juncos and sparrows consume large quantities of seeds. The greatest consumer of leaves is the white-tailed deer. These deer eat so much of the new growth that it damages the forest and affects the patterns of development. Porcupines consume conifers to the
50 point of occasionally killing trees by girdling them. Cedar waxwings flock to any source of fruit.

In the deciduous forests of the southern part of the region, the rich environment of the forest floor is a beehive of animal activity. Frogs, toads, and salamanders feed on insects and are,
55 in turn, eaten by the predators of the forest, such as snakes, skunks, and raccoons.

The Green Mountain National Forest runs north and south in south-central Vermont, enclosing the rocky backbone of the Green Mountains. When settlers first arrived in Vermont, the
60 entire landscape was covered with trees—huge, 250-foot trees, including great white pines as well as fir, spruce, hemlock, beech, birch, maple, oak, and ash. The lumber industry in the region began in New England and the Mid-Atlantic colonies during colonial times. The largest, straightest pines—those with
65 trunks up to five feet in diameter—were harvested and carried to England to be used by the British Royal Navy for ship mast

After the American Revolution, Americans needed wood of all kinds for boats, wagons, tools, containers, fences, charcoal, and fuel. As the population increased, loggers went high up
70 Vermont's mountain slopes to search for wood. As time passed the lumber industry removed the forest and exhausted the soil of the Green Mountains. Like other extractive industries, the lumber industry tried to consolidate and monopolize wood during the late nineteenth and early twentieth centuries. One
75 famous Vermonter who had enough insight to recognize the danger and also had the courage and eloquence to write well about it was George Perkins Marsh, whose book *Man in Natu* was published in 1864. This indictmentof the plundering of the Green Mountains was an international best-seller.

80 In 1909, the Vermont Legislature passed an act creating the position of State Forester and allowing for the purchase of Sta Forests. However, the act neglected to allocate the necessary funds for land purchases. In 1925, Vermont finally turned to the federal government to establish a National Forest in the state
85 In November 1927, heavy rains inVermont fell on barren hillsides and flooded into the rivers, sweeping away roads,

GO ON TO THE NEXT PAGE

bridges, and entire towns. The flood cost the state more than $35 million, an incredible amount for 1927.

90   Ultimately, the need for conservation arose because of the spread of this damage caused by industrial development. Indeed, the economies of many of the states in the eastern region depended largely on extractive industries. The great manufacturing complexes of the area fed on the coal, iron, oil, water, soil, and wood of the region. These industries, along with
95 advanced agriculture, helped create great cities and change the face of the land.

    In the process, however, they badly abused the natural resources and polluted the air and water. It was this situation that created the need for conservation in the United States and
100 action by the federal government.

24.   The main point of the passage is to:

    (A)   give a history of global warming
    (B)   raise concerns about Vermont forests
    (C)   describe the history of the eastern National Forests
    (D)   discuss colonial use of lumber
    (E)   describe forest wildlife

25.   Which of the following titles would be most appropriate for the passage?

    (A)   Lost Lands
    (B)   The History and Value of Federal Forests
    (C)   Lumber and the Colonies
    (D)   Why Vermont is the Green Mountain State
    (E)   Trees of the United States

26.   In line 13, the author uses the expression "veritable explosion" to mean:

    (A)   large variety
    (B)   explosive species
    (C)   small variety
    (D)   tall trees
    (E)   minimal differentiation

27.   In line 16, the author makes which of the following claims regarding the climatic zones of the eastern region?

    (A)   There are vast changes in climate within the region.
    (B)   The entire eastern region is in the temperate climatic zone.
    (C)   There are microclimates within the region.
    (D)   The climate is similar to that of western forests.
    (E)   The climate is similar to that of rainforests.

28.   In lines 22–23, the statement "Naturally, the climates of the higher elevations of the Appalachians and Adirondacks call for hardier plants" implies that:

    (A)   plants in this region must be able to withstand cold temperatures
    (B)   plants in this region readily bloom
    (C)   plants in higher elevations are non-native species
    (D)   all plants naturally grow in higher elevations
    (E)   very few plants grow naturally in higher elevations

29.   In line 31, the word "flourish" means:

    (A)   consume
    (B)   decorate
    (C)   flower
    (D)   thrive
    (E)   thirst

30.   In line 38–39, the author states that "Frogs, toads, and salamanders feed on insects, and are, in turn, eaten by the predators of the forest" in order to:

    (A)   list the species of the forest
    (B)   illustrate the food chain
    (C)   upset the reader
    (D)   highlight predator behavior
    (E)   distress wildlife lovers

31.   Lines 47–48 states that wood was used as:

    (A)   a building block for forms of transportation
    (B)   a heat source
    (C)   both (A) and (B)
    (D)   ship masts
    (E)   none of the above

GO ON TO THE NEXT PAGE

32. The lumber industry had what impact on the Green Mountains?

   (A)   It replenished the soil.
   (B)   It cleaned the air.
   (C)   It restored the forest.
   (D)   It removed the forest but replenished the soil.
   (E)   It removed the forest and exhausted the soil.

33. In line 54–55, the author indicates that George Perkins's book *Man in Nature* was written to:

   (A)   praise the lumber industry
   (B)   sympathize with the lumber industry
   (C)   celebrate the lumber industry
   (D)   castigate the lumber industry
   (E)   capitalize on the lumber industry

34. In line 60, the word "barren" means:

   (A)   without vegetation
   (B)   outrageous
   (C)   frolicsome
   (D)   fruitful
   (E)   ripe

35. The role of the final paragraph is to:

   (A)   repeat the author's earlier statements
   (B)   summarize the author's entire argument
   (C)   distance the author from the historical situation
   (D)   provide a happy ending
   (E)   recant previous statements

GO ON TO THE NEXT PAGE

SAT TEST

The passage below is followed by questions based on its content. Answer the questions on the basis of what is <u>stated</u> or <u>implied</u> in the passage and in any introductory material that may be provided.

Questions 1–13 are based on the following passages.

This passage is from "Impressions of an Indian Childhood" by Gertrude Simmons Bonnin, also known as Zitkala-Sa. A Yankton Sioux from South Dakota, she was born in 1876. This memory from her childhood was published in the Atlantic Monthly in 1900.

"Where is your mother, my little grandchild?" were his first words.

"My mother is soon coming back from my aunt's teepee," I replied.

5　"Then I shall wait awhile for her return," he said, crossing his feet and seating himself upon a mat.

At once I began to play the part of a generous hostess. I turned to my mother's coffeepot. Lifting the lid, I found nothing but coffee grounds in the bottom. I set the pot on a heap of cold
10　ashes in the center, and filled it half full of warm Missouri River water. During this performance I felt conscious of being watched. Then breaking off a small piece of our unleavened bread, I placed it in a bowl. Turning soon to the coffeepot, which would never have boiled on a dead fire had I waited forever, I
15　poured out a cup of worse than muddy warm water. Carrying the bowl in one hand and cup in the other, I handed the light luncheon to the old warrior. I offered them to him with the air of bestowing generous hospitality.

He nibbled at the bread and sipped from the cup. I sat back
20　against a pole watching him. I was proud to have succeeded so well in serving refreshments to a guest all by myself. Before the old warrior had finished eating, my mother entered. Immediately she wondered where I had found coffee. Answering the question in my mother's eyes, the warrior remarked, "My
25　granddaughter made coffee on a heap of dead ashes, and served me the moment I came."

They both laughed, and mother said, "Wait a little longer, and I shall build a fire." She meant to make some real coffee. But neither she nor the warrior, whom the law of our custom
30　had compelled to partake of my insipid hospitality, said anything to embarrass me. They treated my best judgment, poor as it was, with the utmost respect. It was not till long years afterward that I learned how ridiculous a thing I had done.

This passage is from the memoirs of Henry Morton Stanley, who was born in 1841 in Wales as John Rowlands. Born out of wedlock, he grew up partly in the charge of reluctant relatives, partly in St. Asaph Workhouse. Here is his recollection of seeking a family member to take him in after leaving the Workhouse.

Nothing is clear to me but the interview, and the appearance of two figures, my grandfather and myself. It is quite unforgettable.

I see myself standing in the kitchen of the Llys, cap in hand,
5　facing a stern-looking, pink-complexioned, rather stout old gentleman, in a brownish suit, knee-breeches, and bluish-grey stockings. He is sitting at ease on a wooden settee, the back of which rises several inches higher than his head, and he is smoking a long clay pipe.
10　I remember that he asked who I was, and what I wanted, in a lazy, indifferent way, and that he never ceased smoking while he heard me, and that, when I concluded, he took his pipe from his mouth, reversed it, and with the mouth piece pointing to the door, he said, "Very well. You can go back the same way you
15　came. I can do nothing for you, and have nothing to give you."

The words were few; the action was simple. I have forgotten a million things, probably, but there are some few pictures and some few phrases that one can never forget. The insolent, cold-blooded manner impressed them on my memory, and if I have
20　recalled the scene once, it has been recalled a thousand times.

In the afternoon, I paid a visit to Uncle Moses, who was now a prosperous butcher. They gave me a meal, but married people with a houseful of children do not care to be troubled with the visits of poor relations, and the meaning conveyed by their
25　manner was not difficult to interpret.

I next visited the "Golden Lion" kept by Uncle Thomas, but here also the house was full. Early on the following morning I was on my way to Brynford, to interview Moses Owen, the school-master.
30　Brynford is a hamlet situated in the midst of a moory waste, about half an hour from Holywell, and about five minutes' walk from Denbigh. The district is mostly given up to lead mining. I stopped in front of a new National Schoolhouse, and the master's residence. Mycousin was my last chance. If he refused
35　his aid, my fate must necessarily be that of a young vagabond, for Wales is a poor country for the homeless and friendless.

I was first admitted by a buxom woman of decided temper,

GO ON TO THE NEXT PAGE ➜

whose first view of me was with an ill-concealed frown. But as I
requested to see Mr. Owen, the school-master, she invited me in,
40 gazing curiously at the strange garb of what she took to be a
new pupil.

On being shown to the parlor, a tall, severe, ascetic young
man of twenty-two or twenty-three years demanded my
business. As he listened to me, an amused smile came to his
45 face, and when I had concluded, he reassumed his pedagogic
severity and cross-examined me in my studies. Though he gave
me several hard questions which I was unable to answer, he
appeared pleased and finally agreed to employ me as pupil-
teacher—payment to be in clothing, board, and lodging.

1. In the first passage, the grandfather's attitude toward his
   grandchild is:

   (A) indulgent
   (B) scornful
   (C) sad
   (D) pitying
   (E) oblivious

2. In the second passage, the attitude of the grandfather
   toward his grandchild is:

   (A) mild
   (B) ingratiating
   (C) cruel
   (D) calm
   (E) soothing

3. Bonnin would describe her childhood recollection as:

   (A) bitter
   (B) happy
   (C) vague
   (D) wrenching
   (E) anguished

4. Stanley would describe his childhood recollection as:

   (A) vague
   (B) tolerable
   (C) satisfying
   (D) painful
   (E) superficial

5. In line 12, Bonnin refers to her grandfather as an "old
   warrior" in order to:

   (A) establish his role in the community
   (B) denigrate his age
   (C) annoy the reader
   (D) provide another narrator
   (E) foreshadow a war

6. In line 16, the phrase "answering the question in my
   mother's eyes" implies that:

   (A) the mother is angry
   (B) the mother is sad
   (C) the mother is confused
   (D) the mother is hopeless
   (E) the mother is complicated

7. In line 20, when Bonnin describes her hospitality as
   "insipid," she means that it was:

   (A) tasty
   (B) savory
   (C) elegant
   (D) flavorless
   (E) inspired

8. The grandfather views his granddaughter's efforts in
   passage one as:

   (A) ridiculous
   (B) improper
   (C) a sign of ignorance
   (D) a risk
   (E) a sign of respect

9. In line 8 of the second passage, Stanley describes his
   grandfather's demeanor by saying, "that he never ceased
   smoking." This description implies that the grandfather is

   (A) deaf
   (B) a careful listener
   (C) not interested at all
   (D) apoplectic
   (E) nervous

10. In line 14–15, Stanley writes, "if I have recalled the scene
    once, it has been recalled a thousand times" to express:

    (A) the impact of the memory
    (B) the feel of the moment
    (C) the hope of the future
    (D) the burying of the past
    (E) his forgiveness of his family

GO ON TO THE NEXT PAGE

11. In line 29, the expression "ill-concealed frown" means that the woman was:

(A) trying to hide a smile
(B) laughing
(C) frowning
(D) neutral
(E) placid

12. The tone of the second passage can best be described as:

(A) bleak
(B) worried
(C) contrary
(D) pretentious
(E) blank

13. Which of the following words best describes the difference between the ways in which these two writers remember their grandfathers?

(A) implicit
(B) sensitive
(C) meager
(D) paltry
(E) significant

S T O P

IF YOU FINISH BEFORE TIME IS CALLED, YOU MAY CHECK YOUR WORK IN THIS SECTION ONLY.
DO NOT TURN TO ANY OTHER SECTION IN THE TEST.

Practice Test 1
Answers and Explanations

Answers to SAT Verbal Workbook Practice Test 1

Question Number	Correct Answer	Right	Wrong	Question Number	Correct Answer	Right	Wrong	Question Number	Correct Answer	Right	Wrong
				Section (30)							
1.	B			11.	C			21.	E		
2.	D			12.	E			22.	A		
3.	A			13.	A			23.	C		
4.	B			14.	C			24.	A		
5.	E			15.	B			25.	C		
6.	B			16.	B			26.	E		
7.	E			17.	C			27.	C		
8.	A			18.	E			28.	D		
9.	B			19.	C			29.	D		
10.	E			20.	D			30.	B		
				Section 2 (35)							
1.	C			13.	A			25.	B		
2.	A			14.	D			26.	A		
3.	C			15.	E			27.	B		
4.	D			16.	C			28.	A		
5.	D			17.	A			29.	D		
6.	D			18.	D			30.	B		
7.	B			19.	B			31.	C		
8.	A			20.	C			32.	E		
9.	A			21.	B			33.	D		
10.	B			22.	B			34.	A		
11.	E			23.	D			35.	B		
12.	B			24.	C						
				Section 3 (13)							
1.	A			6.	C			11.	C		
2.	C			7.	D			12.	A		
3.	B			8.	E			13.	E		
4.	D			9.	C						
5.	A			10.	A						

SECTION 1

Sentence Completion

1. **(B)**   One-Word Direct   *Moderate*
The missing word in the sentence describes the way that "Laura seemed." Because Laura covers her face with her hands when told bad news, it should be obvious that Laura seems this way because she is upset about the bad news. You can immediately eliminate *nonchalant,* because if Laura were nonchalant, then she would not have reacted at all to the bad news. You should also be able to rule out *ecstatic* and *exuberant*, since neither word makes any sense in reference to receiving bad news. That leaves *poised* and *distraught.* Because Laura covered her face with her hands, she would probably not be considered *poised* or composed in this situation. Therefore, **distraught** is a better answer because it fits perfectly with the receipt of bad news.

2. **(D)**   One-Word Direct   *Moderate*
The missing word in the sentence describes the way Allie's face appeared. Because Allie cannot stop her husband's embarrassing behavior, it should be clear that Allie appears this way because of her lack of control over the situation. You can immediately eliminate *aloof* because if Allie were aloof, she would not have tried to stop her husband's behavior at all. You should also be able to rule out *confident* and *cheerful,* for this situation would not encourage either of these states of being. Because the behavior is embarrassing, Allie probably would not be *animated*, which means "full of movement." **Mortified** is the best answer because it means that Allie was embarrassed.

3. **(A)**   Two-Word Contrast   *Difficult*
The sentence states that Benjamin Franklin was the son of a poor candle maker. Therefore, immediately dismiss (B), (C), and (E) as incorrect answers because each includes a first word that contradicts "poor" in some way. In looking at the remainder of the sentence, it is clear that Franklin enjoyed the presence of France's upper class. Thus, Franklin's beginnings in a poor family contrast with the lifestyle of the upper class. Keeping this in mind, eliminate (D) because those of the upper class are usually not *servile.* The logical answer is then (A), **meager...cosmopolitan**.

4. **(B)**   One-Word Direct   *Moderate*
Because Andrea has lost many friends as a result of her sense of humor, one may assume that it is not a pleasant one. So, answers (A), (C), (D), and (E), which offer positive terms, may be eliminated. The only word in the group that has a negative meaning that would fit in this sentence is (B), **acerbic**, which means "biting or harsh."

5.   **(E)**   One-Word Direct   *Moderate*

Since Aretha Franklin is said to be "the queen of soul music," her vocals must be out-standing in a positive way. So, (A), (B) and (C) can be eliminated immediately since these words carry negative meanings. Choice (D) might need a second look. After all, *strident* means "loud." However, that choice does not seem to fit with the rest of the sentence, which describes Franklin's music as "heartfelt." So, the obvious answer is (E), **evocative**, which means "inducing a powerful emotional response."

6.   **(B)**   Two-Word Contrast   *Moderate*

At a first glance, because of the "Although" structure of this sentence, it seems that the blanks should be completed with words that have opposite meanings. Answer (C) makes no sense, because one's comments are not usually described as *emollient*, or softening. Answer (E) can also be eliminated because friendliness does not fit in the context of this sentence about conflict between nations. Answer (D) can be thrown out because of the word *affable*, or friendly, does not fit for the same reason that (E) does not work. That leaves (A) and (B). Answer (A) is not the best choice because the two words are not exact opposites, whereas in answer choice (B), a speech might seem **innocuous**, meaning "harmless," while it is really **insidious**—enticing but harmful.

7.   **(E)**   Two-Word Contrast   *Moderate*

Because of the "Although" in this sentence, the two blanks should be filled with words of opposite meanings. (A) must be discarded immediately, since both *fallacious* and *specious* have similar meanings. (B) will not work for the same reason; *astute* and *inge-nious* are too close in meaning. Likewise, in (C) *perceptive* and *adroit* are relatively similar in meaning. (D) does not fit because both words loosely mean "shrewd." Thus, (E) is the answer that fits, since **spurious** means "worthless or false," while **shrewd** means "clever."

8.   **(A)**   One-Word Direct   *Moderate*

Since Ellie seems like a typical, motivated businesswoman, (B), *slovenly*, meaning "lazy," and (D), *bellicose*, meaning "quarrelsome," are immediately ruled out. Like-wise, (E), *pompous*, meaning "pretentious," does not describe a hard-working busi-nesswoman. So, (A) is the best answer. Ellie is the prototype or model, the **archetypal** businesswoman.

9.   **(B)**   One-Word Direct   *Moderate*

In this sentence, choice (A) does not fit, because one does not use *bolstering*, or boost-ing, to incite fear. Likewise, (C), *annihilating*, or destroying, does not logically work, because the missing word describes a desired practice. (D), *eschewing*, does not work, because it is a synonym for avoiding something. (E), *proffering*, will not fit since one does not proffer, or present, fear. Thus, (B), **inculcating,** or putting fear in the people, is the best answer.

Analogies

1.　**(E)**　Function / Purpose　　　　　　　　　　　　　　　*Moderate*
"The function of an ABBREVIATION is to SHORTEN something" is the most specific sentence you can make with this stem pair. Similarly, the function of a **ruler** is to **measure** something. In choices (A) and (C), the meaning of the first word is opposite of the second word in function or purpose. Choice (B) is a pair of synonyms rather than a function or purpose relationship, and choice (D) does not have a clear or necessary relationship.

2.　**(C)**　Function / Purpose　　　　　　　　　　　　　　　　*Easy*
"The function of an INSTRUCTION is to DIRECT people to do something" is the most specific sentence you can make with this stem pair. Similarly, the function of an **announcement** is to **inform** people of something. The word pairs in choices (A) and (D) do not have a clear or necessary relationship. In choices (B) and (E), the first word performs the opposite function of the second word.

3.　**(E)**　Part / Whole　　　　　　　　　　　　　　　　　　　*Easy*
"A CONGREGATION is comprised of PARISHIONERS" is the best sentence you can make with this stem pair. Similarly, a **team** is comprised of **players**. This stem pair requires you to recognize that the second word in the pair is comprised of the first. Choices (A), (B) and (D) have meaningful relationships; however, the second word is not comprised of the first. Choice (C) is a pair of synonyms.

4.　**(A)**　Part / Whole　　　　　　　　　　　　　　　　　*Moderate*
"A TRUNK is part of a TREE" is a logical sentence that can be made from this stem pair. Similarly, a **seat** is a part of a **chair**. Choice (B) is a pair of synonyms. Choice (C) is a pair of words often used in the same context, but an *injunction* is not part of a *law*. The word pair in choice (D) has no meaningful or necessary relationship, and in choice (E), the function of a *scale* is to determine the *weight* of something.

5.　**(C)**　Characteristic Action　　　　　　　　　　　　　　*Difficult*
"A HEDONIST is one who seeks PLEASURE" is a logical sentence that can be produced with this stem pair. Likewise, a **mediator** seeks **reconciliation**. The word pairs in choices (A) and (E) are not related in any significant manner. Similarly, the word choices in (B) and (D) are pairs of opposite actions: an *irritant* does not *mollify,* or

soothe; a *mendicant,* which means a beggar or an ascetic, does not seek *affluence,* or wealth

6. **(B)** Characteristic Action   *Moderate*

"A characteristic action of a PROFESSOR is to TEACH" is the most specific sentence that can be constructed with this stem pair. In the same way, a characteristic action of a **illusionist** is to **deceive**. Choices (A) and (E) are placed in the question to confuse you, unless you know the specific definitions of *engender* (to cause, produce, or give rise to) and *expatriate* (immigrant or refugee). The word pair in choice (C) represents an opposite action, and the word pair in choice (D) has no meaningful or necessary relationship.

Reading Comprehension

1. **(B)** Main Theme, Idea, or Point   *Easy*

This question tests your general understanding of the passage. The passage does not discuss all of the activities of the GPO during the 1940s, but rather, it focuses more specifically on the reasons why it had difficulty obtaining enough paper. (A) can be discarded because the passage only discusses the GPO's need for paper, not its many printing jobs. (D) is incorrect because the passage also includes information about international suppliers of papermaking materials. (E) can quickly be eliminated because the passage does not discuss recycling.

2. **(C)** Main Theme, Idea, or Point   *Moderate*

While details gathered from the passage point out that mass papermaking is a large industrial undertaking, the main emphasis of the passage is on the limits of goods as a result of the war. (A) can be discarded since the passage does not provide an example of a government grinding to a halt due to a lack of paper. (B) and (D) are general statements but are not the main point. (E) is factually inaccurate.

3. **(E)** Understanding Words in Context   *Easy*

(E) is correct, as currency is a synonym for money. (A) and (B) may be misleading because of their use of words such as "royal" and "realm," but they are incorrect. (C) is wrong, as ration stamps were used as utilitarian objects, not as artwork. (D) is wrong, because ration stamps were used as currency, not as passports.

4. **(C)** Implied Information   *Moderate*

The government took steps to prevent counterfeiting of ration steps because it anticipated that people would attempt such counterfeiting. (A) is incorrect, as counterfeit-proof paper was a necessity in order to produce effective ration stamps. (B) and (D) are claims that the passage does not make. (E) is a statement of opinion rather than an implied observation from the passage.

5.   **(D)**   Understanding Words in Context   *Difficult*
Answer (D) is correct. If you did not know that the definition of *commandeer* is "to seize for military or government use," you should have been able to choose this answer from the context of the passage. While (A) and (E) may seem to fit in the sentence, they do not imply use of government authority. From the previous discussions about the need for paper, it should be clear that paper stocks would be consumed, so answer (C) cannot be correct. (B) is also incorrect, as commandeering goes beyond identifying to procuring.

6.   **(E)**   Main Theme, Idea, or Point   *Easy*
The author uses most of the passage to describe how the *Cairo* was raised out of the river and what kind of items were found onboard the boat, so the correct answer is (E). In the fifth paragraph, the author describes how the items found onboard altered historians' understanding of naval life during the Civil War, but because this topic is not the passage's focus, choice (D) is incorrect. The other answer choices are not discussed in the passage.

7.   **(A)**   Author's Attitude or Tone   *Easy*
If none of the answer choices immediately strikes you as right, you can find the correct answer through a process of elimination. You can rule out choices (B) and (C), which suggest that the author is taking a negative stance toward the subject. Choice (D), "dramatic," is too strong a word to describe the author's tone. Although the author seems to respect the people working on the project and the goal of raising the boat, the tone is never deferential enough to be described as "reverent." The best answer is choice (A).

8.   **(C)**   Specific Information   *Easy*
This question asks for specific information from the beginning of the passage. In the first paragraph, the author states: "The New England Naval and Maritime Museum . . . began a thirty-day survey to determine the condition of the *Cairo*'s structure in order to see if it might be possible to raise the ship. Every beam and structural support they tested was sound." Choice (C), which states that the museum was trying to determine whether the boat was in good enough condition to be raised, is the correct answer.

9.   **(A)**   Words in Context   *Moderate*
If you don't know that "sound" means "undamaged," you can answer this question by substituting the answer choices into the sentence. Choice (B), "noise," does not make

sense in the context of the passage. Choice (C), "decayed," does not make sense either. If the boat's beams and structural supports had been decayed or significantly damaged, then the project to raise the boat would not have taken place. Because choice (D), "rotten," also suggests that the boat was damaged, you can eliminate it as well. Choice (E), "healthy," is the opposite of "decayed" and "rotten"; it suggests that the boat's beams and supports were in good condition. But because "healthy" generally applies to humans and animals, choice (E) is not as good an answer as choice (A), "undamaged," which applies to objects.

10. **(C)** Understanding Themes and Arguments   *Moderate*
The author uses the phrase "great adventure" to suggest that the salvage project was exciting and risky. You may be tempted to pick choice (A) since it uses the word "risk," but (A) is wrong because the author never suggests that the project was frivolous or unnecessary. The best answer is choice (C), "an exciting project."

11. **(E)** Implied Information   *Moderate*
At the end of the third paragraph, the author writes: "Again, the cables strained, and the hulk moved, but with a sickening noise, two of the cables cut deeply into the wooden hull. All hope of raising the boat intact was gone." These sentences imply that the boat could not be raised intact because of the damage that occurred to the boat when the cables cut into its wooden hull. The correct answer is choice (E), which summarizes what happened by saying that the boat "was damaged during the second attempt to raise it."

12. **(C)** Understanding Themes and Arguments   *Moderate*
The author states that once raising the *Cairo* intact was no longer an option, the engineers decided that cutting the boat into three sections was the best possible method for "saving as much of the historic vessel as possible." According to the author, raising the boat in one piece was the ideal method, but raising the boat in three pieces was the best method available once raising the boat intact was no longer an option. The correct answer is choice (C).

13. **(D)** Understanding Themes and Arguments   *Difficult*
The sentence quoted in the question explains how existing models and drawings of the *Cairo* had to be changed once the boat was raised and new information was discovered about its structure and its contents. This sentence does not suggest that all existing models and drawings of historical objects are incorrect, so you can rule out choice (A). You can also rule out choice (B) for being too strong; (B) claims that every discovery will result in the rewriting of museum literature. Choice (E) should immediately stand out to you as wrong, for the passage never discusses computer modeling. You may be

tempted to pick choice (C), but the passage does not imply that the existing models had been done "sloppily" or carelessly. Instead, it suggests that the models had been based on the information available at the time they were made, but this information ultimately proved to be insufficient. Choice (D), which says that discoveries can lead to the revision of history, is the best answer to this question.

14. **(D)**   Specific Information   *Moderate*
Answering this question correctly simply is a matter of going back to the fifth paragraph, in which the author lists items discovered aboard the *Cairo*. The correct answer is choice (D) because the author never says that biscuits were found on the wreck. Instead, the author mentions the discovery of a rolling pin, which suggests that biscuits and pastries had been made on the *Cairo*.

15. **(B)**   Words in Context   *Moderate*
Artifacts are manmade items preserved from the past. If you do not know this definition, you can reach the answer by substituting the answer choices back into the sentence. The sentence says, "A large selection of the artifacts removed from the gunboat is on display at the Cairo Museum in the park." You can immediately throw out choices (A) and (D) because the passage never mentions plastic objects or works of art. You can also eliminate choice (C) because it would not make sense to remove the "body of the boat" from the gunboat. Choice (E) does not work because "models of items found on the *Cairo*" would not have been removed from the *Cairo*. The best answer to this question is choice (B), "recovered items."

SECTION 2

Sentence Completion

1.   **(C)**   Two-Word Direct   *Moderate*
Because Narcissus cannot love anyone but himself, one may infer that he is selfish. So, answers (A) and (D) can immediately be eliminated because of their first words; *amity* means "friendship," and *benevolent* means "full of good will." Choice (B) can also be disregarded because Narcissus' behavior is not necessarily *insipid*, or uninteresting. (E), *contemptuous*, would be a good choice, but the word *gullibility*, meaning "easily fooled," does not work, for a curse does not imply *gullibility*. Choice (C), **cavalier...egotism**, is the correct answer; *cavalier* means "disdainful," while *egotism* means "self-absorbed."

2.   **(A)**   Two-Word Direct   *Moderate*
(B) and (D) may immediately be omitted, for the task of the gymnast is not easy or *facile*, nor is it *serendipitous,* a matter of pure luck. (C) does not work because the word *triumphantly* does not make sense in the second blank. (E) does not fit because of the word *eminently*, which does not fit logically in the sentence. Answer (A), **formidable**, meaning "huge or daunting," and **simultaneously**, meaning "at the same time," is the best choice.

3.   **(C)**   One-Word Direct   *Moderate*
Choices (A) and (D) will not fit because Mark is not forcing Rita to do anything. Rita is not being put down, or (B), *denigrated*, as far as we know. Neither does Mark yell at her, so she is not (E), *lambasted* by him. Thus, she is (C), **flabbergasted**, or stunned, because of shock of his appearance.

4.   **(D)**   One-Word Direct   *Moderate*
Because Anna's comment is rude, John is probably not having an (A), *amenable*, or agreeable, reaction. He is also not reacting in an *erudite*, (B), or intelligent manner just because his face turns red. His behavior is not (C), *magnanimous*, either, which means "generous or gracious." Also, since his face turns red, he is certainly not completely calm, or (E), *placid*. Thus, he is most likely (D), **incensed,** or angry.

5.   **(D)**   One-Word Direct   *Easy*
In this question, (A), *ire*, or anger, would not be a respected quality. Neither would (B), *audacity*, meaning "boldness," or (E), *belligerence*, which means "animosity." In addition, *reverence* does not fit the context at all since there is nothing for Alan to be reverent toward. Thus, choice (D), **fortitude**, or strength, fits the blank best.

6.   **(D)**   One-Word Direct   *Easy*
Because the second part of the sentence states that many musicians are also stage actors and movie stars, one may assume that such people show variation in their talents. Thus, (A), *stagnancy*, (B), *rigidity*, and (E), *invariability,* can immediately be omitted as possible answers, because all mean "staying the same." (C), *fluidity*, seems to be a possibility, but (D), **multiformity**, is a better choice, for the word implies talent that can exist in many forms.

7.   **(B)**   Two-Word Direct   *Moderate*
Since Carver produced so many uses for the peanut, one can assume that his inventions were important. Thus, choices (A), (C), and (D) may be ruled out because the first word in these pairs implies unimportant inventions. The word *inconsequential*, or unimportant, in choice (E) removes it as a viable option. (B) is the correct answer

because both Carver's invention and the uses of the peanut are **ingenious** and **propitious,** or advantageous.

8.   **(A)**   Two-Word Direct   *Moderate*
Because paintings usually shed light on their subject matter, several choices can be eliminated. In (B), *obfuscate* means "to make something more complicated than it really is." (C) offers two words that negate the sense of the sentence, and (E), *invalidate,* means "to weaken or lessen the force of." Since a narrative is not usually considered *obtuse*, (D) can be omitted. Thus, answer (A) is correct; the triptych style is an attempt to **illuminate**, or shed light on, a **prominent**, or important, narrative.

9.   **(A)**   Two-Word Direct   *Moderate*
Since Thoreau refers to "noble" men, one may infer that the beliefs of such men would be positive. So, answers (B), (D), and (E) can be eliminated. Because the government is errant, it can be assumed that the dealings of a noble man with such a flawed government would be difficult, at best. So, answer (C) does not seem correct; such a man's response would most likely not be *ambiguous,* or undecided. Clearly, answer (A) is correct. A man with **meritorious**, or good beliefs, would hold them as **paramount**, or of extreme significance, in his dealings with the government.

10. **(B)**   One-Word Direct   *Moderate*
Since the teacher does not appear to be a fun-loving person, *sanguine*, or playful and happy, would not fit her demeanor. *Obsequious* does not exactly fit either, for it means "meek." Likewise, *obdurate* can be ruled out because the quality of stubbornness does not necessarily dictate that a person cannot be fun-loving. *Jocund*, or "blithe and happy," definitely would not fit a person who seems to dislike fun. The correct answer is that the teacher is **melancholic**, or sad.

Analogies

1.   **(E)**   Relative Size and Degree   *Moderate*
"To INCINERATE something is to BURN it completely" is the best sentence that can be made with this stem pair. Similarly, to **obliterate** something is to **destroy** it completely. In choice (A), a person may *aspire* to *succeed*, but there is no degree of relationship. Choice (C) is a pair of opposites. The words in choice (B) are synonyms, and the words in choice (D) do not share a necessary or meaningful relationship.

2.   **(B)**   Relative Size and Degree   *Moderate*
"Something that is HILARIOUS is very COMICAL" is the most specific sentence that you can make with this stem pair. Equally, something that is who is **repulsive** is

extremely **unpleasant**. Choices (A) and (C) are pairs of synonyms, and if you are familiar with the vocabulary, you will see that the word pairs in (D) and (E) share no necessary or meaningful relationship.

3.   **(A)**   Type   *Easy*
"A SOFA is a type of FURNITURE" is the simplest sentence that can be constructed with this stem pair, just as a **ruby** is a type of **gemstone**. While the vocabulary in choices (B) and (D) have meaningful relationships, *bridges* and *trucks* are not types of *water* or *garages*. In choice (C), an *obstacle* stands in the way of *success*. The words in choice (E) are synonymous.

4.   **(D)**   Type   *Easy*
"A JET is a type of AIRCRAFT" is the best sentence that can be made with this stem pair. Similarly, **television** is a type of **media**. In choices (A) and (C), *desk* is characteristically located in an *office,* and building a *dam* is a typical activity for a *beaver*. In choice (B), a *typewriter* has *keys*; however, a *key* is not a type of *typewriter.* The words in choice (E) are synonymous.

5.   **(E)**   Characteristic Location   *Easy*
"MONEY is kept in a BANK" just as **food** is kept in a **pantry**. The first word in each pair is somehow contained by the second word in each pair. The first word in choices (A), (B) and (C) is not contained within in the second word. The words in choice (D) share no meaningful or necessary relationship.

6.   **(C)**   Attribute   *Moderate*
"Being DISREPUTABLE is a characteristic of a SCOUNDREL" is the best sentence that you can make with this stem pair. Likewise, being **greedy** is a characteristic of someone who is a **glutton**. In word pair (A), an *aesthetician* makes something *beautiful*. By definition, in choice (B), a *cad* lacks *sensitivity*. In choice (D), an *egotist* is conceited, not *elusive*. In choice (E), the word pair has no meaningful or necessary relationship.

7.   **(A)**   Descriptive Pair   *Moderate*
"If a MEMBRANE is IMPERMEABLE, nothing can pass through it" is the most specific sentence that you can make with this stem pair. Similarly, if a **fortress** is **impregnable**, nothing can enter it. In choices (B), (C), and (D) the words in the pairs have meaningful relationships, but not in the same manner as the stem pair. In choice (E), a *border* that is *guarded* may be difficult to cross, but not necessarily

8.   **(D)**   Descriptive Pair   *Moderate*

"EXHAUSTIVE RESEARCH is research that is thorough or complete" is the most specific sentence that you can make with this stem pair. Likewise, **comprehensive analysis** is analysis that is thorough or complete. Although the word pairs in all the other choices have meaningful relationships, they do not share the same relationship as the words in the stem pair.

9.   **(B)**   Cause and Effect   *Moderate*

"TWILIGHT is the onset of DARKNESS" is the a logical sentence that you can make with the stem pair. Similarly, **adolescence** is the onset of **adulthood**. In choices (A), (C) and (E), the first word does not necessarily cause the second word. Choice (D) contains a pair of words that are opposite in meaning.

10.   **(C)**   Other   *Moderate*

"WATER is necessary for HYDRATION" is a logical sentence that you can make with this stem pair. In the same manner, **literacy** is necessary for **reading**. In choices (A) and (B), the first word is not necessary for the second word. Choice (D) contains a pair of synonyms, and in choice (E), there is no necessary or meaningful relationship.

11.   **(B)**   Lack   *Difficult*

"Something that is INTRACTABLE lacks FLEXIBILITY" is the most specific sentence that you can develop from this stem pair. Likewise, something that is **amorphous** lacks **shape**. The words in choice (A) do not have a clear or necessary relationship. You should be able to eliminate choices (C), (D), and (E), because each of these responses offers pairs of synonyms rather that pairs that identify a lack of something.

12.   **(B)**   Lack   *Moderate*

By definition, to be MOROSE is to lack HAPPINESS. Similarly, to be **desultory** is to lack **direction**. Each of the other choices relies on your knowledge of the difficult vocabulary. Choices (A), (D) and (E) are synonyms, and the words in choice (C) maintain no clear or meaningful relationship.

13.   **(D)**   Characteristic Use   *Difficult*

"A CATECHISM (lesson) is used to INSTRUCT" is the most specific sentence that you can make from this stem pair. In the same way, a **diatribe**, or bitter and abusive condemnation, is used to **denounce**. In choice (A), an *effigy,* or representation, is not used to *ameliorate,* or improve. Choices (B) and (C) are pairs of opposite meanings, and the words in choice (E) have no meaningful relationship.

Reading Comprehension

1. **(C)**   Main Theme, Idea, or Point   *Easy*
This question tests your general understanding of the passage. (D) and (E) can quickly
be eliminated since they are specific points made in the passage. (A) can be discarded
because the passage does not discuss global warming. (B) may seem correct, but the
main point of the passage is broader than just the forests of Vermont.

2. **(B)**   Author's Attitude or Tone   *Difficult*
(B) is the best answer because the author conveys the value of the forests by describing
their history and the variety of plant and animal species in them. (A) is misleading
because the forests have been restored rather than lost. (C) is a specific point that is
mentioned in the passage but not the focus of the author's concern. (D) is not discussed
in the passage, and (E) is a statement too broad to accurately summarize the passage.

3. **(A)**   Words in Context   *Moderate*
This vocabulary question presents you with one logical replacement. Neither (B) nor
(E) makes sense in context. (C) is incorrect, and (D) is inappropriate, as they focus on
the size of trees rather than their species.

4. **(B)**   Specific Information   *Moderate*
(A) may be distracting because the passage does discuss climate changes. However, (B)
can be found nearly verbatim in a prominent spot—the first sentence in the paragraph.
(C) is not discussed in the passage, nor are the claims made in (D) and (E).

5. **(A)**   Implied Information   *Difficult*
If you did not know that the Appalachians and Adirondacks are mountain ranges, you
should be able to guess their identity from the phrase "higher elevations." Therefore,
plants growing in mountain ranges must be able to withstand the colder climates. (B) is
incorrect, as the passage does not imply that the climate of higher elevations results in
additional blooms. (C) is incorrect, as hardiness is not usually a characteristic of a non-
native species. (D) and (E) use absolute terms that make these answers unacceptable.

6. **(D)**   Words in Context   *Moderate*
(D) is the most logical replacement, as *thrive* is a synonym for "flourish." (A), (B), (C),
and (E) do not make sense in this context.

7. **(B)** Understanding Themes and Arguments   *Moderate*
(B) is correct, as the author is making a point about the natural environment of animals in the forest. (A) is incorrect because the species the author mentions is by no means meant to be exhaustive. (C) and (E) are incorrect, as the author does not use overly graphic or disturbing imagery. (D) is also incorrect, as the passage focuses on the interactions among all the members of the food chain, not merely predators.

8. **(C)** Specific Information   *Moderate*
The passage states that wood was used in building boats and wagons, as forms of transportation, and as charcoal and fuel, which provide heat, so (C) is the best answer. (D) may be distracting because some tall trees were used as masts, but it does not fully answer the question. (E), "none of the above," cannot be correct because (C) is indeed an appropriate answer.

9. **(E)** Understanding Themes and Arguments   *Moderate*
Careful reading reveals that the lumber industry not only removed the forest but also exhausted the soil. (A) and (D) are incorrect, for *replenished* is the opposite of "exhausted." (B) and (C) are factually incorrect.

10. **(D)** Words in Context   *Moderate*
If you did not know that *castigate* shares the same negative implication as *indictment*, the word "plundering" in this line should help you realize that Perkins' book was a negative portrayal of the lumber industry. (A), (B), (C), all share the quality of promoting the industry. (E) is also incorrect in this context.

11. **(A)** Words in Context   *Easy*
The information preceding this question should have already established that the trees and soil in the forest had been destroyed, making it possible to guess that there was no vegetation on the hillsides. Other clues should be that (B) and (C) are nonsensical in this context. (D) and (E) are antonyms of barren.

12. **(B)** Structure and Technique   *Easy*
(B) is the best answer since the author returns to the larger picture of the entire Eastern Forest Region to summarize the importance of federally mandated conservation. (A) is incorrect because the paragraph does more than repeat earlier statements. (C), (D), and (E) are not accurate statements of the final paragraph's role.

SECTION 3

Reading Comprehension

1. **(A)** Understanding Arguments and Themes   *Moderate*
Even though the grandfather is aware that his granddaughter does not know how to make coffee, he indulges her by playing along and accepting her hospitality. If you did not know the meaning of indulgent, it is possible to eliminate (B) as obviously incorrect. (C) and (D) cannot be correct, as the grandfather's actions do not convey a sense of sadness or pity. (E) is incorrect, as the grandfather is interacting with the child.

2. **(C)** Understanding Themes and Arguments   *Easy*
The grandfather's refusal to acknowledge his grandchild can only be described as cruel. (A) and (B) can easily be discarded. (D) and (E) do not illustrate the heartlessness of the grandfather's reply to his grandson.

3. **(B)** Implied Information   *Easy*
While Bonnin does not make obvious statements, the way in which she describes her family implies that her memory of this event is a happy one. (A), (D), and (E) can be eliminated, as they are all opposites of pleasant. (C) is incorrect, as the memory has many specific details.

4. **(D)** Implied Information   *Easy*
Stanley clearly remembers this childhood rejection as a painful memory. (A) is incorrect, for the narrative is filled with details. (B) is wrong since tolerable implies a level of acceptability. (C) is clearly not the right answer. In contrast to (D), (E) is not a good answer, either.

5. **(A)** Understanding Themes and Arguments   *Moderate*
Describing the grandfather as an old warrior clarifies his status in the community as a respected elder and a survivor. It is not stated to (B), denigrate his age, or (C), annoy the reader. This description does not provide another narrator, so (D) is incorrect. The description is used to provide a better picture of the character rather than foreshadow events, so (E) is also incorrect.

6. **(C)** Implied Information   *Easy*
The phrase shows that the mother is confused by describing her eyes as "questioning." The previous line also indicates that the mother wonders how the daughter could have

served coffee. "Questioning" does not necessarily imply "angry" or "sad," so (A) and (B) are incorrect. Through a process of elimination, (D) and (E) can also be discarded.

7. **(D)**   Words in Context   *Moderate*
If you did not know that *flavorless* is a synonym for "insipid," then by plugging the other words into the sentence in place of *insipid*, you should have been able to guess correctly. The previous descriptions of the water with coffee grounds should help you realize that the hospitality offered was not ideal.

8. **(E)**   Main Theme, Idea, or Point   *Moderate*
This question requires you to analyze the grandfather's response to his granddaughter. (A) is incorrect because "ridiculous" is the word Bonnin uses to describe herself. (B) is not the right answer, as the grandfather was pleased with his granddaughter's efforts to serve him a meal. He does not take it as (C), ignorance, or (D), a risk, but rather, as a show of respect for him and his culture, even though she is too young to properly carry it out.

9. **(C)**   Implied Information   *Easy*
Stanley is able to convey that the grandfather is not at all interested in his grandson by describing how the old man does not even bother to put down his pipe. (A) is incorrect, for the grandfather participates in the conversation. (B) is also incorrect because there is no evidence to suggest that he is a careful listener. The attributes of (D) and (E) are not implicitly or explicitly assigned to this character. In (D), *apoplectic* means "highly excited or frenetic."

10. **(A)**   Understanding Themes and Arguments   *Moderate*
The answer must be (A), as the writer emphasizes the impact of his memory by revealing the number of times he has relived it. He focuses on this constant recollection rather than (B), the feel of the moment. (C), (D), and (E) are not reflected in the passage.

11. **(C)**   Understanding Words in Context   *Moderate*
If you do not know that *ill-concealed* means "still visible," you might be able to guess from the rest of the passage and how he has generally been treated so far that the woman is not pleased to see the narrator. (A) and (B) are incorrect, for there is nothing in the passage to suggest that she is pleased to see the boy. (D) and (E) do not convey a sense of displeasure.

12. **(A)**   Author's Attitude or Tone   *Easy*

The author's description of his many rejections is bleak. (B) and (C) do not correctly summarize the tone since the narrator is not anxious or difficult. (D), *pretentious,* is not an appropriate description of the weary, sad narrator. (E), *blank,* is also inappropriate because the writer's sense of despair is obvious.

13. **(E)**   Relating Two Passages   *Moderate*

The two writers remember their grandfathers in significantly different ways, which is clear from the contrasting descriptions of the men. (A) and (B) do not make sense as a measure of difference. (C) and (D) could be used as a measure of difference, but neither is the correct answer to this question.

SAT Verbal
Practice Test 2

SAT VERBAL PRACTICE TEST ANSWER SHEET

VERBAL SECTION 1	VERBAL SECTION 2	VERBAL SECTION 3
1. Ⓐ Ⓑ Ⓒ Ⓓ Ⓔ	1. Ⓐ Ⓑ Ⓒ Ⓓ Ⓔ	1. Ⓐ Ⓑ Ⓒ Ⓓ Ⓔ
2. Ⓐ Ⓑ Ⓒ Ⓓ Ⓔ	2. Ⓐ Ⓑ Ⓒ Ⓓ Ⓔ	2. Ⓐ Ⓑ Ⓒ Ⓓ Ⓔ
3. Ⓐ Ⓑ Ⓒ Ⓓ Ⓔ	3. Ⓐ Ⓑ Ⓒ Ⓓ Ⓔ	3. Ⓐ Ⓑ Ⓒ Ⓓ Ⓔ
4. Ⓐ Ⓑ Ⓒ Ⓓ Ⓔ	4. Ⓐ Ⓑ Ⓒ Ⓓ Ⓔ	4. Ⓐ Ⓑ Ⓒ Ⓓ Ⓔ
5. Ⓐ Ⓑ Ⓒ Ⓓ Ⓔ	5. Ⓐ Ⓑ Ⓒ Ⓓ Ⓔ	5. Ⓐ Ⓑ Ⓒ Ⓓ Ⓔ
6. Ⓐ Ⓑ Ⓒ Ⓓ Ⓔ	6. Ⓐ Ⓑ Ⓒ Ⓓ Ⓔ	6. Ⓐ Ⓑ Ⓒ Ⓓ Ⓔ
7. Ⓐ Ⓑ Ⓒ Ⓓ Ⓔ	7. Ⓐ Ⓑ Ⓒ Ⓓ Ⓔ	7. Ⓐ Ⓑ Ⓒ Ⓓ Ⓔ
8. Ⓐ Ⓑ Ⓒ Ⓓ Ⓔ	8. Ⓐ Ⓑ Ⓒ Ⓓ Ⓔ	8. Ⓐ Ⓑ Ⓒ Ⓓ Ⓔ
9. Ⓐ Ⓑ Ⓒ Ⓓ Ⓔ	9. Ⓐ Ⓑ Ⓒ Ⓓ Ⓔ	9. Ⓐ Ⓑ Ⓒ Ⓓ Ⓔ
10. Ⓐ Ⓑ Ⓒ Ⓓ Ⓔ	10. Ⓐ Ⓑ Ⓒ Ⓓ Ⓔ	10. Ⓐ Ⓑ Ⓒ Ⓓ Ⓔ
11. Ⓐ Ⓑ Ⓒ Ⓓ Ⓔ	11. Ⓐ Ⓑ Ⓒ Ⓓ Ⓔ	11. Ⓐ Ⓑ Ⓒ Ⓓ Ⓔ
12. Ⓐ Ⓑ Ⓒ Ⓓ Ⓔ	12. Ⓐ Ⓑ Ⓒ Ⓓ Ⓔ	12. Ⓐ Ⓑ Ⓒ Ⓓ Ⓔ
13. Ⓐ Ⓑ Ⓒ Ⓓ Ⓔ	13. Ⓐ Ⓑ Ⓒ Ⓓ Ⓔ	13. Ⓐ Ⓑ Ⓒ Ⓓ Ⓔ
14. Ⓐ Ⓑ Ⓒ Ⓓ Ⓔ	14. Ⓐ Ⓑ Ⓒ Ⓓ Ⓔ	
15. Ⓐ Ⓑ Ⓒ Ⓓ Ⓔ	15. Ⓐ Ⓑ Ⓒ Ⓓ Ⓔ	
16. Ⓐ Ⓑ Ⓒ Ⓓ Ⓔ	16. Ⓐ Ⓑ Ⓒ Ⓓ Ⓔ	
17. Ⓐ Ⓑ Ⓒ Ⓓ Ⓔ	17. Ⓐ Ⓑ Ⓒ Ⓓ Ⓔ	
18. Ⓐ Ⓑ Ⓒ Ⓓ Ⓔ	18. Ⓐ Ⓑ Ⓒ Ⓓ Ⓔ	
19. Ⓐ Ⓑ Ⓒ Ⓓ Ⓔ	19. Ⓐ Ⓑ Ⓒ Ⓓ Ⓔ	
20. Ⓐ Ⓑ Ⓒ Ⓓ Ⓔ	20. Ⓐ Ⓑ Ⓒ Ⓓ Ⓔ	
21. Ⓐ Ⓑ Ⓒ Ⓓ Ⓔ	21. Ⓐ Ⓑ Ⓒ Ⓓ Ⓔ	
22. Ⓐ Ⓑ Ⓒ Ⓓ Ⓔ	22. Ⓐ Ⓑ Ⓒ Ⓓ Ⓔ	
23. Ⓐ Ⓑ Ⓒ Ⓓ Ⓔ	23. Ⓐ Ⓑ Ⓒ Ⓓ Ⓔ	
24. Ⓐ Ⓑ Ⓒ Ⓓ Ⓔ	24. Ⓐ Ⓑ Ⓒ Ⓓ Ⓔ	
25. Ⓐ Ⓑ Ⓒ Ⓓ Ⓔ	25. Ⓐ Ⓑ Ⓒ Ⓓ Ⓔ	
26. Ⓐ Ⓑ Ⓒ Ⓓ Ⓔ	26. Ⓐ Ⓑ Ⓒ Ⓓ Ⓔ	
27. Ⓐ Ⓑ Ⓒ Ⓓ Ⓔ	27. Ⓐ Ⓑ Ⓒ Ⓓ Ⓔ	
28. Ⓐ Ⓑ Ⓒ Ⓓ Ⓔ	28. Ⓐ Ⓑ Ⓒ Ⓓ Ⓔ	
29. Ⓐ Ⓑ Ⓒ Ⓓ Ⓔ	29. Ⓐ Ⓑ Ⓒ Ⓓ Ⓔ	
30. Ⓐ Ⓑ Ⓒ Ⓓ Ⓔ	30. Ⓐ Ⓑ Ⓒ Ⓓ Ⓔ	
31. Ⓐ Ⓑ Ⓒ Ⓓ Ⓔ	31. Ⓐ Ⓑ Ⓒ Ⓓ Ⓔ	
32. Ⓐ Ⓑ Ⓒ Ⓓ Ⓔ	32. Ⓐ Ⓑ Ⓒ Ⓓ Ⓔ	
33. Ⓐ Ⓑ Ⓒ Ⓓ Ⓔ	33. Ⓐ Ⓑ Ⓒ Ⓓ Ⓔ	
34. Ⓐ Ⓑ Ⓒ Ⓓ Ⓔ	34. Ⓐ Ⓑ Ⓒ Ⓓ Ⓔ	
35. Ⓐ Ⓑ Ⓒ Ⓓ Ⓔ	35. Ⓐ Ⓑ Ⓒ Ⓓ Ⓔ	

SAT TEST

Time—30 Minutes
30 Questions

For each question in this section, select the best answer from among the choices given and fill in the corresponding oval on the answer sheet.

Each sentence below has one or two blanks, each blank indicating that something has been omitted. Beneath the sentence are five words or sets of words labeled A through E. Choose the word or set of words that, when inserted in the sentence, <u>best</u> fits the meaning of the sentence as a whole.

Example:

Medieval kingdoms did not become constitutional republics overnight; on the contrary, the change was ----.

(A) unpopular
(B) unexpected
(C) advantageous
(D) sufficient
(E) gradual

Ⓐ Ⓑ Ⓒ Ⓓ ●

1. Amy's sweet smile concealed her ---- feelings toward Leigh.

   (A)   inimical
   (B)   benevolent
   (C)   amiable
   (D)   saccharine
   (E)   propitious

2. Although Bob's manner of speaking seems ---- because it was learned in the Amish country, his views are surprisingly ----.

   (A)   prosaic...puerile
   (B)   quaint...cosmopolitan
   (C)   eclectic...sophomoric
   (D)   sublime...spurious
   (E)   colloquial...provincial

3. Because of the scientist's ----, he had a personal bodyguard with him at all times.

   (A)   notoriety
   (B)   anonymity
   (C)   nonchalance
   (D)   perspicacity
   (E)   meekness

4. Allie's beaming face during Tom's speech indicated her ---- feelings about the subject matter.

   (A)   doleful
   (B)   wrathful
   (C)   ebullient
   (D)   nonchalant
   (E)   lugubrious

5. Thomas Paine was a person with little formal schooling and ---- education; nevertheless, his political pamphlets ---- the revolution in the American colonies.

   (A)   negligible...incited
   (B)   copious...stifled
   (C)   nominal...deterred
   (D)   profuse...bolstered
   (E)   meager...dissuaded

GO ON TO THE NEXT PAGE

6. John accomplished an impressive ---- when he beat all his opponents in the senatorial election.

   (A)   coronation
   (B)   coup
   (C)   edict
   (D)   increment
   (E)   antecedent

7. Schizophrenia is a ---- disease, but there is hope for those who have it to improve somewhat.

   (A)   deliberate
   (B)   degenerative
   (C)   decorous
   (D)   innocuous
   (E)   pacific

8. Even though Ruth smiles often, she never talks and is described by friends as ----.

   (A)   taciturn
   (B)   garrulous
   (C)   raucous
   (D)   boisterous
   (E)   animated

9. Despite his claims to enjoy a(n) ---- lifestyle, fancy cars, clothes, and homes indicated Josh's love of ----.

   (A)   frugal...opulence
   (B)   parsimonious...indigence
   (C)   affluent...aesthetics
   (D)   unassuming...modesty
   (E)   unpretentious...monotony

GO ON TO THE NEXT PAGE

Each question below consists of a related pair of words or phrases, followed by five pairs of words or phrases labeled A through E. Select the pair that best expresses a relationship similar to that expressed in the original pair.

Example:
CRUMB : BREAD ::

(A) ounce : unit
(B) splinter : wood
(C) water : bucket
(D) twine : rope
(E) cream : butter

10. BUCKLE : BELT ::

(A) pendant : chain
(B) shoe : heel
(C) brim : hat
(D) shirt : sleeve
(E) umbrella : galoshes

11. WORDS : DICTIONARY ::

(A) factory : assembly
(B) books : library
(C) museum : artwork
(D) closet : coat
(E) humidor : cigar

12. RATIONALE : EXPLAIN ::

(A) knife : cut
(B) hint : summarize
(C) exhibition : conceal
(D) system : avert
(E) subordinate : dominate

13. SHEEP : FLOCK ::

(A) hills : caste
(B) dogs : canine
(C) pastures : field
(D) relatives : family
(E) jackpots : premium

14. PROPONENT : ADVOCATE ::

(A) champion : dissuade
(B) nuisance : delight
(C) traditionalist : permit
(D) vagabond : remain
(E) dissenter : oppose

15. CAREFUL : METICULOUS::

(A) mundane : ordinary
(B) nonplussed : baffled
(C) disordered : pandemonious
(D) peripheral : interior
(E) perfunctory : cursory

GO ON TO THE NEXT PAGE

SAT TEST

The passage below is followed by questions based on its content. Answer the questions on the basis of what is <u>stated</u> or <u>implied</u> in the passage and in any introductory material that may be provided.

Questions 16–20 are based on the following passage.

The following excerpt discusses the methods by which astronomers categorize stars. Other important and often unconsidered properties of stars are also analyzed. The selection gives special focus to the naming of stars.

Astronomers are able to categorize and describe stars on the basis of a number of properties. The most essential property is a star's simple location in the sky. The coordinates of objects in the sky are given in terms of the celestial equivalents of latitude
5 and longitude, which are known as "declination" and "right ascension," respectively This coordinate system is organized around "celestial poles" defined by a line extending through space and in the direction of the Earth's axis of rotation, and a "celestial equator" defined by a plane running through the
10 Earth's equator.

Declination and right ascension are given in degrees, with declination ranging from 0 degrees at the celestial equator to 90 degrees at the celestial poles. Right ascension ranges from 0 to 360 degrees, increasing to the east, with the zero coordinate in
15 the direction of the constellation Pisces.

The Earth's direction of spin is not fixed. The Earth's spin has a "wobble" or "precession" that causes the poles to move around a circle in the sky once every 26,000 years. This wobbling means that the coordinates of stellar objects in terms
20 of declination and right ascension vary over time. Therefore, properly declination and right ascension must be given along with a date.

Astronomers have formally organized the sky into 88 constellations, with well-defined boundaries between the
25 constellations. However, stars themselves are not fixed in space. The constellations tens of thousands of years from now will not resemble the star groupings we see today. Although the brightest stars in the night sky, such as Sirius, Procyon, Rigel, and Betelgeuse, have names of their own, most stars are given
30 names relative to the constellations in which they are found. Stars within constellations are designated with Greek letters in order of brightness. The brightest star in the Southern Cross (Crux in Latin) is Alpha Crucis, the second brightest in Beta Crucis, and so on. A star may have both a formal name and
35 constellation designation. For example, Sirius is Alpha Canis Majoris because it is the brightest star in the constellation Canis Major. Once the Greek alphabet is used up, pairs of Roman characters are used instead.

Other stars discovered in more recent times are often just
40 named after their discoverer, such as Barnard's Star, or have catalog entries and are usually designated with the initials of the catalog and their celestial coordinates. There are a large

number of such celestial catalogs, with the most famous being Messier's list of nebulas and the New General Catalogue (NGC
45 which despite its name dates from the late nineteenth century

Other properties of stars include their rate of angular motion, or proper motion, across the sky; their velocity along a line of sight to the Earth, or radial motion, as determined by the Doppler shift of its spectrum; its color, which implies its
50 temperature; and its luminosity, or brightness.

16. According to line 4, declination refers to

(A) brightness
(B) latitude
(C) angle
(D) spectrum
(E) longitude

17. Which of the following is *not* one of the brightest stars mentioned in the selection?

(A) Sirius
(B) Rigel
(C) Polaris
(D) Betelgeuse
(E) Procyon

18. In lines 18–20, the passage states that

(A) more constellations will appear in the future
(B) all current constellations will remain for infinity
(C) current constellations will change form
(D) no constellations will exist at all
(E) it is likely that scientists may discover additional constellations

GO ON TO THE NEXT PAGE

19. Which of the following is *not* a property of a star mentioned in the selection?

    (A) size
    (B) angular motion
    (C) color
    (D) proper motion
    (E) luminosity

20. Which of the following best states one of the main ideas of the passage?

    (A) Ideally, science should not focus on stars.
    (B) Stars should be the most studied of the heavenly bodies.
    (C) Very little work has been done with stars and their activities.
    (D) The methods used to categorize stars are outdated and should be replaced.
    (E) The methods used to categorize stars are time-tested and valuable.

GO ON TO THE NEXT PAGE

SAT TEST

The passage below is followed by questions based on its content. Answer the questions on the basis of what is <u>stated</u> or <u>implied</u> in the passage and in any introductory material that may be provided.

Questions 21–30 are based on the following passage.

The excerpt below is from the autobiography of Zitkala-Sa, a Sioux woman born in 1876. Zitkala-Sa is recognized for writing down many of the legends of the Sioux tribe.

I loved best the evening meal, for that was the time old legends were told. I was always glad when the sun hung low in the west, for then my mother sent me to invite the neighboring old men and women to eat supper with us. Running all the way
5 to the wigwams, I halted shyly at the entrances. Sometimes I stood long moments without saying a word. It was not any fear, that made me so dumb when out upon such a happy errand; nor was it that I wished to withhold the invitation, for it was all I could do to observe this very proper silence. But it was a sensing
10 of the atmosphere, to assure myself that I should not hinder other plans. My mother used to say to me, as I was almost bounding away for the old people: "Wait a moment before you invite any one. If other plans are being discussed, do not interfere, but go elsewhere."
15 The old folks knew the meaning of my pauses; and often they coaxed my confidence by asking, "What do you seek, little granddaughter?"

"My mother says you are to come to our tepee this evening," I instantly exploded, and breathed the freer afterwards.
20 "Yes, yes, gladly, gladly I shall come!" each replied. Rising at once and carrying their blankets across one shoulder, they flocked leisurely from their various wigwams toward our dwelling.

My mission done, I ran back, skipping and jumping with
25 delight. All out of breath, I told my mother almost the exact words of the answers to my invitation. Frequently she asked, "What were they doing when you entered their tepee?" This taught me to remember all I saw at a single glance. Often I told my mother my impressions without being questioned. At the
30 arrival of our guests I sat close to my mother, and did not leave her side without first asking her consent. I ate my supper in quiet, listening patiently to the talk of the old people, wishing all the time that they would begin the stories I loved best. At last, when I could not wait any longer, I whispered in my
35 mother's ear, "Ask them to tell an Iktomi story, mother."

Soothing my impatience, my mother said aloud, "My little daughter is anxious to hear your legends." By this time all were through eating, and the evening was fast deepening into twilight.
40 As each in turn began to tell a legend, I pillowed my head in my mother's lap; and lying flat upon my back, I watched the stars as they peeped down upon me, one by one. The increasing interest of the tale aroused me, and I sat up eagerly listening for

every word. The old women made funny remarks, and laughed
45 so heartily that I could not help joining them.

The distant howling of a pack of wolves or the hooting of an owl in the river bottom frightened me, and I nestled into my mother's lap. She added some dry sticks to the open fire, and the bright flames leaped up into the faces of the old folks as they sat
50 around in a great circle.

On such an evening, I remember the glare of the fire shone on a tattooed star upon the brow of the old warrior who was telling a story. I watched him curiously as he made his unconscious gestures. The blue star upon his bronzed forehead
55 was a puzzle to me. Looking about, I saw two parallel lines on the chin of one of the old women. The rest had none. I examined my mother's face, but found no sign there.

After the warrior's story was finished, I asked the old woman the meaning of the blue lines on her chin, looking all the
60 while out of the corners of my eyes at the warrior with the star on his forehead. I was a little afraid that he would rebuke me for my boldness.

Here the old woman began: "Why, my grandchild, they are signs—secret signs I dare not tell you. I shall, however, tell you
65 a wonderful story about a woman who had a cross tattooed upon each of her cheeks."

It was a long story of a woman whose magic power lay hidden behind the marks upon her face. I fell asleep before the story was completed.

21.   The author's attitude toward the village elders could best described as

    (A)   amused
    (B)   respectful
    (C)   fearful
    (D)   venerating
    (E)   impatient

GO ON TO THE NEXT PAGE

22. In line 6, why does the author hesitate to invite "the old people" to dinner?

   (A) To make sure there was someone in the wigwam
   (B) To listen and see if "the old people" were talking about her mother
   (C) To make sure "the old people" didn't already have plans for the evening meal
   (D) To quiet her fears about speaking to "the old people"
   (E) To make sure she wasn't interrupting a conversation in the wigwam

23. Why is the writer of this passage referred to as "little granddaughter" in line 12?

   (A) It is a term of endearment and acceptance used by "the old people"
   (B) She is not actually called by this name; it is just a term the author chose to use for the autobiography
   (C) The people in the wigwam are her grandparents
   (D) Granddaughter is a generic term used by all the village elders when referring to a younger person
   (E) She is small in stature and often teased about her size

24. The author claims which of the following regarding the question her mother asked in line 20?

   (A) The author could not be trusted to keep secrets
   (B) It made the author aware that she and her mother were outcasts, as they did not arrange their teepee as the village elders did
   (C) Her mother had to nag the author to remember what the elders said in response to the invitation for a meal
   (D) It educated the author to be keenly and swiftly observant
   (E) Her mother was interested in what the village elders were doing in their teepees

25. The metaphor in paragraph 8 serves to

   (A) let the reader know that someone is watching the writer of the passage in this scene
   (B) set the surrealistic tone for the upcoming paragraphs, which begin to describe the legend telling process
   (C) show that the author was frightened by what she saw as "eyes in the night"
   (D) demonstrate how children interpret things in nature that they do not understand
   (E) let the reader know how the Sioux revered the heavens

26. Which of the following most clearly expresses what the author means in line 42 when she says "I examined my mother's face but found no sign there."

   (A) The writer's mother was showing no signs of interest in the stories and legends being told by the village elders
   (B) The writer's mother had no tattoo nor any expression of explanation as to why other Sioux did
   (C) The writer and her mother had developed an interpersonal means of communication through a system of signs
   (D) The writer's mother had been disfigured and was not able to communicate via facial expression
   (E) The writer's mother was giving the writer a reproachful look because she was not paying attention to the stories being told

27. The word "rebuke" in line 45 most nearly means

   (A) offend
   (B) punish
   (C) admonish
   (D) banish
   (E) alienate

28. The tone of the passage might be best described as

   (A) cautiously optimistic
   (B) slightly mocking
   (C) bittersweet
   (D) alarmingly frightening
   (E) peacefully reminiscent

GO ON TO THE NEXT PAGE

29. The author narrates the story in the first person in order to

    (A) make the story easier to read
    (B) explain difficult concepts in the passage
    (C) make the story more intimate and personal
    (D) demonstrate Sioux conversation patterns
    (E) distance the reader from the subject matter

30. The primary purpose of the passage is to:

    (A) describe the day-to-day life of the nineteenth-century Sioux
    (B) examine the communication practices between tribe members
    (C) raise concerns about the invalid legends told by village elders
    (D) describe a Sioux child's memory of community and heritage
    (E) prompt historians to reexamine the roles of women in Sioux culture

GO ON TO THE NEXT PAGE

SAT TEST

Time—30 Minutes
30 Questions

For each question in this section, select the best answer from among the choices given and fill in the corresponding oval on the answer sheet.

Each sentence below has one or two blanks, each blank indicating that something has been omitted. Beneath the sentence are five words or sets of words labeled A through E. Choose the word or set of words that, when inserted in the sentence, <u>best</u> fits the meaning of the sentence as a whole.

Example:
Medieval kingdoms did not become constitutional republics overnight; on the contrary, the change was ----.

(A) unpopular
(B) unexpected
(C) advantageous
(D) sufficient
(E) gradual

1. Although the small child's bad behavior was ---- to the patients in the waiting room, they still smiled at him.

(A) winsome
(B) vexatious
(C) quixotic
(D) impeccable
(E) conciliatory

2. The couple rushed into a(n) ---- marriage; as a result, they learned many ---- lessons about each other.

(A) irascible...rigorous
(B) heedless...facile
(C) impetuous...arduous
(D) prudent...serendipitous
(E) asinine...felicitous

3. The pained look on Ellie's face and her broken leg convinced the other girls that she was indeed ----.

(A) ludicrous
(B) ravenous
(C) afflicted
(D) dissembling
(E) duplicitous

4. The Nobel Peace Prize winner John Nash ---- with his schizophrenia for most of his adulthood; nevertheless, he ---- his mental and emotional strength by returning to Princeton University as a professor.

(A) wrangled...invalidated
(B) skirmished...suppressed
(C) grappled...evinced
(D) flourished...hindered
(E) waned...decimated

5. Although Andrea was annoyed by Tom's ---- "hello" as he ran out of the office, she did not show it.

(A) amiable
(B) brusque
(C) congenial
(D) jubilant
(E) poignant

6. Even though Lila threw away all unhealthy foods when she began her diet, her ---- sweet tooth still ---- her desire to lose weight.

(A) incorrigible...thwarted
(B) compliant...abetted
(C) obstinate...placated
(D) nominal...sanctioned
(E) notorious...vindicated

7. All of Michael's teachers knew from his superior writing that he was ----; however, they also knew that his ---- habit of making fun of other students would ruin his bright academic future.

(A) ignorant...loquacious
(B) insipid...insolent
(C) mediocre...fortuitous
(D) astute...appalling
(E) obtuse...baleful

GO ON TO THE NEXT PAGE

8. Sharon has a(n) ---- smile, but her attitude ruins her physical beauty.

   (A) censorious
   (B) querulous
   (C) atrocious
   (D) beguiling
   (E) ostentatious

9. The teacher banned the student from the classroom for his loud catcalls, laughter, and generally ---- behavior.

   (A) obstreperous
   (B) orthodox
   (C) palatable
   (D) punctilious
   (E) prudent

10. The students viewed the professor as ---- in his field; in addition, they disliked his continual ---- jokes concerning past students.

    (A) inconsequential...caustic
    (B) competent...deprecating
    (C) negligent...vulgar
    (D) miniscule...congenial
    (E) proficient...jovial

GO ON TO THE NEXT PAGE

Each question below consists of a related pair of words or phrases, followed by five pairs of words or phrases labeled A through E. Select the pair that best expresses a relationship similar to that expressed in the original pair.

Example:

CRUMB : BREAD ::

(A) ounce : unit
(B) splinter : wood
(C) water : bucket
(D) twine : rope
(E) cream : butter

11. APPLE : PEAR ::

(A) dagger : pestle
(B) wool : cotton
(C) stallion : steed
(D) parade : procession
(E) interstate : highway

12. FEVER: ILLNESS ::

(A) noise : uproar
(B) cataclysm : disaster
(C) hiatus : tribute
(D) silence : tranquility
(E) pain : injury

13. LUSH : FOLIAGE ::

(A) opulent : lavish
(B) forest : sylvan
(C) verdant : roots
(D) sumptuous : banquet
(E) sparse : vegetation

14. SYNOPSIS : SUMMARIZE ::

(A) forecast : visualize
(B) foreword : introduce
(C) innovation : regress
(D) separation : converge
(E) excerpt : scrutinize

15. SOOTHSAYER : PROPHECIES ::

(A) escort : galas
(B) charlatan : lies
(C) tactician : provocations
(D) megalomaniac : denunciations
(E) soldier : barracks

16. VIRULENT : POISONOUS ::

(A) pervasive : permeating
(B) ponderous : superficial
(C) pragmatic : practical
(D) precocious : immature
(E) gargantuan : sizable

17. RAIN: PRECIPITATION ::

(A) flood: aridity
(B) silence : articulation
(C) loam : soil
(D) decoration : affiliation
(E) hound : bovine

18. CAMOUFLAGE : OBSCURE ::

(A) constraint : amend
(B) provocation : defuse
(C) satire : promenade
(D) acquittal : conviction
(E) rally : enliven

19. JUDAISM : RELIGION ::

(A) postcard : correspondence
(B) hypothesis : theorem
(C) branch : tree
(D) asset : liability
(E) emotion : anger

GO ON TO THE NEXT PAGE

20. ELITIST : EXCLUSIONARY ::

(A) insurrectionist : exact
(B) traditionalist : adventurous
(C) criminal : moral
(D) connoisseur : discriminatory
(E) extremist : flexible

21. AMORAL : ETHICS ::

(A) hostile : fractiousness
(B) notorious : renown
(C) effusive : susceptibility
(D) disheartened : hope
(E) reserved : restraint

22. BACTERIA : INFECTION ::

(A) fertilizer : growth
(B) grain : fermentation
(C) violence : strength
(D) spice : blandness
(E) anesthesia : surgery

23. DEBILITATED : STRENGTH ::

(A) stable : steadiness
(B) gauche : tact
(C) obstinate : inertia
(D) standardized : uniformity
(E) importunate : determination

GO ON TO THE NEXT PAGE

SAT TEST

The passage below is followed by questions based on its content. Answer the questions on the basis of what is <u>stated</u> or <u>implied</u> in the passage and in any introductory material that may be provided.

Questions 24–35 are based on the following passage.

The excerpt below is adapted from the reminiscences of Paul Jennings, a slave in James Madison's household. After Madison's death, Jennings purchased his freedom and eventually began work for the Department of the Interior. His memoir was published in 1865.

When Mr. Madison was chosen as President, we came on and moved into the White House; the east room was not finished, and Pennsylvania Avenue was not paved but was always in an awful condition from either mud or dust. The city
5 was a dreary place.

After the War of 1812 had been going on for a couple of years, the people of Washington began to be alarmed for the safety of the city, as the British held Chesapeake Bay with a powerful fleet and army. Everything seemed to be left to General
10 Armstrong, then Secretary of War, who ridiculed the idea that there was any danger. But, in August 1814, the enemy had got so near, there could be no doubt of their intentions. Great alarm existed, and some feeble preparations for defense were made. Well, on the 24th of August, sure enough, the British reached
15 Bladensburg, and the fight began between eleven and twelve. Even that very morning General Armstrong assured Mrs. Madison there was no danger. Mrs. Madison ordered dinner to be ready at three, as usual; I set the table myself, and brought up the ale, cider, and wine, and placed them in the coolers, as all
20 the Cabinet and several military gentlemen and strangers were expected.

At just about three, James Smith, a free colored man who had accompanied Mr. Madison to Bladensburg, galloped up to the house, waving his hat, and cried out, "Clear out, clear out!
25 General Armstrong has ordered a retreat!" All then was confusion. Mrs. Madison ordered her carriage, and passing through the dining-room, caught up what silver she could crowd into her old-fashioned reticule, and then jumped into the chariot with her servant girl Sukey; the British were expected in a few
30 minutes. People were running in every direction. John Freeman drove off in the coach with his wife, child, and servant; also a feather bed lashed on behind the coach, which was all the furniture saved, except part of the silver and the portrait of Washington (of which I will tell you by-and-by). I will here
35 mention that although the British were expected every minute, they did not arrive for some hours; in the mean time, a rabble, taking advantage of the confusion, ran all over the White House, and stole lots of silver and whatever they could lay their hands on.

40 It has often been stated in print that when Mrs. Madison escaped from the White House, she cut out from the frame the large portrait of Washington (now in one of the parlors there), and carried it off. This is totally false. She had no time for doing it. It would have required a ladder to get it down. All she carried
45 off was the silver in her reticule, as the British were thought to be but a few squares off, and were expected every moment. John Suse, then doorkeeper, and Magraw, the gardener, took it down and sent it off on a wagon.

Mrs. Madison was a remarkably fine woman. She was
50 beloved by everybody in Washington. In the last days of her life, before Congress purchased her husband's papers, she was in a state of absolute poverty, and I think sometimes suffered for the necessaries of life. While I was a servant to Mr. Webster, he often sent me to her with a market-basket full of provisions and
55 told me whenever I saw anything in the house that I thought she was in need of, to take it to her. I often did this, and occasionally gave her small sums from my own pocket, though I had years before bought my freedom of her.

Mr. Madison, I think, was one of the best men that ever
60 lived. He was temperate in his habits. I don't think he drank a quart of brandy in his whole life. He ate light breakfasts and no suppers, but rather a hearty dinner, with which he took invariably but one glass of wine. When he had hard drinkers at his table, who had put away his choice Madeira pretty freely, in
65 response to their numerous toasts, he would just touch the glass to his lips, or dilute it with water, as they pushed about the decanters. For the last fifteen years of his life he drank no wine at all.

I have heard Mr. Madison say that when he went to school,
70 he cut his own wood for exercise. He often did it also when at his farm in Virginia. He was very neat, but never extravagant, in his clothes. He always dressed wholly in black—coat, breeches, and silk stockings, with buckles in his shoes and breeches. He never had but one suit at a time. He had some poor relatives
75 that he had to help, and wished to set them an example of economy in the matter of dress.

I was always with Mr. Madison till he died and shaved him every other day for sixteen years. For six months before his death, he was unable to walk and spent most of his time reclined
80 on a couch; but his mind was bright, and with his numerous visitors he talked with as much animation and strength of voice as I ever heard him in his best days. I was present when he died. That morning Sukey brought him his breakfast, as usual. He

GO ON TO THE NEXT PAGE

could not swallow. His niece, Mrs. Willis, said, "What is the
85 matter, Uncle James?" "Nothing more than a change of mind,
my dear." His head instantly dropped, and he ceased breathing
as quietly as the snuff of a candle goes out. He was about eighty-
four years old, and was followed to the grave by an immense
procession of people.

24. The primary purpose of this passage is to

(A) reveal previously unknown facts about the
Madisons' personal life

(B) support the antislavery movement by
demonstrating the intelligence and humanity of
a former slave

(C) argue that James Madison was the best man
who ever lived

(D) describe the Madisons from the viewpoint of
someone inside their household

(E) provide an accurate historical account of the
War of 1812

25. The tone of the passage can best be described as

(A) moralizing

(B) academic

(C) conversational

(D) defensive

(E) passionate

26. In his description of Washington in the first paragraph, the
author states all of the following about the city EXCEPT:

(A) The architecture of the city was considered
modern at the time

(B) Pennsylvania Avenue was unpaved

(C) The decoration of the White House was not yet
complete

(D) The city had a gloomy atmosphere

(E) Mud and dust could make road conditions in
the city bad

27. The author's discussion of General Armstrong in the second
paragraph suggests that

(A) Armstrong had the complete trust of Madison,
who gave the general sole authority to call up
troops

(B) before she was interrupted by the British
attack, Mrs. Madison was planning to honor
Armstrong at dinner

(C) Armstrong was a competent military leader
who correctly sensed changing tides during the
war

(D) Armstrong underestimated the danger posed by
the British and failed to prepare the city
adequately against attack

(E) Armstrong played an insignificant role in the
development of the War of 1812

28. As it is used in line 19, the word "reticule" most likely
means:

(A) chariot

(B) horse

(C) skirt

(D) bag

(E) hands

29. In line 25, what is the meaning of the word "rabble"?

(A) the British army

(B) a mob of people

(C) Army deserters

(D) an organized gang

(E) the working class

30. In the passage, what misconception about events during the
War of 1812 does the author attempt to correct?

(A) Mrs. Madison removed a painting of George
Washington from the White House.

(B) The warning of attack was a false alarm, so the
White House was never evacuated.

(C) Mrs. Madison took the silver as she evacuated
the White House.

(D) The gardener and the doorkeeper stole the
painting of George Washington during the
British attack.

(E) The British never invaded the White House.

GO ON TO THE NEXT PAGE

SAT TEST

The passages below are followed by questions based on their content. Answer the questions on the basis of what is <u>stated</u> or <u>implied</u> in the passages and in any introductory material that may be provided.

Questions 1–13 are based on the following passages.

The following passages discuss two events in the history of submarines. Passage 1 is an account of the invention of the first viable submarine by David Bushnell in the eighteenth century. Passage 2 is an account of the use of German U-boat submarines against the British Navy during World War I, at the beginning of the twentieth century.

Passage 1

The first submarine that was actually worthy of the name was the *Turtle,* designed during the American Revolution by David Bushnell, a student at Yale who was involved in the resistance against the British. The precise details of Bushnell's
5 submarine design are unknown, since all that remains is a written description of his work. The most commonly-accepted illustration of the *Turtle* was drawn over a century after the submarine was built, and it was based solely on Bushnell's description. The accuracy of this illustration is questionable;
10 some of the submarine features that this illustration shows are clearly implausible.

The one-man craft described by Bushnell resembles in many ways the modern submarines with which we are familiar. The *Turtle* was shaped like two bowls joined together at the lip. On
15 top of the submarine, there was a brass "conning tower" with portholes that allowed the operator to see. The submarine carried a 150-pound black powder charge, or mine, that was intended to disable enemy ships. Bushnell designed the charge to attach to an enemy warship with a screw driven in by
20 the submarine operator. A clockwork timing mechanism would then detonate the charge and damage the enemy ship.

The operator of the submarine had to take care of multiple tasks simultaneously. The submarine was propelled by hand-driven horizontal and vertical propellers. The operator could
25 make the craft sink by letting water into a tank, and rise again by pumping the water out. He obtained air through pipes with valves that closed when the submarine submerged completely under water. There was enough air to allow the operator to stay submerged for approximately a half an hour. The *Turtle* was
30 steered by a rudder, and had a compass and barometer for navigation. Handling the propellers, rudder, and all the other gears kept the operator extremely busy.

Bushnell proposed to use the *Turtle* to attack British vessels that were blockading American ports. Although Bushnell
35 himself wanted to pilot the craft, he fell ill, and substitute operators had to be found. In August 1776, Sergeant Ezra Lee of the American Army took the *Turtle* to sea. The little submarine was towed toward the British blockaders by two longboats, and

then released to move forward with the tide. The tide swept him
40 past his target, the British warship *HMS Eagle,* so Lee had to wait for the tide to reverse before he could make his way to his target. The screw used to attach the charge to the warship could not penetrate the copper sheathing covering the warship's hull and Lee was forced to give up the attack.

45 While he was struggling to return the *Turtle* to shore, the British noticed the strange little vessel bobbing on the surface of the water and sent out a boat to investigate. Lee released the charge, activating the clockwork timer. The charge exploded, and the British decided to give up the chase. Lee escaped, but
50 the *Turtle* never managed to get close to another British warship; it was eventually found by the British and sunk.

Bushnell rebuilt the *Turtle* during the War of 1812, and used it once more in unsuccessful attacks on British blockaders Despite its failure in combat, another submarine pioneer, John
55 P. Holland, wrote in the early twentieth century that the *Turtl* was "the most perfect thing of its kind constructed before 1880 Considering the technology available, the design of the little submarine was remarkably clever and well thought out.

Passage 2

On August 6, 1914, two days after Britain declared war on Germany to start World War I, ten German U-boat submarines left their base in Heligoland to attack Britain's Royal Navy warships in the North Sea.
5 It was the first submarine war patrol in history, and it got off to a rough start. One of the U-boats was sunk in a minefield Another, the "U-15," fired torpedoes at several British warship and missed each time. The U-15 was later rammed and sunk b the Royal Navy cruiser *Birmingham* while the U-boat was
10 trapped on the ocean's surface because of mechanical troubles.

Despite these debacles, the U-boats continued to follow British war patrols. They finally attacked successfully on September 5, 1914, when a U-boat commanded by Lieutenant Otto Hersing torpedoed the Royal Navy light cruiser *Pathfinde*
15 The cruiser's magazine exploded, and the ship sank in four minutes, taking 259 of her crew with her. It was the first comba victory of the modern submarine.

The German U-boats enjoyed even greater success later in the month. On September 22, a lookout on the conning tower o
20 the "U-9," commanded by Lieutenant Otto Weddigen, spotted a

GO ON TO THE NEXT PAGE

31. The author states that he gave Mrs. Madison money "though I had years before bought my freedom of her" (lines 38–39) primarily in order to:

    (A) argue that the abolition of slavery would benefit slave owners
    (B) describe how demanding Mrs. Madison was of everyone around her
    (C) show that he had become wealthy
    (D) demonstrate his willingness to be Mrs. Madison's loyal servant
    (E) emphasize his affection for her

32. Of the following, the best synonym for "temperate" in line 40 is:

    (A) grouchy
    (B) irascible
    (C) lukewarm
    (D) docile
    (E) moderate

33. The discussion of Madison's habits in lines 47–52 is used to:

    (A) emphasize Madison's modest behavior
    (B) illuminate Madison's humble origins
    (C) show how meanly Madison treated his poor relatives
    (D) describe the poverty into which the Madisons descended after leaving the White House
    (E) provide a physical description of Madison for posterity

34. The author's main purpose in stating that Madison was "followed to the grave by an immense procession of people" (lines 60–61) is to

    (A) describe the large number of deaths that occurred after Madison's death
    (B) chastise the organizers of Madison's funeral for inviting too many people
    (C) deny claims that few people attended Madison's funeral
    (D) show the amount of respect and affection Madison was given until his death
    (E) convey the grave atmosphere at Madison's funeral

35. Which of the following titles best summarizes the passage?

    (A) The Presidency of James Madison
    (B) Memoirs of a Servant
    (C) Reminiscences of James and Dolly Madison
    (D) The Role of Slaves in the War of 1812
    (E) The Private Life of James Madison

GO ON TO THE NEXT PAGE

vessel on the horizon. Weddigen ordered the U-boat to submerge immediately, and the submarine went forward to investigate.

At closer range, Weddigen discovered three old Royal Navy light cruisers, the *Aboukir*, the *Cressy*, and the *Hogue*. Not only
25 were these three vessels antiquated, but also they were staffed mostly by reservists. In fact, these ships were so vulnerable that a decision to withdraw them was already filtering up through the bureaucracy of the British Admiralty. The order didn't come soon enough. Weddigen sent one torpedo into the *Aboukir*. The
30 captains of the *Hogue* and *Cressy* assumed the *Aboukir* had struck a mine and came up to assist. The U-9 put two torpedoes into the *Hogue,* and then hit the *Cressy* with two more torpedoes as the cruiser tried to flee.

The U-9 sank three British cruisers in less than a hour,
35 killing 1,460 British sailors. Three weeks later, on October 15, Weddigen also sank the old cruiser *Hawke*. The crew of the U-9 became national heroes. Each was awarded the Iron Cross Second Class, except for Weddigen, who received the Iron Cross First Class.
40 Weddigen was simply lucky. The U-9 was a small, obsolescent submarine powered by kerosene engines, not nearly as powerful as the diesel-powered U-19 class vessels, and the U-9 was of marginal combat utility. The captains of the British cruisers had been careless, and it was unlikely the U-9 would
45 have caught them if they had been alert.

The sinking of these ships was a wake-up call to the British Admiralty. The Royal Navy base at Scapa Flow in the Orkney Islands, just north of Scotland, seemed clearly vulnerable to enemy attacks. The Admiralty was also increasingly nervous
50 about mines, which had sunk the light cruiser *HMS Amphion* off the Thames Estuary during the first week of the war and the battleship *HMS Audacious* on October 17 in the Irish Sea. Most of the crew of the *Audacious* survived, but the sinking was still a major humiliation.
55 The fleet was sent to wait in Ireland and on the western coast of Scotland until adequate defenses were installed at Scapa Flow. This evacuation, in a sense, was a more significant victory for the Germans than the sinking of a few old British cruisers. The German submarine had forced the world's most
60 powerful fleet from its home base and into hiding.

1. In Passage 1, the author's description of the *Turtle* as "the first submarine that was actually worthy of the name" (lines 1) suggests that

    (A) Bushnell was the first person to attempt to build an underwater vessel
    (B) many successful attempts had been made to build submarines before Bushnell
    (C) the *Turtle* was the best submarine ever made
    (D) the *Turtle* was the first vessel that resembled the modern submarine
    (E) the *Turtle* passed the test by which submarines are judged

2. The word "implausible" in line 8 most nearly means

    (A) believable
    (B) ingenious
    (C) scientific
    (D) unbelievable
    (E) workable

3. According to the third paragraph, the operator of the *Turtle* was responsible for all of the following EXCEPT

    (A) pumping water out of the submarine's tank
    (B) driving the vertical and horizontal propellers
    (C) firing torpedoes at enemy ships
    (D) navigating the submarine
    (E) using the rudder to steer the craft

4. In Passage 1, how does the second paragraph function in relation to the first?

    (A) It refutes the claims made in the first paragraph.
    (B) It focuses the broad claims of the first paragraph.
    (C) It presents generalizations based on the information given in the first paragraph.
    (D) It qualifies the statements made in the first paragraph.
    (E) It extends the arguments made in the first paragraph to their logical limit.

5. The author's tone in Passage 1 can best be described as

    (A) mocking
    (B) angry
    (C) interested
    (D) indifferent
    (E) ambivalent

6. Which of the following titles best summarizes Passage 1 ?

    (A) The *Turtle:* A Crushing Maritime Failure
    (B) The History of David Bushnell's *Turtle*
    (C) The Manufacture of Submarines in the Eighteenth Century
    (D) David Bushnell: Triumphant Inventor
    (E) The Rise of the Submarine

GO ON TO THE NEXT PAGE

7.   In Passage 2, the author states that the German submarine patrol "got off to a rough start" because

(A)   through the carelessness of their captains, three of the U-boats were destroyed
(B)   two of the U-boats were destroyed, and the patrol failed to damage Royal Navy ships
(C)   the U-boats were able to destroy only one British cruiser
(D)   the charges that the Germans attached to British ships failed to detonate
(E)   the Royal Navy surrounded and trapped the U-boat patrol

8.   Which of the following is the best synonym for the word "debacles" as it is used in line 9?

(A)   setbacks
(B)   successes
(C)   damages
(D)   disasters
(E)   triumphs

9.   The author of Passage 2 bases his argument that "Weddigen was simply lucky" (lines 30) on the fact that

(A)   the British Admiralty had failed to withdraw its cruisers
(B)   the U-9 was not powerful enough to take on full-strength British cruisers
(C)   British cruisers did not normally travel in groups of three
(D)   the lookout on Weddigen's submarine was unusually talented
(E)   the captains of the British cruisers had been careless

10.   Which of the following does the author of Passage 2 give as the most significant success of the German submarine patrol?

(A)   The submarine patrol killed thousands of British sailors.
(B)   The submarine patrol destroyed key vessels in the British fleet.
(C)   The submarine patrol gained control of British bases in Ireland and western Scotland.
(D)   The submarine patrol proved that submarines were assets in modern naval warfare.
(E)   The submarine patrol drove the British fleet from its base.

11.   With which of the following statements would the authors of the passages most likely agree?

(A)   Submarines are foolish inventions.
(B)   Submarines are useful, ingenious inventions.
(C)   Submarines never function according to their designs.
(D)   Submarines are only as good as the men operating them.
(E)   Pacifists regretted the invention of the submarine.

GO ON TO THE NEXT PAGE

12. Which of the following most accurately describes a similarity between the two passages?

    (A) The passages describe how the submarine is useless in warfare.
    (B) The passages describe significant moments in the history of the submarine.
    (C) The passages describe how the submarine was invented.
    (D) The passages describe how the operation of submarines has evolved.
    (E) The passages describe how submarines have affected the way in which war is conducted.

13. How would the author of Passage 1 most likely view the submarine's success as described in Passage 2 ?

    (A) He would disbelieve it.
    (B) He would disagree that it was a success.
    (C) He would be indifferent toward it.
    (D) He would be pleased.
    (E) He would be scornful of it.

S T O P

IF YOU FINISH BEFORE TIME IS CALLED, YOU MAY CHECK YOUR WORK IN THIS SECTION ONLY.
DO NOT TURN TO ANY OTHER SECTION IN THE TEST.

Practice Test 2
Answers and
Explanations

Answers to SAT Verbal Workbook Practice Test 2

Question Number	Correct Answer	Right	Wrong	Question Number	Correct Answer	Right	Wrong	Question Number	Correct Answer	Right	Wrong
Section (30)											
1.	A			11.	B			21.	D		
2.	B			12.	A			22.	C		
3.	A			13.	D			23.	A		
4.	C			14.	E			24.	D		
5.	A			15.	C			25.	B		
6.	B			16.	B			26.	B		
7.	B			17.	E			27.	C		
8.	A			18.	C			28.	E		
9.	A			19.	A			29.	C		
10.	C			20.	E			30.	D		
Section 2 (35)											
1.	B			13.	B			25.	C		
2.	C			14.	B			26.	A		
3.	C			15.	B			27.	D		
4.	C			16.	E			28.	D		
5.	B			17.	C			29.	B		
6.	A			18.	E			30.	A		
7.	D			19.	A			31.	E		
8.	C			20.	D			32.	E		
9.	A			21.	D			33.	A		
10.	B			22.	A			34.	D		
11.	E			23.	B			35.	C		
12.	D			24.	D						
Section 3 (13)											
1.	D			6.	B			11.	B		
2.	D			7.	B			12.	B		
3.	C			8.	D			13.	D		
4.	B			9.	E						
5.	C			10.	B						

Section 1

Sentence Completions

1. **(A)** One-Word Direct   *Moderate*
In this sentence, the words *amiable, benevolent* and *saccharine* may be immediately eliminated as possible answers because these all refer to kind or friendly feelings. *Propitious* may also be eliminated because it refers to favorable feelings. Thus, **inimical**, which means hostile, is the correct answer.

2. **(B)** Two Words   *Easy*
The answer choice with *sublime* as the first word may be immediately eliminated because it does not fit in the context of the sentence. In looking at the second word in each pair, *puerile* may be eliminated since it means childish. Likewise, *sophomoric,* or foolish, *spurious,* or false, and *provincial,* or limited, may be dismissed as possible answers because they do not fit with the clue word *surprisingly.* Thus, (B) is the best answer.

3. **(A)** One-Word Direct   *Easy*
In this sentence, *anonymity, nonchalance,* and *meekness* do not seem to fit as reasons for a scientist to have a bodyguard. Also, *perspicacity* or intelligence does not fit. Thus, the answer is (A), **notoriety**.

4. **(C)** One-Word Direct   *Moderate*
Since Allie is beaming or smiling, one can infer that she is happy. Thus, the words *doleful*, meaning sad, and *wrathful*, or angry, can immediately be dismissed. Also, *nonchalant* would indicate neither happiness nor sadness, so it also may be eliminated. Likewise, *lugubrious* indicates an exaggerated feeling of sorrow that would not fit in this case. The answer is **ebullient**, which means very happy.

5. **(A)** Two Words   *Moderate*
Since Paine is said to have little formal schooling, it follows that his education was limited. Thus, the first words *copious*, or abundant, and *profuse*, meaning lavish, do not fit. Thus, choices (B) and (D) may be eliminated. In the remaining choices, the second word of the pair must be examined. Since Paine's writings neither *dissuaded* nor *deterred* the American revolution, these choices may be dismissed. The word "nevertheless" gives the clue that this word must be a word in opposition to the first choice. The correct answer is (A).

6.   **(B)**   One-Word Direct   *Moderate*
In this sentence, *coronation* may be immediately eliminated since it refers to a crowning of a ruling official and does not fit in the sentence. Also, the word *edict* may be dismissed as a choice because John has given no command to a group of people. Likewise, *increment*, or addition, and *antecedent*, meaning cause, simply do not fit as solutions. So, the answer is **coup**, a political strike or blow.

7.   **(B)**   One-Word Direct   *Moderate*
The words *decorous,* or mannerly, *innocuous,* meaning harmless, and *pacific,* or calm, do not fit as descriptors of a disease. Neither does the word *deliberate* describe a disease. So, the answer is **degenerative** since schizophrenia worsens over time.

8.   **(A)**   One-Word Contrast   *Difficult*
Garrulous may be eliminated since it refers to a talkative person. *Raucous, boisterous,* and *animated* may also be eliminated since they all refer to the actions of a talkative, outgoing person. So, the correct answer is **taciturn** which describes a quiet person.

9.   **(A)**   Two-Word Contrast   *Difficult*
The choice with the word *affluent* may be immediately eliminated because it does not fit in the sentence. In the other pairs, the second words *indigence,* which means poverty, *modesty,* and *monotony* may be deleted as choices since they indicate the opposite of the sentence's implications. So, choice (A) is the correct answer.

Analogies

1.   **(C)**   Part / Whole   *Easy*
"A BUCKLE is part of a BELT" is the most specific sentence you can make with this stem pair. Similarly, a **brim** is part of a **hat**. All of the other choices have items that are related, but the word order is backward—a *pendant* is not part of a *chain,* a *shoe* is not part of a *heel,* and so on.

2.   **(B)**   Characteristic Location   *Easy*
"WORDS are located in a DICTIONARY, just as **books** are located in a **library**. The first word in each pair is contained in the second word in each pair. In each of the other choices, the words are listed in the wrong order. For example, assembly may take place in a factory, and a cigar may be kept in a humidor, but not vice versa.

3.   **(A)**   Function / Purpose   *Moderate*
"The function of a RATIONALE is to EXPLAIN something" is the most specific sentence you can make with this stem pair. Similarly, the function of a **knife** is to **cut**

something. In choices (B) and (D), the meanings of the word pairs do not have a clear or necessary relationship. The words in choices (C) and (E) are opposite in function or purpose.

4.   **(D)**   Part / Whole   *Moderate*
"A group of SHEEP is called a FLOCK" is the best sentence that can be made from this stem pair. Similarly, a group of **relatives** is called a **family**. The word pairs in choices (A) and (E) do not share meaningful or necessary relationships Choice (B) is a pair of synonyms. Choice (C) is a pair of words that are often used in the same context, but a *pasture* is not a group of *fields*.

5.   **(E)**   Characteristic Action   *Difficult*
"A PROPONENT ADVOCATES a cause or action" is a logical sentence that can be produced with this stem pair. Likewise, a **dissenter opposes** a cause or action. If you know your vocabulary, it is evident that the word pairs in choices (A) and (C) are not related in any significant manner. The word choices in (B) and (D) are pairs of opposite actions.

6.   **(C)**   Relative Size and Degree   *Difficult*
"Someone who is very CAREFUL is considered METICULOUS" is the most specific sentence that you can make with this stem pair. Equally, something that is very **disordered** is considered **anarchic**. Choices (A), (B) and (E) are pairs of synonyms, and if you are familiar with the vocabulary, you will see that the words in choice (D) are antonyms. Unfamiliar vocabulary may include these words: *nonplussed*, which means baffled, and *peripheral*, meaning located on the outermost boundary.

Reading Comprehension

1.   **(B)**   Understanding Words in Context   *Moderate*
To answer this word-in-context question, you should first go back to line 4 and read the sentence in which the word is contained. In this case, the word "respective" later in the sentence indicates that the correct answer is the first word, which is (B) latitude. "Longitude," although contained in the same sentence as "latitude," is the incorrect word. In astronomical terms, it is known as "right ascension." The major clue in the sentence is the word "respectively."

2.   **(E)**   Specific Information   *Easy*
Answers (A), (B), (D), and (E) are all clearly indicated as being among the brightest stars, so those answers may be eliminated as correct. The only star not mentioned in lines 20–21 is Polaris. Thus, the correct answer is logically (C).

3. **(C)** Implied Information   *Difficult*

Because lines 18–20 state that current constellations will be unrecognizable in the future, answers (A), (B), (D) and (E) may be removed as options. The answer is (C) because that is all one can say with certainty after learning that current constellations will have changed their forms. While it is certainly possible that scientists may discover more constellations in the future (E), and new one may appear (A), these ideas are not stated in the passage in regard to the movement of stars through the sky.

4. **(A)** Specific Information   *Moderate*

The only choice not stated in the passage as a property of stars is its size. Angular motion, color, proper motion, and luminosity, are all stated in the last paragraph of this selection.

5. **(E)** Main Theme, Idea, or Point   *Difficult*

Answer choices (A) and (C) may be immediately eliminated since they do not reflect the obviously intense study that has been given to stars. Answer (B) is a strong assertion but is nowhere found in the excerpt itself; neither is the idea implied. Answer (D) is not a valid answer since many of the old methods for naming stars have been replaced. So, the correct answer is (E).

6. **(D)** Author's Attitude or Tone   *Difficult*

The writer of this passage seems to describe many feelings regarding the village elders. Of the choices listed, answer (A) can be eliminated because the writer is obviously more than amused by the elders. And, while she holds a deep respect (B) for them, the context regarding her excitement about interaction with the village elders implies there is more than just respect. Line 5 specifically states that has no fear of them (C), and while it is difficult for the writer of the passage to wait for the legends to be told, impatient (E) is not her overriding feeling toward them. Overall, the author's attitude toward the village elders is veneration, defined as a deep esteem edged with awe.

7. **(C)** Implied Information   *Easy*

While all of the answers would be logical reasons to hesitate before entering the wigwam and rendering an invitation, you should be able, from context, to determine the actual reason for the writer's hesitancy at the door of the wigwam. The mother of the author had advised the writer to "Wait a moment before you invite any one. If other plans are being discussed, do not interfere, but go elsewhere." The mother wanted to make sure she was not intruding on plans already made—answer (C). While answers (A) and (E) seem logical, neither are specifically stated or implied in the text. Also, there is no mention or implication that the writer or the mother had thoughts that "the old people" might be speaking ill of them, thus eliminating answer (B). The text specifically states that it was not fear that made the writer hesitate (line 4), eliminating answer (D).

8. **(A)** Implied Information   *Moderate*
Because the tone of the passage indicates that this is a happy and nurturing memory for the writer, you can assume that "the old people" were fond of the writer and enjoyed her antics (A). There is no evidence given in the passage to undermine the truthfulness of the writer's memories, so answer (B) can be eliminated. Because there is no familial history given in the passage except for the mother-daughter relationship, answers (C) and (D) can be eliminated. Answer (E) has no evidence in the passage to support it.

9. **(D)** Specific Information   *Easy*
In lines 8–10, the author states that her mother was subtly teaching her to be observant (D). Answers (A), (B), and (C) have no contextual or implied support in the passage. Answer (E) may or may not have been true. However, the author did not claim it in the passage, so this answer is incorrect.

10. **(B)** Structure and Technique   *Moderate*
The mythological tone of the paragraph contains the "stars" metaphor and sets the tone for the upcoming paragraphs, in which the Sioux legends start to be told (B). In answer (A), the metaphor is taken too literally to be valid. Answer (C) can be eliminated as line 5 shows no indication by context or dialogue that the child is afraid. Answer (D) is not correct because the context of the paragraph is descriptive, not interpretative. (E) is also incorrect and lacks support in the text.

11. **(B)** Understanding Themes and Arguments   *Difficult*
Answer (B) most clearly describes the dual meaning of the sentence. The writer is looking at her mother not only to see if she has markings on her face but also to see if she can interpret the meaning of the markings on other tribe members' faces. Answer (A) does not work because it is by the mother's invitation that the village elders come for a meal and to share stories; in fact, the mother even asks the elders to tell stories to her daughter. Neither context or dialogue support answers (C), (D), or (E).

12. **(C)** Words in Context   *Easy*
"Rebuke," as can be derived from the context, most nearly means admonish. Definitions of the other answers reveal they are not synonymous with "rebuke."

13. **(E)** Author's Attitude or Tone   *Difficult*
The tone of this passage is not cautious, mocking, or frightening, which eliminates answers (A), (B), and (D). Answer (C) is also incorrect, as the author gives no indica-

tion via dialogue or context implications that these are good, yet sad memories, as answer (C) would imply. The tone is peaceful and the passage is, in fact, a reminiscence (E).

14. **(C)** Structure and Technique   *Moderate*
Answer (C) is correct. The author's use of first person narration (writing from the point of view of "I" rather than "she") makes the narrative voice more personal. It does not necessarily (A), make the story easier to read, and does not (B), explain difficult concepts to the reader. Moreover, the point of view of the story does not have anything to do with the conversation patterns of its characters, (D). Choice (E) is incorrect because, if anything, the use of a first person voice brings the reader closer to the subject matter rather than distancing the reader from it.

15. **(D)** Main Theme, Idea, or Point   *Moderate*
As an excerpt from an autobiography, the writer is relying on memories as she describes the community she lived in and how she learned about her Indian heritage (D). Answer (A) cannot be true, as this passage is only one account from one person's perspective, and it is based upon memory and interpretation, not research. In (B), although some communication practices are, in fact, described in the passage, they are not the main focus, nor are they are analyzed in the passage. Choice (C) does not work because only one brief legend was discussed in the passage, and the validity of the legend is not questioned, nor is the content of the legend central to the theme of the passage. In fact, the legend is not even finished by the time the passage ends. Answer (E) can be eliminated on the grounds that although the central character is a woman (or girl), the gender of the writer, as a participant in the passage, is not central to the passage

Section 2

Sentence Completions

1. **(B)** One-Word Contrast   *Difficult*
The child's behavior is described as "bad," so it stands to reason that the word that best fits as an answer will be one with negative meaning. Thus, *winsome* and *impeccable* can be immediately ruled out as possibilities, for they imply pleasing behavior. Also, *quixotic,* meaning enthusiastic and generous, may be eliminated. Likewise, *conciliatory* may be removed as an option since the boy's actions are in no way consoling or pacifying. The answer is (B), **vexatious**, meaning annoying.

2. **(C)** Two-Word Direct *Moderate*

The first words, *prudent*, meaning wise, and *irascible*, meaning angry, may be eliminated since these words do not work with the meaning of the sentence. Thus, the answer is (B), (C), or (E). (B) may be eliminated because lessons learned in such a marriage would not be *facile*, or easy. (E) may also be removed as a choice because such lessons would probably not be *serendipitous*, or a fortunate but accidental discovery. So, the answer is (C), meaning the lessons were difficult.

3. **(C)** One-Word Direct *Easy*

(A) and (B) may be eliminated because it is clear that the girl is neither *ludicrous*, meaning totally unbelievable, or *ravenous*, meaning starving. (D) and (E) may also be removed as options because both words mean dishonest: *dissembling* and *duplicitous*. Obviously the girl is **afflicted**, or injured, and the correct answer is (C).

4. **(C)** Two-Word Contrast *Moderate*

Because Nash's return to a teaching position at Princeton implies that he regained his mental and emotional strength, the word in the second blank is likely a word with a positive rather than negative connotation. In (C), **evinced** means "demonstrated," which is the only meaning that makes sense in the second blank.

5. **(B)** One Word Contrast *Moderate*

Since Andrea is annoyed by Tom's greeting, it would not be *amiable, poignant, or congenial*. After some consideration, it is also unlikely that such a greeting would be perceived as *jovial*. Thus, the correct answer is **brusque**, meaning short or abrupt.

6. **(A)** Two-Word Direct *Moderate*

The first word *compliant* may be immediately eliminated because Lila's sweet tooth is not agreeing with her. The second word of each pair must then be analyzed since none of the other first words may be eliminated. *Sanctioned, vindicated*, and *placated* suggest positive outcomes, so none of these words will work. Therefore, the answer is (A).

7. **(D)** Two-Word Contrast *Moderate*

Answers (A), (B), (C), and (E) may be immediately eliminated because Michael's writing is superior, an antonym of all of these words. Thus, the answer is (D).

8. **(C)** One-Word Contrast *Moderate*

The sentence implies that Sharon's smile is beautiful, even though the word "however" indicates that her attitude is not. Thus, the correct answer is (C), **beguiling**, meaning charming.

9.   (A)   One-Word Direct   *Difficult*

Since a student would not get into trouble for *orthodox* or normal behavior, (B) may be eliminated. Also, bad behavior is not *palatable* or pleasant. Such a student would not be described either as *punctilious*, meaning well behaved, or *prudent*, meaning wise. Thus, the correct answer is **obstreperous**, which means noisy.

10.   (A)   Two-word Direct   *Difficult*

The first words *inconsequential, negligent*, and *miniscule* may be considered as valid choices since the phrase "in addition" indicates that the students think negatively of the professor's ability in his field. However, the two words in all pairs except (A) do not share the same meaning with regard to the professor's bad teaching and jokes. The correct answer is (A).

Analogies

1.   (B)   Other   *Easy*

"APPLES and PEARS are two varieties of the same thing—fruit" is a logical sentence that you can make with this stem pair. Similarly, **wool** and **cotton** are two varieties of the same thing—fabric or fiber. In choice (A) the words in the pair do not have a meaningful or necessary relationship. In choices (C), (D) and (E), the word pairs are synonymous.

2.   (E)   Cause and Effect   *Easy*

"FEVER is a symptom or sign of ILLNESS" is a logical sentence that you can make with this stem pair. In the same manner, **pain** is a symptom or sign of **injury**. In choices (A), and (D), the first word is not necessarily a sign of the second word. Choice (B) contains a pair of synonyms, and in choice (C), there is no necessary or meaningful relationship.

3.   (D)   Descriptive Pair   *Moderate*

"LUSH FOLIAGE is foliage (greenery) that is abundant or plentiful" is a specific sentence that you can make from this stem pair. Likewise, a **sumptuous banquet** is a banquet that is abundant or plentiful. In (A), *opulent* and *lavish* are synonyms. (B) does not work because *sylvan* is an adjective that means "of the forest." The words in (C) have no clear relationship, and in (E), the words have a relationship similar to the stem pair but opposite in meaning: *sparse vegetation* is the opposite of *lush foliage*.

4.   (B)   Function / Purpose   *Easy*

"The function of a SYNOPSIS is to SUMMARIZE something" is a logical sentence you can make with this stem pair. Similarly, the function of a **foreword** is to **introduce** something. The vocabulary of choices (A) and (E) is straightforward, and the word pairs do not have clear relationships. In choices (C) and (D), the first word performs the opposite function of the second word.

5. **(B)**   Characteristic Action   *Difficult*
"A characteristic action of a SOOTHSAYER (prophet or oracle) is speak PROPHE-CIES" is the most specific sentence that can be constructed with this stem pair. In the same way, a characteristic action of a **charlatan** (fraud) is to speak **lies**. While choices (A) and (E) have word pairs that can often share the same context, an *escort* does not speak *galas*, or festive events, and a *soldier* does not speak *barracks*. The word pairs in choices (C) and (D) represent opposite characteristic actions: a *tactician* is one who plans carefully, while *provocations* are acts designed to bring about a response.

6. **(E)**   Relative Size and Degree   *Moderate*
"Something that is VIRULENT is very POISONOUS" is the best sentence that can be made with this stem pair. Similarly, something that is **gargantuan,** or gigantic, is very **sizable.** The word pairs in choices (A) and (C) are synonyms. The word pairs in choices (B) and (D) are antonyms.

7. **(C)**   Type   *Moderate*
"RAIN is a type of PRECIPITATION" is the simplest sentence that can be constructed with this stem pair, just as **loam** is a type of **soil**. Choices (A) and (B) are pairs of words that have opposite connotations. The words in choice (D) have no meaningful or necessary relationship, in choice (E), a *hound* is a canine, not a *bovine*.

8. **(E)**   Characteristic Use   *Moderate*
"CAMOUFLAGE is used to OBSCURE something" is the best sentence you can make from this stem pair. In the same way, a **rally** is used to **enliven** something. If you know the vocabulary, you can eliminate choices (A) and (C) as these word pairs have no meaningful relationship. Choices (B) and (D) are opposite of characteristic use. Unfamiliar vocabulary may include *constraint,* which means restriction or confinement.

9. **(A)**   Type   *Moderate*
"JUDAISM is a type of RELIGION" is the best sentence that can be made with this stem pair. Similarly, a **postcard** is a type of **correspondence**. In choice (B), a *hypothesis* may lead to a *theorem*, but it is not a type of theorem. In choice (C), a *branch* is part of a *tree*. Choice (D) is a pair of antonyms. In choice (E), the words are listed in the wrong order—*emotion* is not a type of *anger*; however, anger is a type of emotion.

10. **(D)** Attribute *Difficult*

"An ELITIST is EXCLUSIONARY" is the best sentence you can make with this stem pair. Likewise, a **connoisseur** is **discriminatory**. In word pairs (A) and (B), there is no meaningful or necessary relationship. By definition, in choice (C), a *criminal* lacks *morality* and in choice (E), an *extremist* lacks *flexibility*. Unfamiliar vocabulary may include *elitist*, meaning best member of a social group, and *exclusionary*, meaning preventing or keeping from entering a place.

11. **(D)** Lack *Difficult*

"Someone who is AMORAL lacks ETHICS" is the best sentence you can develop from this stem pair. Likewise, someone who is **disheartened** lacks **hope**. You should be able to eliminate choices (A), (B), and (E), because each of these responses offer pairs of synonyms rather that pairs that identify a lack of something. The words in choice (C) do not have a clear or necessary relationship.

12. **(A)** Cause and Effect *Moderate*

"BACTERIA cause INFECTION" is the best sentence you can make with the stem pair. Similarly, **fertilizer** causes **growth**. In choices (B) and (E), the first word does not cause the second word. In choice (C), the words do not share a meaningful or necessary relationship. Choice (D) contains a pair of words opposite in meaning.

13. **(B)** Lack *Difficult*

By definition, to be DEBILITATED is to lack STRENGTH. Similarly, to be **gauche**, or awkward, is to lack **tact**. Each of the other choices counts on your knowing the difficult vocabulary. Choices (A), (D) and (E) are synonyms, and the words in choice (C) maintain no clear or meaningful relationship. *Enervating* means to weaken; *energizing*, which is very similar, means to increase energy or strengthen.

Reading Comprehension

1. **(D)** Main Theme or Idea *Moderate*

The focus of the passage is on the Madison family, so you can quickly eliminate choices (B) and (E), which talk about the anti-slavery movement and the War of 1812, respectively. The author never claims or implies that he reveals any secrets about the Madison family in this passage, so you can also eliminate (A). While the author does say that he considers Madison to be "one of the best men who ever lived," choice (C) ("Madison was the best man who ever lived") exaggerates that statement and inflates the importance of that statement to the passage. The author's opinion about Madison is only part of the picture the passage builds. The overall purpose of the passage is to describe the

Madison household from an insider's, specifically a slave's, perspective, so the correct answer is (D).

2.   (C)   Author's Attitude or Tone   *Easy*
Of the answer choices, (C) is best. The author's tone throughout the passage is chatty and informal. The passage almost reads like a transcription of the author's speech, so "conversational" is the best description of its tone. Although the author expresses affection and respect for the Madisons, his tone never becomes passionate in this passage.

3.   (A)   Specific Information   *Easy*
In the first paragraph, the author describes the city of Washington. He does not mention modern architecture in this paragraph or anywhere else in the passage, so choice (A) is correct. The author does describe the unfinished White House, the unpaved Pennsylvania Avenue, the mud and dust on the road, and the dreariness (or gloominess) of the city.

4.   (D)   Implied Information   *Difficult*
Because the author's tone does not change much throughout the passage, you may have a hard time identifying his opinion of General Armstrong. In the second paragraph, the author sticks to the facts about the British attack on Washington, but he makes sure to say twice that Armstrong underestimated the potential danger posed by the British and to lay the responsibility for the city's safety in Armstrong's hands ("everything seemed to be left to General Armstrong"). He says that even on the day of the attack, Armstrong dismissed the idea of any fighting occurring. The author implies that Armstrong's blindness to the danger compromised the safety of the city, its residents, and the White House, since there were only feeble defenses and little time to evacuate. The answer choice that best captures the author's implicit criticism of Armstrong is (D).

5.   (D)   Words in Context   *Moderate*
You may not know that "reticule" means a woman's drawstring bag, but you should be able to figure out its rough meaning from the context of the paragraph. The passage says that during the evacuation Mrs. Madison "caught up what silver she could crowd into her old-fashioned reticule." From this sentence, you should realize that a reticule is some kind of container. The best answer is choice (D), "bag."

6.   (B)   Words in Context   *Moderate*
"Rabble" means a disorganized, unruly crowd of people, so choice (B), "a mob of people," is the best answer to this question. If you didn't know the definition of "rabble,"

you could use elimination to improve your chances of guessing the right answer. At the end of the third paragraph, the author states that before the British arrived, "a rabble . . . ran all over the White House." You should realize from this sentence that the rabble could not have been the British army, so you can eliminate (A). You could probably eliminate choices (C) and (E) too, since they seem less likely to be right than either (B) or (D).

7.   **(A)**   Specific Information   *Easy*

The author devotes an entire paragraph to denying the claim that Mrs. Madison removed a portrait of George Washington while she fled from the White House. Unless you skipped over the middle section of the passage, you should be able to answer this question easily. The one tricky part is choice (D), which is designed to throw careless readers off track. If you mistakenly interpret the question as asking *how* the author corrected a misconception, then you may be tempted to choose (D), which says that the gardener and the doorkeeper, rather than Mrs. Madison, took the portrait. However, not only is (D) the wrong answer, but it also makes a false claim when it says that the gardener and the doorkeeper *stole* the painting.

8.   **(E)**   Understanding Themes and Arguments   *Difficult*

The author begins the fifth paragraph by saying that "Mrs. Madison was a remarkably fine woman" and then continues on to describe how he tried to help her after her husband's death. The author gave money to Mrs. Madison out of his own pocket, even though he was under no obligation to do so; thus his gifts can best be interpreted as tokens of his affection and respect for her. Choice (E), therefore, is the best answer. If you weren't sure of the right answer, you could improve your chances for guessing by eliminating (A), which discusses the abolition of slavery. Slavery is not a subject in the paragraph on Mrs. Madison, so (A) is unlikely to be right. You could also eliminate (B), since the rest of the paragraph talks about how "remarkably fine" and "beloved" Mrs. Madison was. These descriptions do not suggest that she was "demanding," as (B) claims.

9.   **(E)**   Words in Contest   *Easy*

"Temperate" means "not extreme" or "moderate," so choice (E) is the best answer to this question. If you weren't sure of the definition of "temperate," you could probably figure it out by reading the rest of the sixth paragraph. The author talks about Mr. Madison's habits, which were hardly excessive.

10. **(A)**   Author's Technique   *Moderate*

In the section referred to in the question, the author describes how Madison cut his own wood and dressed conservatively. The purpose of this paragraph is to show the modesty of Madison's behavior, even after he achieved fame and power. You can quickly eliminate choice (C) because the author never says or implies that Madison treated his poor relatives meanly; instead, the author says that Madison wanted to set an example for his relatives by wearing conservative clothes himself. You can also eliminate (D) because the author never states that the Madisons were poor after they left the White House. What he does say is that Mrs. Madison was poor after her husband's death. The author also never implies that Madison came from humble origins, so you can rule out (B). Choice (A) is the correct answer. It is a better answer than (E) because there is no sense that the author is writing specifically for readers in the future.

11. **(D)** Understanding Themes and Arguments   *Easy*
The author is referring to Madison's funeral when he says that Madison was "followed to the grave by an immense procession of people." He includes this sentence to show that many people still honored the president long after his presidency. Thus the best answer to this question is (D).

12. **(C)** Main Theme or Idea   *Moderate*
Since the focus of this passage is on the Madisons, you can eliminate choices (B) and (D). Choice (B) puts too much emphasis on the author, but the author seems to limit discussions of himself throughout the passage, especially considering that he is the narrator. Choice (D) talks about the role of slaves in the War of 1812. This subject is clearly not the focus of the passage. Of the remaining answer choices, (C) is the best choice because it focuses on the Madisons while also justifying the conversational tone of the passage. Choices (A) and (E), while plausible titles, are not as good as (C). Choice (A) puts too much emphasis on Madison's presidency rather than on Madison the man, and both it and (E) exclude Mrs. Madison and the author altogether.

Section 3

Reading Comprehension

1. **(D)** Understanding Themes and Arguments   *Moderate*
This question refers to the first sentence of the passage, where the author states that the *Turtle* was the "first submarine that was actually worthy of the name." In other words, the *Turtle* was the first vessel that resembled a modern submarine, so choice (D) is the best answer to this question. The sentence does not exclude the possibility that there were vessels made before the *Turtle* that were designed to operate underwater, but it does imply that these vessels would not have been recognizable to people now as sub-

marines. Choice (E) is incorrect because the passage does not suggest that the *Turtle* needed to pass a submarine test.

2.   **(D)**   Words in Context   *Easy*

"Implausible" means "provoking disbelief," so choice (D) is the best answer to this question. If you don't know the definition of "implausible," you can try to answer this question through elimination. The sentence says that the "accuracy of this illustration is questionable; some of the submarine features that this illustration shows are implausible." Since the sentence says that the accuracy of this illustration is in doubt, you can infer that the illustration contains "wrong" or "unlikely" details, so you can immediately eliminate choice (A), *believable.* You can also rule out *ingenious*, which means "clever," *scientific,* and *workable* because none of these words works in the context of the sentence. You are left with the correct answer, **unbelievable.**

3.   **(C)**   Specific Information   *Easy*

This question asks you to find the answer that is NOT true, according to the passage. Refer back to the third paragraph to find the responsibilities of the submarine operator. Of the answer choices, the only task for which the operator is not responsible is choice (C), **firing torpedoes at enemy ships.** You can also identify this choice as the right answer since Bushnell's design did not include torpedoes; in fact, torpedoes are not mentioned in Passage 1 at all.

4.   **(B)**   Structure and Technique   *Difficult*

The first paragraph of this passage presents the claim that the *Turtle* is the first vessel recognizable as a submarine. The second paragraph, which begins with the sentence, "The one-man craft described by Bushnell resembles in many ways the modern submarines with which we are familiar," focuses this claim by describing how the structure of the *Turtle* resembles modern submarines. Thus choice (B) is the best answer to this question.

5.   **(C)**   Author's Attitude or Tone   *Easy*

You can eliminate choices (A) and (B) because nothing in the passage suggests that the author is either mocking or angry about his subject. You can also rule out choices (D) and (E) since the author expresses obvious enthusiasm for his subject in the last sentence of the passage: "Considering the technology available, the design of the little submarine was remarkably clever and well thought out." Throughout the passage the author seems engaged with his subject, so choice (C) is the correct answer.

6. **(B)** Main Theme, Idea, or Point   *Moderate*

Since the passage ends on a positive note about Bushnell's invention, you can eliminate choice (A), which suggests that the submarine was a failure. Since the passage deals exclusively with Bushnell's submarine, you can also rule out choice (C), which suggests that the passage discusses submarines in general during the eighteenth century. Choice (D) can be eliminated because the passage focuses more on the submarine itself than on Bushnell. Finally, you can rule out choice (E), since the passage focuses on a single submarine rather than on submarines in general. Choice (B), which focuses on the *Turtle,* is the correct answer.

7. **(B)** Specific Information   *Easy*

The answer to this question is in the third paragraph of Passage 2. In that paragraph, the author describes how two of the U-boats were destroyed (one by a mine and the other by a British cruiser) and how the U-boats failed to hit their targets, despite repeated attempts. Thus choice (B) is the correct answer to this question.

8. **(D)** Words in Context   *Moderate*

The word "debacles" means "great disasters," so choice (D) is the best synonym. However, if you don't know the definition of "debacles," you can improve your chances of guessing the right answer by eliminating some of the answer choices first. Since the word follows a paragraph that describes the initial failure of the U-boats, you can infer that "debacles" has a negative meaning; therefore, you can eliminate answer choices with positive meanings. Choices (C) and (E) have positive definitions, so you can cross them out. Eliminating them improves your odds of guessing the right answer to one in three.

9. **(E)** Understanding Themes and Arguments   *Moderate*

You can answer this question by referring back to the passage. After the author says that Weddigen was lucky, he states that the "captains of the cruisers had been careless, and it was unlikely the U-9 would have caught them if they had been alert." This sentence implies that the British captains' carelessness resulted in the Germans' destruction of the cruisers. Thus the correct answer is (E).

10. **(B)** Specific Information   *Moderate*

In the last paragraph of the second passage, the author discusses the British fleet's retreat to Ireland and western Scotland and says that this "evacuation, in a sense, was a more significant victory for the Germans than the sinking of a few old British cruisers. The German submarine had forced the world's most powerful fleet from its home base and into hiding." These sentences imply that the most significant success of the submarine patrol was driving the British fleet from its base, so choice (E) is the best answer to this question.

11. (B) Author's Attitude or Tone   *Moderate*

Since both of the authors praise the submarines they discuss, the best answer is choice (B). You can eliminate the other answer choices because there is no evidence in either passage to suggest they are true. For instance, you can immediately rule out choice (A) because the author of the first passage states the opposite of (A)—that the submarine he discusses was a remarkably clever invention. You can also quickly rule out (E), since pacifists are not discussed in either passage. While the designs of submarines and the captains of submarines are discussed in the passages, neither of the statements made in choices (C) or (D) can be backed up with evidence from the passages.

12. (B) Main Theme, Idea, or Point   *Difficult*

The similarity between the passages may not be immediately obvious since the passages discuss submarines in different contexts. The first passage discusses the first modern submarine, the *Turtle,* and the second passage discusses the first successful use of the submarine in warfare. Since both of these passages focus on significant moments in the history of the submarine, choice (B) seems to be the best answer. You can confirm this answer by eliminating other choices. Choice (A) is wrong because the second passage clearly discusses the success of the submarine in war. Choice (C) is wrong because the second passage does not discuss the invention of the submarine. Choice (D) is wrong because the passages do not focus on the operation of the submarine. Finally, choice (E) is wrong because the passages do not explicitly deal with the effect of the submarine on the way that war is conducted.

13. (D) Author's Attitude or Tone   *Moderate*

Nothing in Passage 1 suggests that the author would have a negative reaction to Passage 2, so you can eliminate choices (A), (B), and (E). You can also eliminate choice (C): since the author of Passage 1 seems interested in the history of submarines, so it is unlikely that he would be indifferent to the account given in Passage 2. Choice (D) is the best answer.

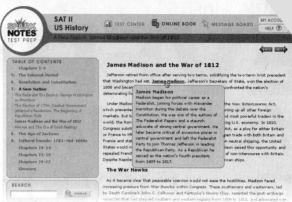

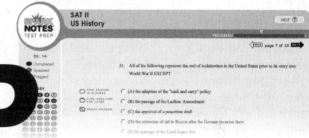

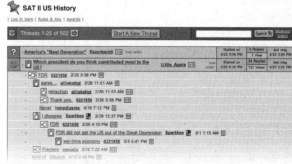

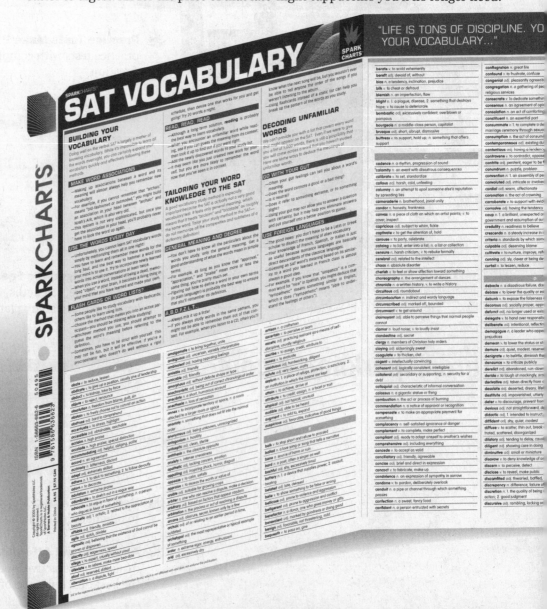

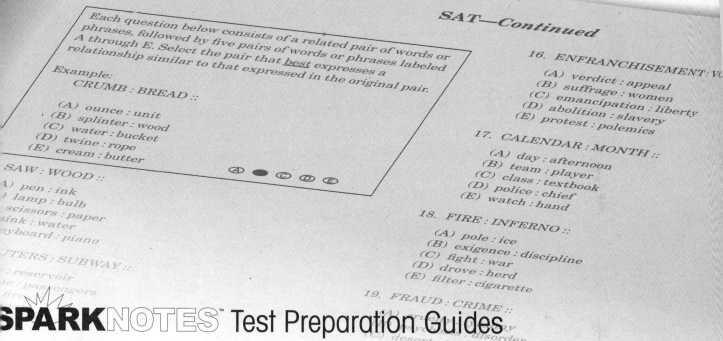